The Theory and Practice of the English Government

BY

THOMAS FRANCIS MORAN, Ph.D.

PROFESSOR OF HISTORY AND ECONOMICS IN
PURDUE UNIVERSITY

The Chautauqua Press
CHAUTAUQUA, N.Y.
MCMVI

Copyright, 1903,
BY LONGMANS, GREEN, AND CO.

UNIVERSITY PRESS · JOHN WILSON
AND SON · CAMBRIDGE, U.S.A.

PREFACE

THE purpose of this book is to place before American readers a concise account of the theory and practice of the English government. An effort has been made to present within reasonable compass a description of the actual working of the English government with some reference to its history and theory.

In the preparation of the book the writer has had the benefit of the advice and criticisms of several scholars both in England and in the United States. There are a few, however, to whom special acknowledgments are due. Mr. Alfred Fellows and Mr. Henry Smyth, of Birmingham, England, and Professor Emma Mont. McRae, of Purdue University, read the entire manuscript, and made many valuable suggestions and corrections both as to form and content. Professor George H. Emmott, of University College, Liverpool, read the manuscript of the earlier chapters, and gave the writer the benefit of his comprehensive historical and legal knowledge of English institutions. Mr. E. W. Kemmerer, of Purdue University, has also rendered a very valuable service by reading the proof-sheets of the entire book.

T. F. MORAN.

CONTENTS

CHAPTER I

THE GENERAL NATURE OF THE ENGLISH GOVERNMENT

England and constitutional government — Written and unwritten constitutions — Powers of the Crown — Heredity — Theory and Practice — English and American institutions — The Crown and the Three Estates of the Realm   3

CHAPTER II

THE SUCCESSION TO THE THRONE AND THE CORONATION

Continuity of the kingly office — The succession — Germanic custom — Anglo-Saxon period — Norman period — Election and heredity — The Act of Settlement — Significance of the coronation — The coronation of Queen Victoria — The coronation oath — The coronation chair   11

CHAPTER III

THE ROYAL PREROGATIVE

Definition of prerogative — Theoretical prerogatives — Theory and practice — Ministerial responsibility — The Crown as the executive — The royal veto — The presence of the Crown in Parliament — Royal messages to Parliament — The Crown and the Foreign Secretary — The Crown as "the fountain of justice" — Pardoning power — Appointing power — Officers of the royal household — Ladies of the household — Crown's private secretary — Abuse of patronage — Power of dismissal — Salaries and pensions — The Crown as Commander-in-chief of the army and navy — Power to declare war — Treaty-making power — The Crown as head of the Church — The Crown as the "fountain of honour" — The sign manual — Theory and practice — Moral influence of the Sovereign   25

CHAPTER IV

The Origin and Early Development of the Cabinet

Importance of the Cabinet — Origin of the Cabinet — The Privy Council — Early history and development of the Cabinet — Stages in Cabinet development 59

CHAPTER V

The Composition of the Cabinet

English and American Cabinets — The Prime Minister and First Lord of the Treasury — Chancellor of the Exchequer — The Lord High Chancellor — The Lord President of the Privy Council — The Home Secretary — The Foreign Secretary — The Colonial Secretary — The Secretary of State for War — The Secretary of State for India — The First Lord of the Admiralty — Other ministers — Size of the Cabinet — Cabinet and Ministry — The Prime Minister — Selection of Premier — Appointment of other members — Premier either a peer or commoner — Premier usually First Lord of the Treasury — Premier a busy man 71

CHAPTER VI

The Fundamental Principles of the Cabinet

Members of the Cabinet in Parliament — Unanimity — Collective resignation — Subordination to a First Minister — Walpole the first Premier — Premier and Cabinet unknown to English law 93

CHAPTER VII

Miscellaneous Provisions relating to the Cabinet

Apportionment of members between the two Houses — Cabinet members re-elected — Meetings — Premier and the Crown — Residences — Pensions 105

Contents

CHAPTER VIII

THE CABINET'S RESPONSIBILITY TO PARLIAMENT

Censure and want of confidence — Defeat on "vital questions" — Appeal to the country — General election — Formation of new Government — Resignations of Lord Salisbury and Mr. Gladstone in 1886 — The fall of the Rosebery Ministry in 1895 — Voluntary dissolution — Lord Salisbury's resignation, 1892 119

CHAPTER IX

THE CABINET IN PARLIAMENT

The King's Speech — The Address in reply to the Speech from the throne — Cabinet control of legislation — Leader of the House of Lords — Leader of the House of Commons — The whippers-in — Answers to questions — The Opposition — The law officers — Theory *versus* practice 137

CHAPTER X

THE ORIGIN, COMPOSITION, AND FUNCTIONS OF THE HOUSE OF LORDS

Its importance — Its origin — The Witan — Composition of the House — Creation of peers — Introduction of new peers — Princes of the royal blood — Irish representative peers — Scotch representative peers — The spiritual Lords — Lords of Appeal — Precedence — Disqualifications — Growth of the House of Lords — The Lord Chancellor — Time of meeting — Quorum — Prayer — Rules of debate — Privileges — Powers and functions — Landed influence of the peers . . . 155

CHAPTER XI

THE PROPOSED REFORM OF THE HOUSE OF LORDS

Reform of the House of Lords a live question — History of the opposition — Reform advocated by the Lords — Theoretical objections — The peers and the Reform Bill of 1832 — The record since 1832 — The tactics of the Lords — "Fifty Years of the House of Lords" — The Lords and the labourers — The proposed changes — Proposals of Lord Salisbury and

x   Contents

Lord Rosebery — Spalding's plan — Indian princes — One chamber — Defenders of the Lords — William C. Macpherson — G. Lowes Dickinson — T. E. Kebbel — "A Sussex Peer" — General conclusion 187

CHAPTER XII

The Origin, Development, and Composition of the House of Commons

Its importance — Origin — Simon de Montfort — Evolution of the House — The Reform Measure of 1832 and the "rotten boroughs" — Defects of representative system — Results of Reform of 1832 — The present situation — University members — American Universities and the state — Contested seats — Vacancies — Disqualifications — Expulsion of members — The franchise — Disqualifications for voting — Nominations — A general election — Women in English politics — Oath of office 221

CHAPTER XIII

The Regulations, Procedure, and Personnel of the House of Commons

Places and seats — Time of meeting — Quorum — Attendance — Payment of members — Strangers in the House — The Speaker — Parties in the House of Commons — The personnel of the House — Strength of the Commons 261

CHAPTER XIV

The Sovereignty, Privileges, and Procedure of Parliament

Composition of Parliament — Sovereignty of Parliament — Privileges of Parliament — Annual meetings — Obstructions — Sunday sessions — Special services — Adjournments — Communications between the two Houses — Communications between Parliament and the Crown — Replies — Methods of procedure — The three readings of a bill — Public and private bills — "Hybrid" bills — Practice and proceedings — Rules of debate — Divisions — Committees — Taxation and supply — The civil list and royal grants — Impeachment — Trial of Warren Hastings — Petitions 289

CHAPTER XV

IMPRESSIONS OF PARLIAMENT

Cards of admission — House of Commons — The "bar" — The galleries — Time of meeting — Good order — Hats on — Attendance — Manner of speaking — Manners of the Commons — Personnel of the Commons — The Opposition — House of Lords — Spiritual peers — Forms and ceremonies — Opening of Parliament — Election of Speaker — Relinquishing a seat — English conservatism 337

BIBLIOGRAPHICAL NOTE 361

Theory and Practice

OF

The English Government

CHAPTER I

THE GENERAL NATURE OF THE ENGLISH GOVERNMENT

REFERENCES: Todd's *Parliamentary Government in England*, i. 1-8; Dicey's *Law of the Constitution*, 37-81; Anson's *Law and Custom of the Constitution*, i. 33-41; May's *Parliamentary Practice*, 1-35; Bagehot's *English Constitution*, 1-67; Courtney's *Working Constitution of the United Kingdom*, 3-23; Creasy's *English Constitution*, 1-11.

ENGLAND has taken the lead in solving the problem of constitutional government; of government, that is, with authority, but limited by law, controlled by opinion, and respecting personal right and freedom. This she has done for the world, and herein lies the world's chief interest in her history." These are the opening words of Goldwin Smith's recent and brilliant work, " The United Kingdom." These two sentences set forth admirably the great debt which the world owes to the English people. As we note the progress of civilisation from its beginnings on the banks of the Nile, the Tigris, and the Euphrates, we are led to the conclusion that every nation has made its peculiar contribution to this progress. Each seems to have contributed something to those forces which tend to civilise, — something to the general good; and we of the present generation are the inheritors of these contributions. The Egyptians and the Chaldeans furnished the humble beginnings of literature, science, and art; the special mission of the Hebrews was to teach religion; the Phœnicians were the merchants, navigators, and colonisers of the Orient; the Greeks excelled in art and the Romans in law. In like manner the solution of the problem of constitutional government has been the great contribution of the English people to the world's civilisation. It is true that England's achievements in agriculture, commerce, and manufacturing are of no mean order and have added much to the welfare of the race; yet her supreme contribution has been along governmental lines. This being the case, a consideration of the English government with some reference to its development can hardly be amiss.

An exposition of the English government must always be attended by difficulties not experienced in a study of American government; because the English Constitution, unlike our own, is exceedingly extensive and largely unwritten. The American form of government is comprised in a definite number of articles and clauses, while that of England is made up of a series of great documents like the Magna Charta, scattered over centuries of time, of Acts of Parliament, of decisions of courts, and of various customs which have slowly crystallised into the law of the land. These various component parts of the English Constitution have never been collected and reduced to writing, and probably never will be. The labour of collecting and unifying these scattered fragments would be a stupendous task, and the work could never be complete even for a single day, as Acts of Parliament affecting the fundamental law of England would still continue to be passed, and the decisions of the courts would still constitute an uninterrupted stream. The American Constitution can be amended only in the two ways specified in the document itself, and changes in our fundamental law are by no means easy. In England, however, no such difficulties present themselves, as Parliament may alter any law with equal facility. As far as the processes of passage, repeal, and alteration are concerned, there is no difference whatever between a law affecting the fundamental principles of the government and any other. As Sir William R. Anson puts it, "Our Parliament can make laws protecting wild birds or shell-fish, and with the same procedure could break the connection of Church and State or give political power to two millions of citizens, and redistribute it among new constituencies."[1] When an Englishman says that a proposed measure is "unconstitutional," he means that it is "opposed to the spirit of the English Constitution," but does not mean to say that it would be void if passed. When an American pronounces an Act of Congress "unconstitutional," he means that it is opposed to the written Constitution of the United States and would be declared null and void in case it were tested in the courts. For these reasons the English Constitution is more variable and intangible than the American, and its exposition correspondingly more difficult.

[1] "Law and Custom of the Constitution," part i. p. 347.

The English government is usually classified by political scientists as a limited or constitutional monarchy. While it is a monarchy in form, in reality it is what Bagehot denominated it a generation ago, — a "disguised republic." This is a fact not always appreciated to the fullest extent. There is a popular misconception in some quarters in respect to the real nature of the English government; and this is particularly true in respect to the powers and prerogatives of the Crown. The idea prevails to some extent that the King or Queen occupies the throne by hereditary right, and is the determining force in directing governmental affairs. As a matter of fact, however, the claim to the throne based on heredity alone is not conclusive, and Parliament may constitutionally refuse at any time to recognise such a claim. This has been done in several instances. It is also true that the Crown at the present time has comparatively little direct participation in the government. The House of Commons, under the leadership of the Cabinet, is the real governing power. The time was when the Parliament was subservient to the Crown and subject to its dictation in most matters. This subserviency and submission are startlingly evident at times during the Tudor period. When Henry VIII. executed Anne Boleyn on one day and married Jane Seymour on the next, the Parliament, being assured in a speech by the Lord Chancellor that these acts of the King were not the result of "any carnal concupiscence," promptly passed an Act "declaring that it was all done 'of the King's most excellent goodness.'" It was during the same reign, in 1529, that a servile Parliament passed an Act releasing the King from all debts due to his subjects, incurred by way of forced loans. This subserviency was carried a step further in 1544 when, after large sums had recently been borrowed by the King, an Act was passed releasing the monarch from all obligation of indebtedness incurred since 1542; and further declaring that all sums already repaid on those debts should be refunded.[1] These and many similar instances of practical absolutism in England in more recent years have conveyed the impression to some extent that the Crown is still the active and controlling force in the government. The fact is, however, that the power of the Crown has gradually decreased, while that of Parliament, or more properly speaking, of the House of Commons, has correspondingly increased. Since the Revolution of 1688 the House of Commons has been practically supreme in the government of England, and no monarch since Queen Anne has exercised the veto power. This important change came about almost imperceptibly and as the result of custom rather than of statute. This fact has given rise to some popular misconception, in the United States at least, respecting the actual power of the Crown, and makes it necessary to distinguish carefully between the theory and the practice of the matter. The Crown possesses in theory many prerogatives not recognised in practice. In theory the Crown may exercise the veto power, but in practice this power has lain dormant for almost two centuries;

[1] It is well, however, to bear in mind in this connection that the retention of the forms of liberty under the Tudors was important, since it favoured the recovery of the reality in later times.

and when George III., as a result of a dictatorial disposition and the maternal exhortation, "George, be King," attempted to revive the veto, Parliament frowned upon the project and shortly after the Commons passed the famous resolution of Mr. Dunning, declaring "that the influence of the Crown has increased, is increasing, and ought to be diminished."

A study of the fundamental principles of the government of England, with some reference to their origin and development, and with a careful distinction between the theory and practice, cannot fail to be of value to an American citizen. American governmental institutions are of English origin, and a consideration of the English government constitutes the best possible preparation for a study of American government. Indeed, such a preliminary survey ought to be considered indispensable to a thorough and intelligent understanding of our political institutions.

In theory the governing power in England is vested in the Crown and the three Estates of the Realm, — the Lords, the Clergy, and the Commons. As a matter of fact, however, the Lords and the Clergy have been merged for centuries, so that there are now only two Estates instead of three.

It will be necessary, then, in a consideration of the English government, to study the powers and prerogatives of the Crown, the functions of the two Houses of Parliament, and the practical working of the Cabinet.

CHAPTER II

THE SUCCESSION TO THE THRONE AND THE CORONATION

REFERENCES: Taswell-Langmead's *English Constitutional History*, 204–235; Anson's *Law and Custom of the English Constitution*, ii. 57–84; *Nineteenth Century and After*, for September, 1902, article on Coronation of King Edward VII., by Sir Wemyss Reid.

ACCORDING to legal theory "the King never dies." By this it is meant that the kingly office is perpetual. The individual may die, but the office continues, and the royal dignity is transferred upon the "demise" of a king to his successor. No recognition is taken of any interval of time which may intervene; for example, the reign of Charles II. is dated in England as beginning in 1649, at the death of his father, instead of in 1660, when he actually began to rule. No recognition is taken of the eleven years constituting the Cromwellian period, or the period of the Commonwealth. The theory is a convenient one and obviates much possible confusion. Its evolution is a matter of interest.

Continuity of the Kingly Office.

The principle of heredity has always played an important part in determining the succession to the English throne. The claim based on hereditary right, however, has not at all times been considered conclusive, and the national assembly, whether Witan or Parliament, has always

The Succession

had the power of electing and deposing kings. King Edward VII. occupies the throne to-day by virtue of an Act passed by Parliament in 1700-1701, and might be set aside by the same authority at any time. Yet the principle of heredity has always been an important factor in determining the succession.

The present English nationality is made up of various elements. The Celts, Danes, Normans, Germans, and others have combined to form the English people. Of these elements the Germanic or Anglo-Saxon is the most important. Says Taswell-Langmead, "The Germanic element has always constituted the main stream of our race, absorbing in its course and assimilating each of the other elements." The Germanic element, too, has an especial importance for the purposes of our discussion, since the governmental institutions of England are of Anglo-Saxon origin. The late Professor Freeman was not dealing with sentiment but with historic reality when he spoke of the English people in its three homes,— Germany, England, and America. The genesis of English institutions is to be sought, then, in the forests of Germany, and Cæsar and Tacitus are the earliest historians of the English people. The King and the Popular Assembly set forth in the pages of Tacitus develop into the King and Parliament of England, and, I might add, into the President and the Congress of the American Republic. Our retrospect should begin, then, with a glance at Saxon times.

During the Anglo-Saxon period, or during that period extending from the Anglo-Saxon conquest

The English Government

to the coming of the Normans in 1066, the English kingship was elective, as it has since continued to be. The Witan, or Witenagemot, the predecessor of the present Parliament, or, more properly, of the House of Lords, was composed of the influential men of the realm and had power to elect the King. The power of the Witan was absolute, and it might elect whomsoever it saw fit, but as a matter of custom it was influenced by several considerations. In the first place the Witan was expected to choose the King from the Royal Family, and did so under ordinary circumstances. The late King's eldest son, other things being equal, had the best chance for election. If he had reached manhood and were not "manifestly incompetent," he was usually chosen to the kingship. In these warlike times, however, when the most important duty of the King was to lead his people in battle, the minor, though next in the order of hereditary succession, was frequently passed by. Thus in 871 the minor children of Ethelred I. were passed over in favor of Alfred, the younger brother of the late King. Neither is this an isolated instance. In several other cases of a similar character the Witan refused to elect the member of the Royal House next in the order of succession. The wisdom of this course was particularly conspicuous in the case of Alfred. An infant king struggling against the waves of the Danish invasion would be not unlike Dame Partington in her contest with the Atlantic Ocean. Also, if an emergency seemed to demand it, the Witan did not hesitate to pass over not only the hereditary claimant, but even the entire

Royal House. Thus in 1066 the Witan passed over Edgar, the hereditary heir, as well as the other members of the Royal Family, and elected Earl Harold to the kingship. The reason is plain. Edgar was an infant, and Harold was the ablest warrior and statesman in England at the time. The Witan was undoubtedly correct in thinking that the strong arm of Harold would be more effective than the impotent one of Edgar in quieting the turmoil then prevalent in England. The times demanded the stern command of the grim warrior and not the idle prattle of the infant. The Royal House did not offer suitable material for the kingship and hence was passed by.

The son born after the father's accession to the throne seemed at times to have a certain peculiar prestige; and the approval of the dying King was not without its influence. Edward the Confessor, appreciating the gravity of the situation in 1066, recommended Harold as his successor, and the latter was duly chosen by the Witan.

We may say, then, that the kingship in England during the Anglo-Saxon period was elective, but that the choice, under ordinary circumstances, was limited by custom to the Royal Family.

The Norman Conquest of 1066 ushered in a new epoch in the history of England and brought in a new line of kings, but it made no change in the matter of the succession to the throne. The kingship continued to be elective with preference given, under ordinary circumstances, to the members of the Royal House. The recommendation of the dying King also continued to have its influence. During the period following the Norman Conquest, however, the doctrine of hereditary right seemed to increase in importance while the matter of election seemed to decrease. Down to the time of Edward II. (1307–1327), there was an interregnum lasting from the death of one king to the coronation or election of his successor. The reign of Edward II., however, is dated as beginning on the day after the death of his predecessor, and he was proclaimed King of England at once "by descent of heritage," no reference being made to any election. From this time, then, the right by heredity is in the ascendency. It seems to have obscured the elective phase of the succession. The eclipse, however, was never total, and Parliament has occasionally exercised and never relinquished the right to regulate the succession to the throne. Before the accession of Edward II. in 1307, we may say that the elective character of the kingship was dominant, but that since that time hereditary succession has been the established rule, subject, however, to regulation by Parliament. This power was exercised in 1327 when Parliament deposed Edward II., the King by whose accession the doctrine of hereditary right was recognised. The deposition of the King was followed immediately by the election of his successor by Parliament. This same Parliamentary supremacy was asserted in the deposition of Richard II. in 1399, and in the immediate election of his successor, Henry IV. Again, as a result of the Revolution of 1688, after James II. had fled from the kingdom, Parliament declared the throne vacant, and by the Bill of Rights of 1689 settled the succession upon William and Mary.

Finally in 1700-1701, Parliament passed the Act of Settlement by virtue of which King Edward VII. occupies the throne of England to-day. This is the last instance in which Parliament exercised its right to regulate the succession to the throne, but it would be expected to do so again in case a proper hereditary claimant were lacking.

We notice, then, that during the Anglo-Saxon period the kingship was elective in character, but that heredity and the recommendation of the dying king influenced the Witan to some extent in making its choice. After the Norman Conquest the elective character of the kingship still continued but gradually decreased in importance while the doctrine of hereditary right grew stronger until 1307, when, by the accession of Edward II., the principle of hereditary succession was established and has since prevailed. During all these years, however, Parliament has never relinquished its right to settle the succession to the throne, and has exercised that right on several conspicuous occasions, the last of which was the passage of the Act of Settlement in 1700-1701, under which the present House of Hanover reigns in England. According to the provisions of this Act, all Roman Catholics are excluded from the throne and any one marrying a Papist becomes thereby ineligible. Had the husband of Queen Victoria been a Roman Catholic, or had she become converted to the Catholic faith, the people of England would have been absolved from all allegiance to her, and the Crown would have been transferred to the next Protestant in the order of hereditary succession as though she " were naturally dead." The Act further provides that every person coming into possession of the Crown "shall joyn in Communion with the Church of England," and shall, in accordance with a previous statute, declare against the doctrine of transubstantiation, at the coronation or on the first day of the session of the first Parliament. These provisions do not now seem to be in harmony with advanced ideas respecting religious toleration, but it should be borne in mind that they were made nearly two centuries ago and were the result of the religious controversies of the seventeenth century. Should Parliament have occasion again to regulate the succession, we would be justified in expecting more liberal provisions.

The coronation usually takes place shortly after the accession to the throne. The ceremony is conducted by the Archbishop of Canterbury and the religious or ecclesiastical element is predominant. As Sir William R. Anson puts it, "The church, in the ceremonial of coronation, gave sacredness to the office, the king was not merely the chosen of the people, he was the anointed of God." The Church thus ratifies and gives religious sanction to the secular title. The coronation of a king or queen is an impressive spectacle, and one which is not witnessed by every generation. The people are anxious to get even a glimpse of the new sovereign, and the greatest of England's citizens count themselves fortunate in being able to view so important and interesting a scene. It is customary for the two Houses of Parliament, if sitting at the time, to repair to Westminster Abbey and attend the ceremonies. The interest of the English people in a coronation is testified to by Pepys in his famous "Diary" when he says: "About four I rose and got to the Abbey, and with much ado did get up into a scaffold across the north end. A great pleasure it was to see the Abbey raised in the middle, all covered with red, and a throne — that is, a chair and footstool — on the top of it, and all the officers of all kinds, so much as the very fiddlers, in red vests." These words were written concerning the coronation of Charles II., and interest in the matter has not abated since that time. According to ancient custom the Archbishop of Canterbury is the master of ceremonies, and these ceremonies, since the time of the Norman Conquest at the latest, have been held in Westminster Abbey.

For the purpose of illustration it will be well, perhaps, to consider as typical the ceremony which took place at the coronation of Queen Victoria.[1] William IV. died in the early morning of June 20, 1837, and before noon of the same day the Lords Spiritual and Temporal and others assembled at Kensington Palace and proclaimed Victoria the Queen of England by hereditary right under the Act of Settlement. After being proclaimed, the Queen entered the room and issued a proclamation continuing in office all those who were serving under her predecessor at the time of his death. This act provided against an embarrassing lapse of official authority.

The Queen's coronation was deferred for more than

[1] For an account of the coronation of King Edward VII., see article by Sir Wemyss Reid in the September number, 1902, of the "Nineteenth Century and After."

The English Government

a year. This ceremony is not considered so essential or so pressing when there is no dispute as to the succession. Elaborate preparations were made for the event, and immense throngs of people came to witness the ceremonies. There is always an intense interest in London and throughout England in any matter which pertains to the Royal Family, and the coronation of the late Queen was the most important event in the recent ceremonial history of England. After the entrance of the Queen the ceremony began with the introduction, or "Recognition," as it is called. The Archbishop, after facing in succession the four points of the compass, spoke as follows: "Sirs, I here present unto you Queen Victoria, the undoubted Queen of this realm: Wherefore all you who are come this day to do your Homage, are you willing to do the same?"

The people then "signify their willingness and joy by loud and repeated acclamations, all with one voice, crying out, 'God save Queen Victoria!'" On this occasion the boys of the Westminster School, located in the rear of the great Abbey and within a stone's throw of the Houses of Parliament, represented the people and took the part in the ceremonies taken by the people in the middle ages.

The most important part of the ceremony was, of course, the Coronation Oath administered by the Archbishop as follows: —

"Will you solemnly promise and swear to govern the people of this United Kingdom of Great Britain and Ireland, and the Dominions thereto belonging, according to the

Statutes in Parliament agreed on, and the respective laws and customs of the same?"

"I solemnly promise so to do."

"Will you to the utmost of your power cause Law and Justice, in mercy, to be executed in all your judgments?"

"I will."

"Will you, to the utmost of your power, maintain the Laws of God, the true profession of the Gospel, and the Protestant reformed religion established by law? And will you maintain and preserve inviolably the Settlement of the United Church of England and Ireland, and the doctrine, worship, discipline, and government thereof, as by the Law established within England and Ireland and the territories thereunto belonging? And will you preserve unto the Bishops and Clergy of England and Ireland, and to the Churches there committed to their charge, all such rights and privileges, as by law do, or shall appertain to them, or of any of them?"

"All this I promise to do."

"After this," says Ewald, "the Queen laying her hand upon the Holy Gospels, said: 'The things which I have here before promised I will perform and keep: so help me God;' and then her Majesty kissed the book."

The chair used at the coronation of Queen Victoria has an interesting history. It is rough, ancient, and dilapidated in appearance, and is preserved with great care in Westminster Abbey in the Chapel of Edward the Confessor. The chair was constructed by order of Edward I. (1272–1307), and in it every English sovereign from his time to the present has been crowned. Edward was waging war in Scotland; and at the Abbey of Scone near Perth he captured the famous "Stone of Destiny," or "Stone of Fate," upon which the Scottish kings had been crowned.

This sacred trophy he took to Westminster Abbey in 1297 and caused the coronation chair to be constructed with the stone beneath the seat. The stone is twenty-six inches long, sixteen inches wide, and eleven inches thick, and is plainly visible from the front of the chair. The Scotch have made numerous efforts to regain their national trophy, but always without success. It has been taken from the Abbey only once since it was placed there in 1297, that occasion being the installation of Oliver Cromwell as Lord Protector. Visitors to the Abbey now view this ancient chair and study its history with absorbing interest. That contempt for ancient historical relics has now, fortunately, passed away which was expressed by Goldsmith's "Citizen of the World," who "saw no curiosity either in the oak chair or the stone; could I indeed behold one of the old kings of England seated in this, and Jacob's head laid upon the other, there might be something curious in the sight." Tradition tells us that this ancient stone is the identical one upon which Jacob laid his head at Bethel; that it was taken into Egypt by the sons of Jacob; that the son of Cecrops, the founder of Athens, conveyed it from Egypt into Spain; that at about 700 B. C. it was taken from Spain to Ireland by an invading army and placed upon the sacred hill of Tara and called the "Stone of Destiny" or the "Stone of Fate" because it sent forth loud groans when the rightful king of Ireland was being crowned upon it, but maintained an ominous silence in the presence of a pretender; that in 330 B. C. it was taken to Scotland, and in 850 A. D. was deposited by King Kenneth in the Abbey of

Scone from which it was taken by King Edward I. of England. All this, tradition tells us; but the unromantic geologist rather effectually punctures a pretty myth by telling us that the stone is a piece of Scotch sandstone, and not of oriental origin. Yet the fact remains that it is now an object of veneration in England as it was for centuries in Scotland. A second coronation chair of less historic interest was constructed in 1689, when the coronation of William and Mary as joint Sovereigns made two chairs necessary.

The coronation of Queen Victoria took place " amid prodigious demonstrations of joy," on June 28, 1838, a little more than a year after her accession. During this interval, however, she was the reigning monarch of England, and had, on the 20th of November of the preceding year, taken the required declaration against the doctrine of transubstantiation in the presence of the two Houses of Parliament.

CHAPTER III

THE ROYAL PREROGATIVE

REFERENCES: Todd's *Parliamentary Government in England*, i. 76–218; Anson's *Law and Custom of the Constitution*, ii. 1–56 and 303–354; Bagehot's *English Constitution*, 101–156; Courtney's *Working Constitution of the United Kingdom*, 123–135; Traill's *Central Government*, 1–11; Taswell-Langmead's *English Constitutional History*, 716–741; Fonblanque's *How We Are Governed*, 18–25; Ewald's *Crown and its Advisers*, The Lecture on the Crown.

PREROGATIVE," says Professor Dicey, "is the discretionary authority of the executive." Adopting this concise statement as a satisfactory working definition, it will be our purpose to determine the extent, in theory and practice, of this "discretionary authority" in so far as we may be able to do so within the limits of a brief discussion. We are sometimes inclined to think that the power of an hereditary monarch must of necessity be very extensive; as a matter of fact, however, the actual participation of the King in the government of England is comparatively slight, — almost insignificant. Neither has the power of the Crown remained the same at all times in the history of England; on the contrary, it has been a very changeable quantity. A consideration of the sources and history of the royal prerogative will not, however, constitute any considerable part of our discussion. Our present concern is with the authority of the Crown as it now exists.

The year 1688 marks an epoch in the history of the royal prerogative. "In outer seeming," says John R. Green in his "Short History of the English People," "the Revolution of 1688 had only transferred the sovereignty over England from James to William and Mary. In actual fact, it was transferring the sovereignty from the King to the House of Commons." The House of Commons at its birth in 1265 was not a very promising infant. Spartan parents might have exposed it in some mountain glen to die. Yet it was carefully nurtured by Englishmen who had faith in its possibilities, and it soon increased in strength. After a struggle between the Crown and the House lasting for centuries, the latter finally and fully triumphed in 1688, and now dominates not only the Crown but also the House of Lords. The Revolution of 1688 did not make any material change in the legal prerogative of the Crown. It did, however, divest the kingship of much power, not conferred upon it by law or by ancient custom, but as the result of the usurpations of the Tudor and Stuart kings. The Revolution was also followed by a series of happy political accidents, which aided in establishing responsible ministerial government and in eliminating the Crown, quite largely, as an active factor in the government. Many of these important changes were the result of custom and not of positive legal action. As a result the prerogative in theory is very different from the prerogative in practice. For example, according to legal theory, King Edward VII. has the undoubted right to veto any bill whatever passed by the two Houses of Parliament, but should he attempt to do so the Parliament and the people would register a most emphatic protest and would carry their point. As a result of this somewhat anomalous condition of affairs, we must distinguish very clearly between theory and practice in connection with the royal prerogative, if we would avoid confusion. Many writers on the subject have not done so. Mr. A. C. Ewald has written a little book, admirable in many respects, entitled, "The Crown and its Advisers," in which this distinction is not clearly and fully made. The reader following it as a guide would certainly conclude that the King is a most powerful factor in the English government in a direct and personal way. This is not true.

It is logical to speak of the theoretical prerogatives first and of the practical ones afterward. Mr. Alpheus Todd, in his excellent work entitled "Parliamentary Government in England," gives a concise statement of the theoretical side of the matter as follows: "The king is, moreover, the head of the legislature, of which he forms an essential constituent part; the generalissimo, or first in command, of the naval and military forces of the state; the fountain of honour and of justice, and the dispenser of mercy, having a right to pardon all convicted criminals; the supreme governor, on earth, of the national church; and the representative of the majesty of the realm abroad, with power to declare war, to make peace, and to enter into treaty engagements with foreign countries." Taswell-Langmead, in his "Constitutional History of England," writes to the same effect when he says: "By the written Constitution the King still retains the supreme Executive and co-ordinate Legislative power. He calls Parliament together, prorogues or dissolves it at pleasure, and may refuse the Royal assent to any Bills. He is the 'Fountain of Justice,' and as such dispenses Royal justice through judges appointed to preside, in his name, over the various Courts of Judicature. As supreme magistrate and conservator of the peace he nominally prosecutes criminals, and may pardon them after conviction. As supreme Military commander, he has the sole power of raising, regulating, and disbanding armies and fleets. As the 'Fountain of Honour,' he alone can create Peers (a power of the highest Constitutional importance) and confer titles, dignities, and offices of all kinds. He is the legal head and supreme governor of the National Church, and in that capacity convenes, prorogues, regulates, and dissolves all Ecclesiastical Synods or Convocations. As the representative of the majesty of the State in its relations with Foreign Powers, he has the sole power of sending and receiving Ambassadors, of contracting Treaties and alliances, and of making War and Peace."

The above quotations constitute an admirable statement of the theoretical powers of the Crown. It will be necessary, however, for us to consider in some detail each of the above powers and to contrast the theory of the matter with the actual practice. We may say at the outset that, according to legal theory, the Crown possesses important and extensive powers, but as a matter of actual practice these powers are exercised only through some responsible minister

The King does not perform any important governmental act whatever upon his own responsibility. He acts solely upon the advice of a responsible minister, and since he is obliged to accept the advice given, the matter amounts to a practical dictation. In theory, then, the act is the act of the Crown; in practice it is the act of a responsible minister. This fact will be obvious after a more detailed discussion of the various prerogatives of the Crown.

It is important at the outset to comprehend fully the theory of ministerial responsibility and of royal irresponsibility. According to Blackstone, **Ministerial Responsibility.** "the King is not only incapable of *doing* wrong, but even of thinking wrong; he can never mean to do an improper thing; in him is no folly or weakness." The maxim that "the King can do no wrong" simply means that the King is not responsible for any act of government, but that there is some minister who is responsible to Parliament for each act. Theoretically the Crown performs many acts of government; practically these acts are performed by responsible ministers. Mr. Todd, in discussing ministerial responsibility, writes as follows: "In a constitutional point of view, so universal is the operation of this rule that there is not a moment in the king's life, from his accession to his demise, during which there is not some one responsible to Parliament for his public conduct; and 'there can be no exercise of the Crown's authority for which it must not find some minister willing to make himself responsible.'" It is only reasonable, then, that the Crown should accept the advice of the minister, since the latter is responsible for the act. If this were not so, it would be impossible to find ministers willing to undertake the government.

According to the theory of the Constitution, the executive power is vested in the Crown; as a matter of practice, however, the Cabinet, or rather the Prime Minister, exercises this power. A more detailed discussion of the principal executive acts will reveal this fact.

The Crown as the Executive.

In theory the Crown has co-ordinate legislative authority. The royal sanction is necessary for the passage of all bills and may, in theory, be withheld at the pleasure of the Sovereign. In practice, however, the granting of the royal assent is a mere matter of form and is now never withheld. The veto power has not been exercised since Queen Anne rejected the Scotch Militia Bill in 1707, and the royal signature is now affixed as a matter of course. Should the King refuse — but he will not — to append his signature to a bill passed by the two Houses of Parliament, the latter would insist that the royal signature be given to the measure, and they would carry their point. Some Englishmen are very reluctant to admit that the veto is a thing of the past. Mr. Gathorne Hardy, a member of the Beaconsfield Cabinet, is clinging to the shadow rather than the substance when he says: "Nor is this veto of the English monarch an empty form. It is not difficult to conceive an occasion when, supported by the sympathies of a loyal people, its exercise might defeat an unconstitutional Ministry and a corrupt Parliament." Mr. Bagehot states the exact truth of the matter in his incisive

The Royal Veto.

The English Government

way when he says: "But the Queen has no such veto. She must sign her own death-warrant if the two Houses unanimously send it up to her. It is a fiction of the past to ascribe to her legislative power. She has long ceased to have any."

Although laws are "enacted by the King's most excellent Majesty, by and with the advice and consent of the Lords Spiritual and Temporal, and Commons," even the presence of the King in Parliament would not now be tolerated except upon a few very special occasions. In early times the King was actually present in Parliament and even took part in the debates as late as the time of Queen Anne. The Sovereign frequently attended the House of Lords as a spectator, but since the accession of the present House of Hanover the practice has been discontinued. George I. and George II. were Germans and knew but little of the language and government of England, and hence took little active part in English affairs. They did not attend Cabinet meetings or the sessions of the House of Lords, and as a result of a custom thus accidentally begun no subsequent monarch has done so. This withdrawal of the first two Georges seems now a "happy accident," since the independence of Parliament and of the Cabinet might otherwise be threatened by the presence of the Crown. The absence of the Sovereign has been favourable to the growth of constitutional liberty and independence. Now, says May, "according to the practice of modern times, the Queen is never personally present in Parliament, except on its opening and prorogation; and occasionally for the purpose of giving the royal assent to bills during a session." In the latter years of Queen Victoria's reign it was her custom to send a commission to Parliament to represent her on the occasions above mentioned, instead of appearing in person. The present King will probably be present in Parliament personally on these special occasions instead of by commission.

Although the Crown is not now ordinarily expected to be present in either House of Parliament, there are occasions, as indicated above, when the royal presence is entirely constitutional. The King may be present, personally or by commission, to open or prorogue Parliament, or to deliver his Speech to the two Houses. He may also be present, personally or by commission, to give his assent to bills passed by Parliament. When so present, the two Houses assemble in one chamber to meet him.

The King may also send a written message to either or both Houses by a member of the Cabinet or by an officer of the Royal Household. The members of Parliament remove their hats during the reading of such a document by the Lord Chancellor or the Speaker. Such messages usually relate to important matters demanding the attention of Parliament, such as the calling out of the militia, the prerogatives of the Crown, or provision for the Royal Family.

Thus while in theory the King possesses the veto power and enacts laws with the advice and consent of Parliament, in practice he cannot withhold his royal sanction from any bill whatever, and his presence in Parliament, even as a spectator, except on special occasions, would not be tolerated.

The English Government

All approaches to the Crown should be made through some responsible minister,—usually a Secretary of State. If a peer wishes an audience with the King he applies to an officer of the Royal Household or to the Secretary of State for the Home Department. The same rule applies to foreign affairs. In theory the Crown represents the kingdom in communication with foreign powers. In practice, however, the business is attended to by the Secretary of State for Foreign Affairs. Here also the Crown is unable to act or even to receive communications except through a responsible minister. The Foreign Secretary, by interview and correspondence, is the real spokesman of the nation. All communications from foreign powers relating to public affairs are addressed to a Cabinet minister and not to the King personally. Also when the King is absent from his usual places of residence, he is accompanied by a Secretary of State, or some other member of the Cabinet, through whom all business of a public nature must be transacted. Should an interview take place between the King and a representative of some foreign power, the Secretary of State for Foreign Affairs must be present. Says Todd: "Private communication between a king of England and foreign ministers is contrary to the spirit and practice of the British Constitution." This is now an invariable rule. Letters addressed by foreign powers to the Crown personally, have sometimes been returned because copies were not sent to the Secretary of State for Foreign Affairs at the same time.

The Crown and the Foreign Secretary.

It follows logically that the Crown should not

reply to foreign governments without the advice of the Foreign Secretary, who is the minister responsible for such acts. The King of Prussia addressed a letter to Queen Victoria personally in 1847 and instructed his Ambassador to deliver it directly to her. Prince Albert, the husband of the Queen, detected the irregularity of the proceeding and caused the communication to be read in the presence of the Secretary of State for Foreign Affairs, by whom it was discussed and by whom the reply was practically dictated. This same rule applied to letters received by the Prince Consort from foreign powers relating to public affairs. All such letters were turned over to the Foreign Secretary or to the Prime Minister.

In theory the Crown participates in judicial, as well as in executive and legislative acts. The Crown is the "fountain of justice." This familiar statement means that it is the prerogative of the Crown to dispense justice to the subjects. The Sovereign is presumed to be present in every British court and to decide cases. The King is not the "author," but the "distributor" of justice. "He is not the spring, but the reservoir, from whence right and equity are conducted by a thousand channels to every individual." This is, of course, a legal fiction; and it is probably not necessary to say that the Crown exercises the prerogative of justice through the instrumentality of the courts. The King personally cannot decide any case whatever. Such decision must be made by the judges of the various courts, and the personal opinion of the Crown has no influence whatever upon the result.

The Crown as the "Fountain of Justice."

The English Government

Neither has the King any personal authority with regard to the organisation of the judiciary. Mr. Todd remarks in this connection that "the Crown cannot of itself establish any new court, or change the jurisdiction or procedure of an existing court, or alter the number of the judges, the mode of their appointment, or the tenure of their office. For all such purposes the co-operation of Parliament is necessary."

The independence of the English judiciary has always been carefully guarded. Royal interference in this respect has been considered illegal for more than five hundred years. There has been such interference, particularly during the Stuart period, but never with the sanction of law. It was the result of usurpation. In order to fortify the independence of the judiciary, the Act of Settlement of 1700-1701 provided that judges of the higher courts should be commissioned to act for life or during good behaviour. Before this time the judges as a rule held office during the pleasure of the King, and were, in a measure, subject to his dictation. As a result, then, of law and custom the power of the Crown at the present time in judicial matters is rather nominal than real. The English people would not tolerate royal interference with the courts of law, and certainly the present King would think of none.

Since the Crown is the fountain of justice, the same power becomes logically the dispenser of pardons. A crime under English law is looked upon as an offence against the King, as in the United States it is considered an offence against the *The Pardoning Power.*

State. It follows, then, that the pardoning power should be vested in the Crown. Such is the theory, but in practice the prerogative of mercy is entirely in the hands of the Secretary of State for the Home Department. The Home Department reviews the case on petition, but almost never retries the prisoner. The facts are usually settled, but mercy is sought. The Secretary may be influenced somewhat by public opinion in regard to the case, and may consider its moral rather than its legal aspects. He sometimes confers with the judge who sentenced the prisoner, but is not obliged to accept his advice. The Secretary has no authority over civil cases, and has no power to increase a sentence considered too lenient. In the latter case Parliament only is competent to review the conduct of the trial judge. The Secretary would not tolerate royal interference. No such interference is now attempted, but was in the early part of the last century. In 1830 a Mr. Comyn was sentenced to death in Ireland. King George IV. wrote to the Lord Lieutenant of Ireland asking to have the sentence commuted. The Home Secretary, Mr. Peel, remonstrated against this as an unwarranted royal interference, and his course was approved by the Prime Minister, the Duke of Wellington. The King withdrew his request and the death penalty was inflicted in the case as originally intended.

Neither should the Secretary allow himself to be biased by personal or political considerations. Lord Brougham, in his work on the "British Constitution," remarks in this connection: "It seems hardly necessary to add that no interference of parties interested, politically or personally, should ever be permitted with the exercising of this eminent function of the executive government. Absolute monarchies offer to our view no more hideous features than this gross perversion of justice. Nor do popular governments present a less hateful aspect when they suffer the interference of the multitude, either by violence, or through the press, or the debate, or any other channel in which clamour can operate, to defeat the provisions of the law."[1]

The Home Secretary is a very busy man. He reviews more than a thousand cases each year in which his mercy is invoked, and each case must have personal and independent consideration.

According to the theory of the English Constitution, the Crown, as the supreme executive authority, has the power to appoint and to dismiss officers of the government. In practice, *Appointing Power.* however, the appointing power can be exercised only upon the advice and with the consent of the Cabinet. In theory, then, the appointing power is in the hands of the Crown; in practice, the Prime Minister and his Cabinet have complete control. In theory, the Crown has the power to appoint the ministers composing the Cabinet and to dismiss them at will. There are, however, some practical restraints upon the exercise of this prerogative. In the selection of a Prime Minister the Crown is practically compelled to appoint the natural leader of the party having a majority in the House of Commons. Should the appointment fall to any one else, he would not be

[1] Quoted in Todd's "Parliamentary Government," vol. i. p. 209.

able to form a Ministry and go on with the government. No one but the acknowledged leader of the dominant party would be able to do so. In short, the Prime Minister must possess the confidence of the majority of the House of Commons; so that, while in theory the Crown exercises its discretion in the appointment, practically the selection is dictated by the Commons and ultimately by the people. The late Queen acknowledged the force of this principle. Sir William R. Anson, in his "Law and Custom of the Constitution," remarks in this connection: "Queen Victoria has invariably accepted the decision of the country as shown by a general election or a vote in the House of Commons. Ministers are the Queen's servants, but they are chosen for her by the unmistakable indication of the popular wishes given at the polling booth or in the division lobby. Legal theory and actual practice here, as elsewhere in our constitution, are divergent." It is the duty of the Prime Minister, immediately after his appointment, to choose the remaining members of the Cabinet. The Ministry could hardly be expected to work in harmony if this were not the case. The list is submitted to the Crown for approval as a matter of form. The Prime Minister is thus the acknowledged head of the administration, and through him the Cabinet communicates with the Crown.[1]

[1] The method of address is rather peculiar. Official etiquette prescribes that the Prime Minister shall refer to himself in the third person and address the Sovereign in the second, as follows: "Mr. Fox has the honour of transmitting to your Majesty the minutes of the Cabinet Council assembled at Lord Rockingham's, 18th May, 1782." Affairs relating to the special departments may be discussed

When a party goes out of power certain officers in the Royal Household go out also, and their places are filled by adherents of the dominant party. This practice began at the close of the reign of George III., and was firmly established during the reign of Queen Victoria. It might seem at first thought that the Cabinet ministers were in rather small business when meddling with the appointment of officers in the King's Household who have nothing to do with the affairs of state. It would seem that they might well turn their attention to the offices strictly political in their nature and leave the management of the Royal Household in the hands of the Crown. It might also seem that an injustice was done when George III. was compelled to dismiss Lord Hertford, his Lord Chamberlain, who had rendered satisfactory service for fifteen years, and at the same time to appoint Lord Effingham — a man personally objectionable to him — to the office of Treasurer of the Household. It might seem, too, at first thought, that politics was obtruding itself unduly into the King's domestic life when the venerable Lord Bateman, the King's personal friend, was compelled to resign as Master of the Buckhounds because of a change of Ministry. Yet a "kitchen Cabinet" has long been all powerful, and the dominant party might be greatly embarrassed in case certain important officials living in semi-confidential relations to the Crown were beyond its control and held office at the pleasure of the King. It has been held, and correctly so,

Officers of the Royal Household.

with the Crown by the various secretaries without the intervention of the Prime Minister.

that "the responsible ministers of the Crown are entitled to advise the Crown in every point in which the royal authority is exercised." The Cabinet ministers are responsible for every act of government, and their influence should not be weakened by any possible advice of an opposite character which an irresponsible partisan might give. It is, then, now a well-established principle that the incoming party has the right to fill certain important offices in the Royal Household.

At the accession of Queen Victoria a new phase of the matter appeared. The question arose, "Should the ladies of the Queen's Household vacate their offices on a change of Ministry?" Sir Robert Peel, when asked to form a Ministry, answered the question in the affirmative. He held that the ladies of the household, including the ladies of the bedchamber, should change with the administration. The Queen objected to this view and contended that she possessed the right to control these appointments absolutely, and expressed her determination to make no change. Peel then declined to form a Cabinet and Lord Melbourne was reinstated, and his Ministry at once declared that in their opinion the principle of change in office upon a change in Ministry should not " be applied or be extended to the offices held by ladies in her Majesty's Household." In later life Lord Melbourne is said to have acknowledged that he made a mistake in this respect. Two years later the Melbourne Ministry went out of power, and Peel became Prime Minister, and we are told that the Queen withdrew her opposition, and that " no difficulties were raised on the bedchamber question." Through the intervention of

Prince Albert, the husband of the Queen, the matter was amicably settled. Those ladies who were related to the members of the retiring Cabinet and who consequently might exert a contrary influence, vacated their offices. The others did not. This stand of Sir Robert Peel is now held to be correct from the constitutional standpoint; and since his time the mistresses of the robes and ladies of the bedchamber, when related to the retiring ministers, have been compelled to vacate their offices upon a change of Ministry, while those ladies not belonging to "political" families have not been disturbed.

English experience has demonstrated the necessity of these precautions. Queen Anne was completely under the sway of Sarah Jennings, Duchess of Marlborough and Mistress of the Robes. It was said that the latter "decided everything, from questions of state to the cut of a gown or the colour of a ribbon, so that it finally grew to be a common saying, 'that Queen Anne reigns, but Queen Sarah governs.'" Mrs. Masham, in the same office, later acquired a like ascendency. These facts gave rise to Hallam's remark that "the fortunes of England were changed by the insolence of one waiting-woman and the cunning of another."

The appointment of ambassadors and other foreign ministers is subject to the same rule which applies to domestic appointments.

It might seem that the King should be left free to appoint whomsoever he saw fit as his private secretary. Such is not the case, however, and for good reasons. The private secretary, *The Private Secretary of the Sovereign.*

is of necessity on very intimate terms with the Crown and might influence his royal master in the affairs of state. For this reason he should be in sympathy with the Government of the day. If it were otherwise, the Cabinet might be placed at a disadvantage.

George III. was the first of the English monarchs to have a private secretary. Before his time one of the secretaries of state rendered the necessary assistance in carrying on the royal correspondence. George III. took upon himself many of the details of government, and when his eyesight failed in 1805, he moved to Windsor away from contact with the Cabinet ministers, and a private secretary became indispensable. The office was accordingly established, and the first incumbent, Col. Herbert Taylor, was appointed on the recommendation of Mr. Pitt, the Prime Minister. A new phase of the question appeared at the accession of Queen Victoria. The new Queen was but eighteen years of age and inexperienced in matters of government, and Lord Melbourne, the Prime Minister, determined that it was not wise to appoint a private secretary for her, as such an officer might have undue influence. The Premier himself undertook to act as royal private secretary. His action in this respect was severely criticised and even characterised as an unconstitutional interference; and after the marriage of the Queen, Feb. 10, 1840, her husband, Prince Albert, became the private secretary with the approval of the Cabinet. The office still remains under the control of the Ministry and is now filled by Lord Knollys.

The English Government

The power of appointment was greatly abused in England as late as a century ago, but public opinion would not now tolerate the shameless corruption existing in the time of George III. Yet the distribution of offices is still partisan to some extent. The candidate's qualifications are carefully scrutinised, but the patronage is distributed in such a way as to strengthen the dominant party. Although a healthy tone pervades English politics, the spirit of the spoilsman is not entirely wanting.

Abuse of Patronage.

The Crown, as the legal head of the Church, has control, in theory, of the ecclesiastical appointments. Bishops, however, and other important officials in the Church are appointed upon the advice of the Prime Minister, while the Lord Chancellor appoints many of the minor officers. The appointment of the rectors and vicars of parish churches is in various hands, and the advowson, or right of presenting or nominating, is now regarded as private property. Political considerations for obvious reasons influence the Cabinet ministers in making appointments of bishops and archbishops.

In making appointments or promotions in the army or navy the ministers of the Crown are expected to relegate partisanship to the background and to act exclusively upon the merits of the case. This they do for the most part.

Again, in making appointments in the diplomatic service, fitness and not politics is supposed to be the primary consideration.

In judicial appointments, however, partisanship is evident. The Lord Chancellor is a member of the

Cabinet and changes with the Ministry; the Chief Justice of the King's Bench is chosen from the dominant party; and other appointments to the judiciary are generally, though not always, partisan.

It follows as a natural consequence that the power to dismiss public officers should be vested in the Crown and be exercised by the Cabinet ministers. It is generally understood, however, that non-political officers should be dismissed for "incompetence or misconduct" only. Any other rule would tend to debauch the civil service. Englishmen are accustomed, and not without some good reason, it must be confessed, to hold up the American Republic as a "horrible example" in this respect. Yet it is sometimes evident that the spirit of the spoilsman, even in England, like Banquo's ghost, will not down.

It is logical that the authority which appoints should also have the power to fix the compensation for official services. This is the case in England. Compensation means not salary alone, but a pension after a certain period of service. We in America are familiar with the pension as connected with the army, but in England the system obtains in all branches of the public service. Says Todd, "That all persons employed by the Crown in the civil service of the United Kingdom are entitled to superannuation allowances after a certain length of service is a principle which, ratified by Act of Parliament, is now 'universally admitted.'" In theory the public officials are servants of the Crown and must look to the Crown for compensation. In practice, however, all salaries except those fixed by Act of

Salaries and Pensions.

Parliament are determined by the Treasury. Heads of departments may make recommendations regarding the salaries of their subordinates, but these recommendations must be passed upon by the Treasury, and not as a mere matter of form. The House of Commons also reviews the estimates.

Pensions are granted upon the advice of the First Lord of the Treasury. The House of Commons, however, reviews the pension list and may give advice and even legislate concerning it. When the Speaker of the House of Commons retires, the Crown confers a peerage upon him and recommends that the Commons grant him a suitable pension. This is done.

We note, then, that the Crown has the right to appoint, compensate, control, and dismiss the officers of the government, but that this power, like other royal prerogatives, is exercised through responsible ministers.

The Crown in theory is the Commander-in-Chief of the military forces of the United Kingdom, but no monarch since George II. has actually led the troops in the field. To do so, says Fischel, "would not accord with modern parliamentary usage." In 1827 George IV. expressed his determination to take the field in person. Lord Liverpool, the Prime Minister, declared that such a step was "preposterous, and that he would never consent to it." Sir Robert Peel characterised it as "almost incredible" and "as pregnant with increasing embarrassment to the Government." The result was that the Iron Duke of Wellington assumed the command instead of the King. Accord-

The Crown as the Commander-in-Chief of the Army and Navy.

ing to the Constitution of the United States, the President is the Commander-in-Chief of the military forces, and as such President Lincoln exercised a very positive and direct control over military affairs. The King of England, however, can act only through some responsible minister, and the Secretary of State for War, under the general supervision of the Prime Minister, has practical control of military affairs.

In theory the right of declaring war is vested exclusively in the Crown. In practice, however, the Cabinet ministers have complete control. The Crown can take no action except upon the advice and through the mediation of the ministers; and for these acts the ministers are responsible and may be censured or even impeached. The consent of Parliament to a declaration of war is not legally necessary, but since that body holds the purse-strings and controls the army and navy, no Ministry would be rash enough to declare war without being assured of the sympathy and co-operation of Parliament. It is customary for the Cabinet to ask the advice of Parliament before opening hostilities. Parliament is, too, in a position to compel the Cabinet to accept its advice. The war in opposition to the American Revolution was brought to a close by the opposition of the House of Commons, and against the will of the King.

Power to declare War.

It is a part of the royal prerogative to negotiate and conclude treaties, but the treaty-making power is actually exercised by the Secretary of State for Foreign Affairs. Neither Parliament nor the Crown has any direct participation

The Treaty-Making Power.

in the matter. In the United States a treaty to be effective must be ratified by a two-thirds vote of the Senate. In England no such ratification by either House is necessary, but it frequently occurs that some legislative enactment is necessary to put a treaty into operation. In such a case the indirect authority of Parliament is very important. That body also may censure or impeach a minister for negotiating an objectionable treaty. Parliament, however, has no initiative in the matter of treaty-making, and has no power to modify a treaty in any way.

In 1534 Henry VIII. caused the English Parliament to pass an Act of supremacy declaring the King to be the supreme earthly head of the Church. Neither that nor subsequent statutes upon the subject are specific in their provisions, but they are sweeping in the changes which they made. "The King," says Macaulay, "was to be the Pope of his kingdom, the vicar of God, the expositor of Catholic verity, the channel of sacramental graces." Since the time of Henry VIII., then, the Crown and not the Pope has been the head of the English Church. The royal declaration accompanying the Thirty-nine Articles of Faith pronounces the Crown the legal head of the Church, the interpreter of the Thirty-nine Articles, the Liturgy, and other church formularies, and the ultimate authority in all ecclesiastical matters. This is the legal theory. In practice the archbishops and bishops of the Church of England, under the general supervision of the Cabinet and Parliament, control ecclesiastical affairs.

The Crown as the Head of the Church.

The power to confer dignities, honours, and titles is vested in the Crown by the theory of the English law.

The Crown as the "Fountain of Honour." This power, however, like all other prerogatives of the Crown, is, in practice, exercised upon the advice of a responsible minister. The Prime Minister wields the real power in this connection, as it is upon his suggestion, or we may say, nomination, that such honours are conferred. Parliament, as a whole, is not expected to make recommendations to the Crown, and does not do so under ordinary circumstances. When a Speaker of the House of Commons retires from office, however, the Commons petition the Crown to confer upon him "some signal mark of royal favour." As a result, the Speaker is granted a peerage. In other instances the creation of peers is by the Crown upon the advice of the Prime Minister, without parliamentary interference.

It is necessary, of course, that the royal signature be affixed to a large number of official documents. **The Sign Manual.** This process has long ceased to be more than a mere matter of form. It would be impossible for the King, even were he so disposed, to acquaint himself with the contents of the various documents demanding his signature. George III. endeavoured, with characteristic industry, to examine a certain class of documents before signing them, until Lord Thurlow bluntly informed him that "it was nonsense his looking at them, for he could not understand them." Mr. Bagehot in his "English Constitution," written thirty or forty years ago, proclaimed against the useless labour devolving upon the Crown at that time in signing documents as a mere matter of form. He says that only one valid argument has been adduced in favour of the practice; namely, "You may have a fool for a sovereign, and then it would be desirable he should have plenty of occupation in which he can do no harm."

It has sometimes happened that the Crown, through some disability, was unable to sign the papers in person. In such a case as this it devolved upon Parliament to authorise an individual or a commission to do the work. George IV. was authorised by Parliament to appoint "one or more persons to affix the royal signature to papers, by means of a stamp," because his impaired health made it practically impossible for him to do the work personally. In 1862 the papers requiring the royal signature became so numerous that the signing became an intolerable burden. At that time the Queen was attempting to sign the commissions of all army and navy officers and of hosts of other officials. This became exceedingly burdensome, and at one time 15,931 commissions were awaiting the royal signature. In many cases men had left the service or had died before their commissions were signed. It was necessary to take some action to relieve the situation, and Parliament accordingly authorised the Queen to have the documents signed by the Commander-in-Chief and a Secretary of State, and to dispense with the royal signature.

The above instances will serve to illustrate the difference between the theory and the practice in respect to the royal prerogative. The personal opinions of the Crown are not

Theory and Practice.

now prominent; not because the opinions of the King are not deemed worthy of respect, but because the government of England is a popular one in which the sovereignty resides ultimately in the people, and not in the Crown. The real facts in the case were stated in an effective and graphic way by the late Prof. Moses Coit Tyler while sojourning in England in 1866. When discussing the theoretical and practical prerogatives of the Queen, he wrote: "Everything in the land is spoken of as hers. It is her Majesty's faithful Commons, her Majesty's army and navy, her Majesty's mails, her Majesty's highways, her Majesty's steamships. Yet everybody else knows, and she cannot help knowing, that all this is but a figure and a fiction — the shadow of a royal authority whose substance was torn away and annihilated in 1688. The navy is not hers: she cannot appoint or remove the smallest middy in all her fleets. The army is not hers: she cannot control the movements of one corporal's squad in all the ranks which swear allegiance to her name. Her steamships will carry her — on payment of the usual fare; her highways are open to her — as they are to the dirtiest peasant who stands gazing at her chariot; her mails will carry her letters — at the rate of one penny the half ounce; and as to her faithful Commons — they would cause the whole island to quake with war and to run with blood before they would yield back to her one iota of all the authority which they fiercely wrested from her ancestors." [1]

The late Queen understood the situation perfectly

[1] "Glimpses of England," p. 211.

and governed herself accordingly. "Since the accession of our present Queen," says Mr. Todd, "the personal predilections of the sovereign in respect to an existing administration have never been brought into public view." The result of this rational and conservative policy greatly endeared the Queen to her subjects. "It is well known," says a recent political writer in the "Edinburgh Review," "that her Majesty has habitually taken an active interest in every matter with which it behooves a constitutional sovereign of this country to be concerned; in many instances her opinion and her will have left their impression on our policy. But in no instance has the power of the Crown been so exercised as to expose it to check or censure or embarrassment of any kind. It may be asserted without qualification that a sense of general content, of sober heartfelt loyalty, has year by year gathered around the throne of Victoria." After quoting the above statement Mr. Todd remarks: "The present writer would add to this his sincere conviction, that attachment to the person and throne of our gracious Queen is not confined to the mother-country, but extends with equal if not greater intensity to the remotest bounds of her immense empire; and that few could be found, even in lands that owe her no allegiance as a sovereign, who would not willingly unite in a tribute of respect and admiration for Victoria, as a woman, a mother, and a queen."

I believe that both of the above statements are easily within the bounds of truth, and that their force will be admitted by any careful American observer whose patriotism is not equivalent to what Bagehot once termed "territorial sectarianism." By accepting the situation as she found it at her accession, by refraining from unwise and futile attempts to revive the royal prerogative, as George III. had attempted to do, and by making her influence felt along moral rather than legal lines, the late Queen not only endeared herself to her own subjects, but won the respect and admiration of the people of the world, and of Americans most of all. There was no dissenting voice when Professor Freeman remarked: "We can wish nothing better for her kingdom than that the Crown which she so lawfully holds, which she has so worthily worn among two generations of her people, she may, like Nestor of old, continue to wear amid the well-deserved affection of a third." And when the end came in January, 1901, the tributes paid to her memory by the American people were not less eloquent and sincere than those of the English people themselves, and the grief of the American nation on that occasion was exceeded only by that of the Queen's own subjects.

Although the Sovereign possesses but little actual governmental authority, it is not difficult to see that his moral influence is of great importance. This fact is observed by the sojourner in England, but is naturally more fully appreciated by British subjects. Mr. Todd testifies to the following effect when discussing this matter: "On the wider field of national and non-political pursuits, wherein the individuality of the sovereign is equally excluded from direct interference, the moral influence of the crown, as a means of promoting the public welfare, is of incalculable weight and value. It properly

The Moral Influence of the Sovereign.

devolves upon the constitutional sovereigns of England to employ this powerful influence for the encouragement of public and private morality, for the advancement of learning, and for the diffusion of civilization among their people. The favour of the monarch is always an object of honourable ambition, and, when worthily bestowed, will nerve the arm and excite the brain to deeds which deserve a nation's gratitude, and bring renown upon the whole empire. . . . Though divested, by the growth and development of our political institutions, of direct political power, the crown still retains immense personal and social influence for good or evil." Notwithstanding the fact that his powers are closely circumscribed, he has " the right to be consulted, the right to encourage, the right to warn. And a king of great sense and sagacity would want no others."

It is easy even for the casual observer to see that even now in the United Kingdom there is still that " divinity which doth hedge a king," and the magic spell of royal rule has not been entirely dissipated by the fierce blasts of modern democracy. Mr. Bagehot, a fearless and incisive critic of existing institutions, recognised the value of the Crown in the English government. In his "English Constitution," he says, "The use of the Queen, in a dignified capacity, is incalculable. Without her in England, the present English Government would fail and pass away. Most people when they read that the Queen walked on the slopes at Windsor — that the Prince of Wales went to the Derby — have imagined that too much thought and prominence were given to little things. But they have been in error; and it is nice to trace how the actions of a retired widow and an unemployed youth become of such importance." The above savours somewhat of irreverence and flippancy, but Mr. Bagehot was serious in regard to the matter, and had a very high appreciation of the Queen as the social and moral head of the nation. He believed that the fiction phase of the matter was not without its value. With refreshing frankness he says that constitutional monarchy " acts as a *disguise*. It enables our real rulers to change without heedless people knowing it. The masses of Englishmen are not fit for an elective government; if they knew how near they were to it, they would be surprised, and almost tremble."

The traveller in England, as he beholds the reverence paid to the King and the other members of the Royal Family, will hardly agree with Napoleon when he characterises a throne as "a piece of wood covered with velvet." In England, at least, it signifies more than that. The late Queen did not live a life of "brilliant idleness." She wielded a very positive influence for good along moral and philanthropic lines. Her appearance or the presence of any member of the Royal Family was the signal for an outpouring of popular jubilation. We may look upon such demonstrations as emotional rather than rational and see in them " a picturesque and amiable weakness; " but the fact remains that the Queen exerted a powerful and beneficial influence upon the people of England. The cynic will smile when he sees the scrawling autograph of Queen Victoria, printed at the age of four, carefully preserved in a glass case in the British Museum, and

The English Government

I doubt not he will sneer when told that the inhabitants of Kirkaldy made a plaster cast from the impression which the Queen's foot made in the sands of their town and treasured it as a priceless memento of the royal visit. The celebration of the Queen's birthday and the observance of the various jubilees had their ludicrous features when viewed by censorious eyes, but they tended to show the sway which Queen Victoria had over the minds of her subjects.

CHAPTER IV

THE ORIGIN AND EARLY DEVELOPMENT OF THE CABINET

REFERENCES: Blauvelt's *Development of Cabinet Government in England;* Todd's *Parliamentary Government in England,* i. 219-252; Traill's *Central Government,* 12-30; Anson's *Law and Custom of the Constitution,* i. 29-31, and ii. 106-118, 141-143; Taswell-Langmead's *English Constitutional History,* 696-706; Freeman's *Growth of the English Constitution,* 111-124.

A THOROUGH knowledge of the functions of the Cabinet is necessary to a correct understanding of the English government. Although the Cabinet is unknown to the English law, it is by far the most important feature of the government. The supreme governing power in England is vested in the House of Commons; and since the Cabinet represents the party dominant for the time in the Commons, obviously the Cabinet is the guiding and determining force in the government. It is composed of the leaders of the party having a majority in the Lower House, and its members have seats either in the House of Lords or the House of Commons. As we have seen, the Crown can perform no act of government except through a responsible minister; and since the most influential and important ministers have seats in the Cabinet and determine the policy for those who do not, the importance of that body in an executive capacity is obvious. Its legislative importance is no less, since practically the entire legislation of Parliament is initiated, shaped, and controlled by the Cabinet. If the House of Commons is the motive power, the Cabinet is the rudder of the ship of state.

In order to view the Cabinet in its proper perspective, it will be necessary to note its origin. The Cabinet originated as a smaller committee, or inner circle of the Privy Council. A detailed account of the history and functions of this latter body does not properly fall within the scope of this discussion; but it should be noted that the Privy Council was, and in theory still is, the legal advisory body of the Crown.[1] The ancient oath of the privy councillor clearly indicates his attitude toward the King. It was in substance as follows: " 1. To advise the king in all matters to the best of his wisdom and discretion. 2. To advise for the king's honour and advantage, and for the public good, without partiality and without fear. 3. To keep secret the king's counsel, and all transactions in the council itself. 4. To avoid corruption in regard to any matter or thing to be done in council. 5. To forward and help the execution of whatsoever shall be therein resolved. 6. To withstand all persons who shall attempt the contrary. 7. And generally to observe, keep, and do all that a good and true councillor ought to do unto his sovereign lord."[2] The modern oath is quite similar in

The Origin of the Cabinet.

---

[1] See G. Barnett Smith's "History of the English Parliament," vol. ii. p. 590.

[2] Todd's "Parliamentary Government in England," vol. i. p. 221.

effect to that anciently administered. It binds the privy councillor to advise the Crown to the best of his ability, and to keep secret those matters intrusted to him. The privy councillors are appointed by the Crown and their number is not limited. Neither are there any qualifications specified for the office except that the privy councillor must be a natural-born subject of Great Britain. Even this requirement is sometimes waived, as was done in the case of Prince Albert, the husband of Queen Victoria.

The privy councillors formerly held office during the life of the Sovereign by whom they were appointed. At present they continue in office for six months after the death of the Sovereign, and as a rule are sworn in again and continue in office under the new monarch. The councillor takes an oath of allegiance as specified in the Act of 1868.

It was from this ancient advisory body that the present English Cabinet originated. It arose because the Privy Council had become too large to discharge its functions properly. It sprang up without the sanction of law, and even at the present time has no legal basis. A Cabinet member, as such, has no legal right to advise the Crown, and certainly no right to insist that his advice be accepted. He has authority and is known to the law as a privy councillor, but not as a Cabinet member. The written law of England contains no reference to the Cabinet; "the names of the noblemen and gentlemen who compose it are never officially announced to the public; no record is kept of its meetings and resolutions, nor has its existence ever been recognised by any Act of Parliament."

In order to understand this anomalous state of affairs, it will be necessary to glance, somewhat more in detail, at the origin and development of the Cabinet. The Cabinet, as noted above, originated as a smaller and more select committee of the Privy Council. For centuries the Privy Council had been the legal adviser of the King on all important matters; but that body became so large that it was impossible to transact business with the necessary speed and secrecy. As a consequence, the King, instead of consulting the entire body, asked the advice of a few of the leading members of the Council, or of those in whose judgment he had confidence. The result was that the Privy Council as an advisory body fell into disuse, and its place was taken by the smaller and less cumbersome one called the Cabinet. The name "Cabinet" arose from the fact that the King consulted its members in a small private room or cabinet in the royal palace. It is a rather peculiar fact that the name which originated as a term of reproach should now designate the most honourable and powerful body in the English government. Macaulay with his customary clearness comments upon the origin of the Cabinet as follows: "Few things in our history are more curious than the origin and growth of the power now possessed by the Cabinet. From an early period the Kings of England had been assisted by a Privy Council, to which the law assigned many important functions and duties. During several centuries this body deliberated on the gravest and most delicate affairs. But by degrees its character changed. It became too large for despatch and secrecy. The rank of privy councillor was often bestowed as an honorary distinction on persons to whom nothing was confided, and whose opinion was never asked. The Sovereign, on the most important occasions, resorted for advice to a small knot of leading ministers."

The fact that the Privy Council, once powerful in affairs of state, is now practically powerless; and that the Cabinet, a body entirely without legal sanction, is the directing force in the English government, well illustrates the force of precedent and custom in the constitutional development of England. The change came about gradually — almost insensibly. At one time "there was," says Sir Harris Nicolas, in speaking of the ancient powers of the Privy Council, "scarcely a department of state which was not in a greater or less degree subject to its immediate control. No rank was too exalted or too humble to be exempt from its vigilance, nor any matter too insignificant for its interference."[1]

Since the rise and establishment of a Cabinet, however, the Privy Council has, as a body, ceased to be important in governmental affairs. In fact, it holds no meetings of a deliberative character. "All that remains to it of the dignity of its ancient place in the constitution is of a merely formal and ceremonial nature."[2] The Cabinet has demonstrated its superior fitness to survive. It is a peculiar fact, too, that the

[1] "Proceedings and Ordinances of the Privy Council," Preface, p. 11.
[2] H. D. Traill's "Central Government," p. 18.

present attitude of the Cabinet toward the Crown is quite different from that of the Privy Council. The latter body is always assembled under the presidency of the King, but he cannot even attend a meeting of the Cabinet. His presence at the Privy Council is indispensable, but at the Cabinet meeting would be unconstitutional.

In order to make the matter more definite and to see more clearly how the transformation above mentioned was brought about, it will be well to view briefly the circumstances attending the origin of the Cabinet, and to note the various stages through which it has passed in the course of its development.

The Early History and Development of the Cabinet.

It was but natural that when the Privy Council became unwieldy the King should consult a few of his more trusted advisers in preference to the entire body. This practice began quite early in the history of the English government; how early it is impossible to determine. Certainly by the time of Henry III. there are traces of this select council, and Bacon says that "King Henry VII., . . . in his greatest business, imparted himself to none, except it were to Morton and Fox." The term "Cabinet Council" was used for the first time in the reign of Charles I. Under the Protectorate of Cromwell there was no Cabinet, for very obvious reasons. When Charles II. came to the throne in 1660 an attempt was made to restore the old Privy Council to its former place in the government. The scheme was soon found to be impracticable, however, and in 1679 the King declared that the "great number of the Council" had "made

The English Government

it unfit for the secrecy and despatch that are necessary in many great affairs." This fact, the King continued, forced him to consult a few of the councillors instead of the entire body. The new Cabinet was very unpopular and the King requested Sir William Temple to devise another plan. He did so, but his scheme was a failure for reasons which we cannot now discuss, and the Cabinet system was left to develop naturally without the assistance of political philosophers. William III. formed a Cabinet of both Whigs and Tories. The result was not good. There was much disputation and no end of wrangling. Finally in 1693, on the advice of the Earl of Sunderland, the King determined to have his Cabinet composed wholly of Whigs — the then dominant party — and by 1696 he had effected changes to that end. This marks an important epoch in the history of the Cabinet. It now begins to take on its modern form. However, there was not yet unity of action in the Cabinet, and the body did not change with the predominating party in the House of Commons. These latter characteristics were developed by the close of the eighteenth century.

It may be well to recapitulate somewhat in order to see clearly the successive steps by which the Cabinet assumed its present form. Mr. H. D. Traill, in his admirable little book entitled "Central Government," notes four distinct stages or periods in the historical development of the Cabinet. These are substantially as follows: —

1. Before the time of Charles I. (1625–1649), there was a small body of confidential advisers whom the

King chose to consult on important matters in preference to the larger and more cumbersome Privy Council. The members of this select body were members of the Privy Council; they gave their advice privately, and no official record was kept of their proceedings. They had no power to perform any act of government without the sanction of the Privy Council. The term "Cabinet" had not yet arisen.

2. During the second period of its existence (reigns of Charles I. and II.) the name "Cabinet" was applied to the body as a term of reproach. There was much opposition to what seemed to be its illegal usurpations, and an effort was made to check its advance. It was to no avail, however, as many had been made members of the Privy Council for purely honorary purposes, and that body had grown too large to be of use in its former capacity. During this period the Cabinet was superseding the Privy Council, but had not yet permanently displaced the latter body as the authoritative adviser of the Crown.

3. During the third period of its existence, in the reign of William III., the Cabinet approached its modern form. It then became the *de facto* advisory body as well as the supreme executive authority, but was not fully accepted in all quarters.

4. "Finally, towards the close of the eighteenth century, the political conception of the Cabinet as a body — necessarily consisting (a) of members of the Legislature (b) of the same political views, and chosen from the party possessing a majority in the House of Commons; (c) prosecuting a concerted policy; (d) under a common responsibility to be

signified by collective resignation in the event of parliamentary censure; and (e) acknowledging a common subordination to one chief minister,— took definite shape in our modern theory of the Constitution, and so remains to the present day."[1]

[1] H. D. Traill's "Central Government," pp. 23-25.

CHAPTER V

THE COMPOSITION OF THE CABINET

REFERENCES: Anson's *Law and Custom of the Constitution*, ii. 144-204; Traill's *Central Government*, 31-153; Dod's *Parliamentary Companion* and English political and statistical almanacs.

THE American observer will note many differences between the English and the American Cabinets. In the United States, for example, we expect every President to appoint eight members — no more and no less — to constitute his advisory body; in England, however, the number of members in the Cabinet varies from time to time. There are ten high officials who always have seats in the Cabinet, and several others, usually from four to ten in number, who may or may not be included. The First Lord of the Treasury, the Chancellor of the Exchequer, the Lord High Chancellor, the Lord President of the Council, the First Lord of the Admiralty, and the five Secretaries of State are necessarily members of every Cabinet.

Before considering the functions of the Cabinet as a whole it may be well to glance for a moment at the departmental duties of the various members.

The Prime Minister, concerning whom we shall have occasion to speak more in detail presently, is usually the First Lord of the Treasury. His duties in this capacity are merely nominal, since the affairs of the Treasury Department are now managed by the

Chancellor of the Exchequer. Since the Prime Minister is the controlling force in the Cabinet, and, of necessity, a very busy man, this combination seems a happy one. At the close of the last Salisbury Ministry, however, the Prime Minister was the Lord Privy Seal, and Mr. A. J. Balfour, one of the strongest men in the Conservative ranks, and successor to Lord Salisbury in the Premiership, was the First Lord of the Treasury and the Leader of the House of Commons. That arrangement, however, was the result of rather exceptional circumstances. When the Salisbury Cabinet was organised in 1895, the Prime Minister assumed control of the Foreign Office. This combination was unusual and laborious, but was made because of Lord Salisbury's peculiar fitness to manage foreign affairs. It was deemed advisable, however, when the Cabinet was reorganised after the last general election in 1900, for the Premier to turn the arduous duties of the Foreign Office over to the Marquis of Lansdowne. This change was made, and the Premier became Lord Privy Seal. The Lord Privy Seal has had a seat in recent Cabinets, but has no specific departmental duties to perform.

The Chancellor of the Exchequer is the responsible head of the Treasury Department. He corresponds, in a general way, to our Secretary of the Treasury, but performs some duties which in the United States fall to the Committee on Ways and Means in the House of Representatives. He must provide for the necessary expenditure of the government, and must control the details of that expenditure. He must first make an estimate of the amount of money necessary to carry on the government for the year, and must then devise methods for raising the required sum. This is the preparation of the famous "Budget." It is considered good financiering to keep the income and the expenditure of the government practically an equation. A deficit would be embarrassing for obvious reasons, and a surplus should not be heaped up needlessly in the treasury vaults. The money should be allowed to "fructify in the pockets of the people." If, after making his estimate of expenses, he finds that the income of the government from present sources will probably be insufficient, it is his duty to recommend the levying of new taxes or the increasing of the old, or, possibly, the negotiation of a loan. In case he finds that the income will probably exceed the expenditure, he must select certain taxes to be abolished or decreased. In this way he keeps the income of the government as nearly equal as may be to the expenditure. It is not always possible, of course, to estimate accurately in advance the expenses and the income of the English government for a year. A discrepancy will sometimes occur. In case of a surplus no serious embarrassment ensues, but a deficit — and one may occur at any time due to sudden and unexpected expenditure — might lead to undesirable results. To avoid this difficulty the government has provided certain permanent funds which may be called upon in cases of emergency. The preparation of the Budget is a very complicated matter, but is sometimes done with almost scientific accuracy. The different kinds of taxes and the various modes of expenditure are numerous. A good many years ago a writer in the

"Edinburgh Review," in commenting on British taxes, wrote as follows: "Taxes upon every article which enters the mouth or covers the back or is placed upon the feet — taxes upon everything which it is pleasant to see, hear, feel, smell, or taste — taxes upon warmth, light, and locomotion — taxes on everything on earth and the waters under the earth — on everything that comes from abroad, or is grown at home — taxes on the raw material — taxes on every fresh value that is added to it by the industry of man — taxes on the sauce which pampers man's appetite and the drug that restores him to health — on the ermine which decorates the judges and the rope which hangs the criminal — on the poor man's salt and the rich man's spice — on the brass nails of the coffin and the ribbons of the bride — at bed or board, *couchant* or *levant*, we must pay; the schoolboy whips his taxed top; the beardless youth manages his taxed horse with a taxed whip on a taxed road; and the dying Englishman, pouring his medicine, which has paid seven per cent, into a spoon that has paid fifteen per cent, flings himself back upon his chintz bed, which has paid twenty-two per cent, makes his will on an eight-pound stamp, and expires in the arms of an apothecary, who has paid a license of an hundred pounds for the privilege of putting him to death. His whole property is then immediately taxed from two to ten per cent. Besides the probate, large fees are demanded for burying him in the chancel; his virtues are handed down to posterity on taxed marble; and he is then gathered to his fathers — to be taxed no more." [1]

[1] Quoted in Ewald's "The Crown and its Advisers," pp. 82-84.

While many of these taxes have been long since discontinued, the remaining ones are still numerous, and the avenues of expenditure are constantly increasing in number; thus the office of Chancellor of the Exchequer is no sinecure. The Chancellor of the Exchequer is always a member of the House of Commons, since money bills must originate in that chamber. The holder of the office is, of necessity, one of the most influential members of the Cabinet. The leadership of the House of Commons was often associated with this office, especially before the press of business became so great as to make such a combination burdensome. The office was held in the last Salisbury administration by Sir Michael Hicks-Beach,[1] and was held in recent Liberal Cabinets by Sir William Vernon-Harcourt, "the colossus of debate" on that side of the chamber.

The Lord High Chancellor of England corresponds to the Chief Justice of the United States Supreme Court in some respects, and to our Vice-President in others. He is the highest judicial officer of the realm, as well as the presiding officer of the House of Lords. The Lord Chancellor, however, has other important functions which the American officials do not possess. He is always a member of the Cabinet, and usually, though not of necessity, a member of the House of Lords. It is customary to elevate a commoner to the peerage when appointed to this office. The post is one of great dignity and carries with it important

[1] Sir Michael Hicks-Beach has since retired. The Cabinet was remodelled somewhat when Mr. A. J. Balfour succeeded Lord Salisbury in the Premiership in the summer of 1902.

patronage. When Parliament is opened by Royal Commission, as was the custom in the reign of Queen Victoria, instead of by the Crown personally, the Lord Chancellor is a member of the Commission and reads the Speech from the Throne. The Lord Chancellor of the last Salisbury administration was the Earl of Halsbury. The office was held by Lord Herschell during the recent Liberal administrations.

The Lord President of the Privy Council is always a Cabinet member, and although the duties of the body over which he presides are not so important as they once were, the presidency is still an office of great dignity and honour. The position was held under Lord Salisbury by the Duke of Devonshire, and was formerly occupied by Lord Rosebery.

There are in England five Secretaries of State; namely, (1) for Home Affairs; (2) for Foreign Affairs; (3) for the Colonies; (4) for War; and (5) for India. These departments developed gradually or were established from time to time as occasion required; the last being that for India, established in 1858. It was formerly customary for the Secretaries of State to live at the royal palace, and one of them now accompanies the King for the transaction of business on his various tours of the kingdom. At least one of the five must sit in the House of Lords, and one must always be in the city of London. The Secretaries for Foreign Affairs, the Colonies, and India may sit in either House, while custom would now seem to require that the Home Secretary should be a commoner. During the early years of the nineteenth century the Home Office was usually held by a peer, but for several decades the Home Secretary has been a commoner. The War Secretary has in recent years generally been a member of the House of Commons, although Lord Lansdowne held that office from 1895 to 1900. He was succeeded by the Rt. Hon. W. St. John Brodrick.

The Home Secretary has duties as heterogeneous as those of the Secretary of the Interior in the United States. He is chief of the constabulary, being charged with the preservation of peace and protection of property; he has charge of prisons, advises the Sovereign regarding the exercise of the prerogative of pardon, issues warrants for the extradition of criminals and registers aliens; he puts the law in motion when it is necessary to regulate labour in mines and factories, inspects coal mines, supervises insane asylums, and attends to scores of other duties imposed upon him either by custom or by statute. His department has to do with affairs concerning which members of Parliament are familiar, and its administration is criticised in the House of Commons with more than the usual severity. The incumbent under the last Salisbury Government was the Rt. Hon. C. T. Ritchie, and the office was held in the last Liberal Cabinet by Mr. H. H. Asquith, one of the most brilliant and forcible debaters that the Commons have listened to in recent years.

The Secretary of State for Foreign Affairs, as his title implies, has charge of all official dealings with foreign powers, under the supervision of the Prime Minister, and under the nominal though not real supervision of the Crown. His duties are far more uniform in character than are those of the Home Secretary. They correspond in a general way to those of the Secretary of State in the United States. As a matter of fact this latter official was styled the Secretary of Foreign Affairs when the office was held by Thomas Jefferson in Washington's first administration. Prior to 1900 the English office was held by Lord Salisbury, the greatest statesman now living in England. He was succeeded by Lord Lansdowne. Under Mr. Gladstone the office was filled with conspicuous success by Lord Rosebery, who afterward became the Premier. The post is a highly honourable one, and we find connected with it many of the most noted names in the recent history of England. The Duke of Wellington, Lord Palmerston, Lord John Russell, George Canning, and Charles James Fox are among the illustrious men who have presided over the affairs of the Foreign Office. The post in recent times has generally been held by a peer, but there is no reason why it could not be held by a commoner. Personal fitness for the delicate affairs of the office must determine the appointment. The suitable and available men are not numerous at any time, and the range of choice is limited.

In 1768 increasing business caused the appointment of a Secretary of State for the Colonial or "American Department," then so-called. The Colonial Office, in its modern form, originated at that time. The head of the department, as would be inferred from his title, has charge of the colonial affairs of the British Empire. Since the marvellous expansion of England the business of this office has been volumi-

The English Government

nous. The present[1] Secretary of State for the Colonies is Mr. Joseph Chamberlain, one of the ablest and best-known men in England. His management of the recent South African difficulty has been so satisfactory to a large part of the English people that he was looked upon by many as the logical successor to Lord Salisbury, when the latter resigned the Premiership. The office in recent years, though not at present, of course, has generally been held by a member of the House of Lords.

The Secretary of State for War corresponds in a general way to the Secretary of War in the American Cabinet. As the wars carried on by England have been frequent and significant, the War Secretary has been an important factor in the Cabinet. He is not a military man, but his under-secretary usually is, and he keeps his chief informed regarding the professional phase of the business. Rt. Hon. W. St. John Brodrick holds the office at the present time,[2] and Sir Henry Campbell-Bannerman, Leader of the Opposition in the House of Commons, was the incumbent during the recent Liberal administrations. The office may be held either by a peer or a commoner, but in recent years it has been found most convenient to have the War Secretary in the House of Commons.

The Secretary of State for India has general supervision of the governmental affairs of that country. He must be ready to defend his administration in Parliament at any time when called upon to do so. The post was established in 1858, and was held in the last Salisbury administration by Lord George Ham-

[1] October, 1902. [2] *Ibid.*

ilton, a member of the House of Commons. The Secretary may sit in either House.

The First Lord of the Admiralty in England corresponds in a general way to the Secretary of the Navy in the United States. He may sit in either House, and if a commoner, he presents and defends the estimates for the navy. If he sits in the Upper House, he is represented in the Commons by a parliamentary secretary. It might be added that each great department of the government is represented in each House of Parliament either by the head of the department or by a parliamentary secretary. The Earl of Selborne was appointed First Lord of the Admiralty after the general election of 1900. Prior to 1900 the office was held by the Rt. Hon. George J. Goshen, now a member of the House of Lords.

The ten ministers whose duties have been briefly described above always have seats in the Cabinet. In addition to these there are several other high officials who may or may not be included. The Lord Privy Seal and the President of the Board of Trade have had seats in recent Cabinets, Liberal and Conservative alike, and may probably be looked upon as permanent members. In the Cabinets of recent years a seat has also been given either to the Lord Lieutenant of Ireland or to the Chief Secretary for Ireland. The President of the Local Government Board, the President of the Board of Agriculture, the Lord Chancellor of Ireland, the Chancellor of the Duchy of Lancaster, the Secretary for Scotland, the Postmaster-General, the First Commissioner of Works, and the Vice-President of the Committee of Council on Education may or may not be accorded seats. The importance of the office at the particular time when the Cabinet is being formed, and the influence of the holder, as well as the personal wishes of the Prime Minister, are factors in the decision of the matter. The Premier may invite a member of Parliament to accept any one of the above offices, and may or may not grant him a seat in the Cabinet. Some of the above-mentioned offices are important in themselves and others are not so. The Lord Privy Seal has practically no duties to perform and usually receives no salary.[1] The post is important in that it usually carries with it a seat in the Cabinet. In 1870 Sir Charles Dilke moved to abolish the office as useless, but Mr. Gladstone opposed the proposition on the ground that it was well to have a man in the Cabinet not burdened by the cares of a department, who could devote his time to the general interests of the Government. The motion was lost by a vote of nearly three to one. The Lord Lieutenant of Ireland is now also largely a figure-head as far as actual governmental duties are concerned. In theory he conducts the executive government of Ireland subject to instructions from the Home Department, but in practice the work is done by the Chief Secretary for Ireland. The Lord Lieutenant represents the pomp, splendour, and ceremony of the government, while his Chief Secretary does the work. Inasmuch as pomp, splendour, and ceremony are expensive luxuries, the Lord Lieutenant receives a magnificent salary of

---

[1] The present incumbent receives a salary of £2000 a year.

£20,000 per year, while the Secretary, who does all the work, receives less than one fourth of that amount, probably on the theory that he is too busy to spend a larger salary. The theoretical functions of the Lord Lieutenant of Ireland are well set forth in Mr. A. C. Ewald's little book, "The Crown and its Advisers;"[1] but should the student desire to know the practice as well as the theory of the matter, he will find Sir William R. Anson's "Law and Custom of the Constitution" a far safer guide.

The English Cabinet, as above noted, is not fixed as to numbers, but varies in size according to the will of the Prime Minister. The general tendency has been for Cabinets to grow steadily larger. The first Cabinet of the reign of George I. consisted of eight members, two or three of whom were not in regular attendance. The first one in the reign of George III. contained fourteen members, while the North Cabinet of 1770 contained only seven. In 1783 the Cabinet of the younger Pitt also consisted of seven members, but immediately after his time we find them growing rapidly larger, consisting of from ten to sixteen members. In 1835 Mr. Peel believed that they were getting too large and expressed his opinion that the government would be "infinitely better conducted" by a Cabinet of nine members than by one of thirteen or fourteen. Mr. Disraeli in 1874 constructed a Cabinet of twelve members, and the number has varied, generally increasing, from time to time since. The present Cabinet is unusually large, containing twenty members. The consequence of the increased size of

[1] Pages 61-62.

the Cabinet has been that the Prime Minister confers more frequently with a few of the leading members than with the entire body. It may be that history is repeating itself and that another "inner circle" may develop as the Cabinet increases in size.

It may be well to note at this time the difference in meaning between the terms "Cabinet" and "Ministry." The terms are often used synonymously, but incorrectly so. The Ministry is broader than the Cabinet. Only certain ones among the ministers are members of the Cabinet. Mr. Gerald Balfour, for example, when Chief Secretary for Ireland, was a member of the Ministry, but not of the Cabinet. He sat on the Ministerial or Treasury Bench in the House of Commons, but did not attend the meetings of the Cabinet. The Ministry includes all of the Cabinet members and some others in addition.

In a subsequent discussion it will be necessary to speak of the historical development of the power of the Prime Minister. A brief statement of his present attributes seems essential at this point.

The Prime Minister.

The Prime Minister is chosen by the Crown, and he in turn selects the remaining members of the Cabinet, subject to the royal approval. In theory the choice is free in each case, but in practice there are many restrictions. Theoretically the Crown may appoint any one whom he wishes as Prime Minister, but as a matter of practical politics he is compelled to appoint that man who can command the support of the majority in the House of Commons. This means that the Crown

The Selection of the Premier.

must appoint, upon the resignation of one Ministry, the leader of the opposite party. No one else could command the support necessary to carry on the government. It is not always easy to determine, however, who the real party leader is. When Mr. Gladstone was in Parliament there was, of course, no question regarding the leadership of the Liberal party; and in the days of Walpole, Peel, the two Pitts, and Lord Palmerston there could be no question regarding the leadership of the party to which these men belonged. So, too, Lord Salisbury was the natural leader of the Conservatives up to the time of his retirement; but when he resigned the Premiership it was not easy to foretell the hands into which the reins of Conservative leadership were destined to fall. Arthur J. Balfour and Joseph Chamberlain both seemed to be in the ascendency, — the former because of his successful leadership in the House of Commons, and the latter because of his able management of the Colonial Office during the recent South African difficulty. In such a case as this it might seem that there would be opportunity for the exercise of discretion on the part of the Crown. However, it is not at all probable that, even in this case, the choice of the Crown was uninfluenced. A parallel instance occurred in 1894. In that year Mr. Gladstone, owing to defective eyesight and other physical infirmities of advanced age, resigned the Premiership. In his absence there was no other man in the Liberal party at the time conspicuously in the ascendant. The two most prominent men were the polished Lord Rosebery and Sir William Vernon-Harcourt, "the fighting Ajax of his party." There was a difference of opinion as to who should succeed, but the Liberal leaders in the two Houses conferred upon the matter and recommended Lord Rosebery to the Queen.[1] He was immediately appointed Prime Minister. A similar case occurring in the future would probably be settled in the same way. In most instances, however, the wheel of time brings some one to the front entitled by natural endowments to the leadership of his colleagues. It is sometimes said that the appointment of the Prime Minister is the only personal act which the Crown now performs in the government. This is undoubtedly true; and when we consider the present practice in regard to this matter, it would seem that the substance is gone and only the empty form remains.

In the same way the Prime Minister is restricted in the selection of his colleagues. Theoretically he is free to choose, except that his appointments must be approved by the Crown as a matter of form; but practically he must appoint those leaders of his party who will strengthen the Ministry and enable him to command and to retain the support of the Commons. When the Conservatives came into power in 1895, the Cabinet was made up by Lord Salisbury; but it was a fact practically assured before the Cabinet was formed that such men as Arthur J. Balfour, Joseph Chamberlain, and Sir Michael Hicks-Beach would be given places. Should the Liberal party come into power and Lord Rosebery be made Prime Minister, he could hardly leave

Appointment of Ministers.

[1] See McCarthy's "History of our own Times," vol. iii. p. 309.

out of his Cabinet such men as John Morley, James Bryce, and Henry Campbell-Bannerman. No Cabinet could do efficient work for any length of time without the services of the recognised leaders of the party which it represents. In both of these instances, then, the Crown and the Prime Minister are greatly restricted in practice in the selection of Cabinet ministers. The simple, ultimate fact is that the will of the people, as indicated by the majority in the House of Commons, now prevails in the English government.

When a parliamentary leader is summoned by the King and intrusted with the formation of a new Ministry, it will take him, as a rule, only a very few days to complete the task. As Mr. Bagehot used to say, there are always some men in the party who cannot be left out and others who cannot be included. The available Cabinet timber is thus somewhat restricted. When the Prime Minister has completed his work, the "London Gazette" announces the fact that certain members of Parliament have been selected to preside over the great departments of state, but no mention is made of the Cabinet in an official way. In fact, there was a time when the membership of the Cabinet was not definitely and generally known by the public; but, of course, no such state of affairs could exist in these days of journalistic enterprise.

The Prime Minister sometimes sits in one House and sometimes in the other. The Marquis of Salisbury was a member of the House of Lords, while Mr. Gladstone, of course, during his various terms of office held a seat in the Commons. Canning held that for purposes of expedi-

Premier either a Peer or Commoner.

ency the Prime Minister should always be a member of the Commons. Sir Robert Peel expressed himself to the same effect, but in the latter part of his career came to the conclusion that the Prime Minister should sit in the House of Lords, and thus escape that vexation of spirit which is ever present in the House of Commons,—the storm centre of the English political world. As a matter of fact, the choice cannot as a rule be made arbitrarily. The Prime Minister must be the real leader of his party, the strong man of the majority, whether a peer or a commoner. In the early days of the Premiership the majority of the Prime Ministers were members of the House of Lords, but since the accession of George III. the time has been quite equally divided between the peers and the commoners.

The Prime Minister is now almost invariably the First Lord of the Treasury. The Chancellor of the Exchequer is now the working head of the Treasury Department, and the First Lord of the Treasury has almost no departmental duties to perform. *Premier usually the First Lord of the Treasury.* This being the case, the Premier may devote his time and energies to the work of general supervision. During the early history of Cabinet government the office of First Lord of the Treasury was not so intimately associated with the Premiership as at present, but since 1762 the Prime Minister had invariably held that office down to the first Ministry of Lord Salisbury in 1885. Lord Salisbury had a remarkably strong grasp upon foreign affairs, and preferred to preside over the Foreign Office, although its duties were exacting, until failing strength and advancing years made it advisable for him to assume a post whose duties were not so arduous. He became Lord Privy Seal in 1900.

Even a casual survey of the duties of the Prime Minister must lead to the conclusion that he is a very busy man. The testimony of the Prime Ministers themselves serves to fortify this opinion. A suggestion of the manifold duties which devolve upon the Prime Minister will be found in the following words of Sir Robert Peel, himself one of the greatest of the Premiers: "Take the case of the Prime Minister. You must presume that he reads every important despatch from every foreign court. He cannot consult with the Secretary of State for Foreign Affairs, and exercise the influence which he ought to have with respect to the conduct of foreign affairs, unless he be master of everything of real importance passing in that department. It is the same with respect to other departments; India, for instance; how can the Prime Minister be able to judge of the course of policy with regard to India, unless he be cognisant of all the current important correspondence? In the case of Ireland and the Home Department it is the same. Then the Prime Minister has the patronage of the Crown to exercise, which you say, and justly say, is of so much importance and of so much value; he has to make inquiries into the qualifications of the persons who are candidates; he has to conduct the whole of the communications with the Sovereign; he has to write, probably with his own hand, the letters in reply to all persons of station who address themselves to him;

he has to receive deputations on public business; during the sitting of Parliament he is expected to attend six or seven hours a day, while Parliament is sitting, for four or five days in the week; at least he is blamed if he is absent."

In the light of these manifold and important duties it seems well that the Premier should be First Lord of the Treasury, or hold some other sinecure office in the Cabinet. Even in this case he must avail himself as largely as possible of the services of others, and thus avoid the depressing effect of an avalanche of details, if he would give his best thought and energies to matters of governmental policy. "If you chain a man's head to a ledger," said the late Walter Bagehot, "and keep him constantly adding up, and take a pound off his salary whenever he stops, you can't expect him to have a sound conviction on Catholic emancipation, tithes, and original ideas on the Transcaucasian provinces."[1] When you hold a man's nose to the grindstone you cannot expect his horizon to be broad and his vision unerring.

[1] "English Constitution," p. 442.

CHAPTER VI

THE FUNDAMENTAL PRINCIPLES OF THE CABINET

REFERENCES: Todd's *Parliamentary Government in England*, i. 253–290, and ii. 1–24; Anson's *Law and Custom of the Constitution*, ii. 118–136; Bagehot's *English Constitution*, 69–100; Courtney's *Working Constitution of the United Kingdom*, 123–135; Ewald's *Crown and its Advisers*, Lecture on *Ministers*, Syme's *Representative Government in England*, 61–94 and 130–158.

IT will be noted from what has been said that the Cabinet consists of members of Parliament; that its members belong to the party dominant in the House of Commons and hence agree in political views; that they settle upon a definite policy before going before Parliament; that they resign when they lose the confidence of the majority in the Commons; and that they are dominated by a First or Prime Minister. These fundamental principles of the modern Cabinet were slow in being established, and a glance at their development may facilitate our investigation.

Before the rise of parliamentary government in England, and while the King had real and practical authority in the affairs of state, there was a decided objection on the part of the members of the House of Commons to permitting those who held office under the Crown to hold seats in that chamber. There was a feeling, not without foundation, that such officials might degenerate into mere tools of the King. Attempts were

Members of the Cabinet in Parliament.

made from time to time to exclude such "place-men" from the popular branch of the legislature. Finally in the Act of Settlement (1700-1701) it was provided "That no person who has an office or place of profit under the King, or receives a pension from the Crown, shall be capable of serving as a member of the House of Commons." This clause, if enforced, would, of course, prevent the Cabinet from assuming its present form. It was repealed, however, before it came into operation, and no mischief was done. The clause was inserted with the best of intentions, and there was reason for it at the time of its enactment; but after the power of the King became merely nominal, there was no valid reason for its retention. In fact, there were weighty reasons why some officers of the Crown, Cabinet members at any rate, should have seats in the House of Commons and thus be in a position to explain and to defend the acts of the Government. Such members could no longer be tools of the King, since after the rise of parliamentary government, the Crown ceased to have any effective control over legislation. The repeal of the clause which was intended to prevent the officers of the Crown from sitting in the House of Commons was accompanied by an Act passed in 1707, whereby a member of the Lower House, upon assuming a place in the Cabinet, vacated his seat, but was allowed to present himself to his constituents for re-election. This arrangement prevails at the present time.

Since the peers have always been looked upon as the hereditary advisers of the Crown, there could be no logical objection to the presence of officers of the

Crown in the House of Lords, and members of the Cabinet have always had seats in that chamber without objection. At present Cabinet members are not only allowed but expected to have seats in Parliament. The exceptions to this rule in recent years have not been important. Mr. Gladstone was appointed Secretary of State for the Colonies in Sir Robert Peel's Cabinet, and was defeated when standing for re-election to the House of Commons. He continued, however, to serve in the Cabinet without a seat in Parliament, until the resignation of the Ministry in 1846, six months after his appointment. This is an exceptional case and was commented upon as such in the Commons at the time.

In the early days of parliamentary government it seemed best, or at least expedient, to have the Cabinet composed of men of opposing political views. The early Cabinets of William III. **Unanimity.** were constituted in this way, but the evil results of the political discord thus engendered were not long in displaying themselves, and the King came to the conclusion that a Cabinet composed entirely of Whigs would be more aggressive and in every way more satisfactory. He made changes gradually until his object was attained, and the experience of two centuries testifies to the wisdom of the innovation. However, the plan once introduced was not consistently adhered to. In some of the subsequent Cabinets of William, as well as in those of Queen Anne, we find men of opposite political beliefs. The same state of affairs continued in the reigns of George I. and II., except when the masterful spirit of Robert Walpole dominated the entire government and produced a political unity, which probably would not have otherwise existed. After the fall of Walpole, discord again prevailed and continued until the younger Pitt became Prime Minister in 1783. Here again a master hand moulded the affairs of state after its own fashion, and the supremacy of Pitt caused a political unity in the Cabinet until his death in 1806. After the death of Pitt affairs were somewhat complicated by the customary interference of George III., but during one of his periods of insanity political unity in Cabinet affairs was recognised as an established governmental principle. In 1812 it was proposed to construct a Cabinet composed of both Whigs and Tories. The proposition was declined on the ground that such a Ministry could not pursue a " uniform and beneficial course of policy." Such had certainly been the experience of the past. The governmental leaders had seen the disadvantages of mixed Cabinets and had determined to have no more of them. From this time (1812), then, to the present the Cabinets have been composed of men of the same political beliefs. They have not always been of the same party, but have agreed to act together in all important matters. Mr. Joseph Chamberlain, for example, the present Secretary of State for the Colonies, is a Liberal Unionist and holds a place in a Conservative Cabinet. This is not inconsistent with the principle of political unity in Cabinet affairs, as the Liberal Unionists are at present acting with the Conservatives in much the same way that the Silver Republicans are co-operating with the Democratic party in America. A

Cabinet may be formed by the coalition of two or more political parties, but there must be unity of action. When a policy has been decided upon by the Cabinet, each member is bound to defend and to explain the measures requisite for the working out of this ministerial policy. There are, it is true, certain matters which the Cabinet agrees to consider "open questions." In these cases there may be a disagreement among the members without violating the principle of unanimity. Should a minister vote against a Government measure, however, not an open question, he should place his resignation in the hands of the Prime Minister at once. The Prime Minister may then advise the acceptance of the resignation or may continue the member in office, as he chooses.

In the early days of parliamentary government changes in the membership of the Cabinet were made gradually, and the simultaneous resignation of the entire body, so familiar in later years, was unknown. *Collective Resignation.* At present, as soon as the Cabinet loses the confidence of the House of Commons the members resign in a body and are replaced by an entirely new Cabinet representing the party dominant in the Lower House. This custom began in 1782, when the Ministry of Lord North resigned because a vote of want of confidence in the Commons was inevitable. This is the first instance of such collective resignation, and since that time every Cabinet has come to an end when it has ceased to command the support of the majority of the House of Commons. In such a case a change is inevitable, and the change, since 1782, "has invariably been simultaneous and complete."

The ascendency of the Prime Minister marks an exceedingly important step in the development of the Cabinet. The disappearance of the King from the Cabinet meetings was followed by the appearance of the Premier.

Subordination to a First or Prime Minister.

When the early Hanoverians habitually absented themselves from meetings of the Cabinet, there was need of a guiding and controlling hand. In such a state of affairs it was inevitable that some strong man in the Cabinet should attain a pre-eminence over his colleagues. Sir Robert Walpole was that man. He dominated the Cabinet and has the distinction of being the first Prime Minister of England, in the modern sense of that term. When the House of Hanover came to the throne in 1714 parliamentary government had been fully established, but not perfected as we know it now. The government was carried on at the time through the various departments in a more or less independent way. It was not centralised. There was no Chief Minister whose supremacy was recognised by his colleagues, and as a consequence there was a conspicuous and lamentable lack of unity in action. This state of affairs continued until the transcendent genius of Sir Robert Walpole elevated him above his fellows. Walpole served under the first two Georges, being First Lord of the Treasury from 1715 to 1717, and again from 1721 to 1742. During much of this time his sway was practically unlimited, and he was First Minister in fact, but not in name. The title "Prime Minister" had not been adopted at the time, although it was clearly seen that Walpole was such in reality. There was a strong prejudice against the elevation of a minister above his colleagues, and in 1741 Walpole himself resented "the title of Prime Minister as an imputation." However, his attitude towards the title did not change the facts, and during the greater part of his term of office, Robert Walpole was a Prime Minister in the modern sense of the term. He was a leader because Nature intended him to be one. He was endowed to a remarkable degree with the masterful traits of leadership. The man who was described by Lord Campbell as being probably the most dexterous party leader in the history of England could not long be kept in a secondary place. His genius would not down. Walpole's position, however, was somewhat in advance of his time. The sentiment of the country was not entirely in favour of submitting to the sway of a First Minister. A protest signed by thirty-one members of the House of Lords declared "that a sole, or even a first minister, is an officer unknown to the law of Britain, inconsistent with the Constitution of this country, and destructive of liberty in any government whatever." The protest asked the removal of Walpole as a "minister dangerous to the King and the kingdom." At the same time a motion made in the Commons condemned him because he had "grasped in his own hands every branch of government; had attained the sole direction of affairs; monopolised all the powers of the Crown; compassed the disposal of all places, pensions, titles, and rewards,"— exactly what the present Premier is doing and is expected to do. As the orthodox sermons of to-day would have been rank heresy a generation ago, so the powers of the Premier, which are now considered constitutional, savoured of despotism and usurpation a century and a half ago. Walpole ran counter to the tide of public opinion as expressed in the House of Commons, and in 1742 he resigned his office and retired to that haven of rest, — the House of Lords.

Not every generation, however, produces a Walpole; and his immediate successors in the Treasury Office being men of smaller calibre, exercised only a dubious sort of leadership. The Pitts, however, were real leaders, and when the younger man became Prime Minister in 1783, his authority over his colleagues in the Cabinet was fully recognised. The office of Prime Minister was now an accepted fact, and it was evident that his great power had sprung up from the ruins of the royal prerogative. Lord North recognised the true status of things when he said in 1783, "The King ought to be treated with all sort of respect and attention, but the appearance of power is all that a king of this country can have." Lord North was somewhat in advance of his time in making the above statement, but the tendency was strongly in that direction, and gradually the personal power of the Crown vanished, and for it the supremacy of the Prime Minister was substituted.

After being able to impose his will upon his colleagues in the Cabinet, it only remained that he should have the power of appointing them to make his supremacy complete. This came about during the latter part of the reign of George III. At that time it was generally agreed that the Sovereign should appoint the Prime Minister, while the latter should select the other members of the Cabinet. This arrangement still obtains, subject to some practical restrictions to be noted later. The force of precedent and the process of evolution are well exemplified in the development of the power of the Prime Minister. According to legal theory the Premier is simply a privy councillor and has no more power than any one of a hundred others; but practically the members of the Cabinet have been raised in importance far above their fellow councillors, and the Prime Minister has gained by custom a supremacy over his colleagues in the Cabinet. This supremacy, too, is real and not nominal. The Prime Minister may insist upon the adoption of his views by his colleagues or may resign; which event, *ipso facto*, dissolves the Cabinet. It is a rather peculiar fact that while the Prime Minister is still unknown to the law his hand is the guiding and controlling force in governmental affairs. No other officer in England compares with him in actual ruling power. The authority of the Sovereign is a mere shadow in comparison. As long as the Premier can command the support of the people as represented in the House of Commons, there is almost no limit to his governmental power; but as soon as he forfeits this popular confidence, he is reduced to the ranks, and another rules in his stead.

CHAPTER VII

MISCELLANEOUS PROVISIONS RELATING TO THE CABINET

REFERENCES: Bryce's *American Commonwealth*, i. 81–91; Todd's *Parliamentary Government in England*, ii. 25–51; Taswell-Langmead's *English Constitutional History*, 706–715.

IT is quite essential that the great departments of state should have members in each House authorised to represent them. When the head of a department sits in one House there is a parliamentary secretary or other officer in the other House to answer questions, and to defend and to explain the policy of the department. Thus while Lord Lansdowne, the Secretary of State for Foreign Affairs, sat in the House of Lords, his under-secretary, Viscount Cranbourne, the eldest son of Lord Salisbury, had a seat in the Commons and represented the Foreign Office in that chamber. Viscount Cranbourne was thus the official spokesman for the Salisbury Government in the Commons as far as foreign affairs were concerned. He might be called upon at any time to speak for the Foreign Office. A cablegram from London bearing the date August 4, 1900, brought the information that the Rt. Hon. St. John Brodrick, then under-secretary for the Foreign Office, had announced in the Commons a definite program of action in regard to the

Apportionment of Members between the two Houses.

"Boxer" disturbance then prevailing. Lord Salisbury was Secretary of State for Foreign Affairs at the time.

There can be no fixed rule regulating the apportionment of the Cabinet members between the two Houses. Obviously, the Prime Minister must get the best men available regardless of the Houses in which they happen to sit. In the early days of parliamentary government the large majority of Cabinet members came from the House of Lords. In fact, some Cabinets were composed almost exclusively of peers. In recent years the proportion has been changed, owing to the increased importance of the House of Commons.

The first Cabinet of the reign of George III. consisted of fourteen members, thirteen of whom had seats in the House of Lords. In 1783, the younger Pitt, then Prime Minister, was the only commoner in the Cabinet. The Addington Cabinet of 1801 was more evenly divided, — five being peers and four commoners. In 1822 Lord Liverpool's Cabinet consisted of nine peers and six commoners. Since the passage of the Reform Bill of 1832 the division has been more nearly equal, the preponderance in some cases going to the House of Commons. Lord Palmerston's Cabinet of 1859, for example, consisted of ten commoners and five peers. No attempt has been made to fix the apportionment by rigid rule, but Mr. Disraeli in 1864 gave it as his opinion that the Secretary of State for War, the First Lord of the Admiralty, a majority of the Secretaries of State, and a "great majority" of the administration officers should have seats in the House of Commons. Some subsequent Cabinets have been constructed according to this general plan. Law and custom, particularly the latter, afford some guidance in the case of specific offices. According to the law at least one of the five Secretaries of State must sit in the Upper House; and the Lord Chancellor, the Lord President of the Council, and the Lord Privy Seal are practically always peers, although Mr. Gladstone was Lord Privy Seal in his fourth Cabinet, constructed in 1892. In recent years the Cabinet members have been quite equally divided between the two Houses. The last Salisbury Cabinet contained twenty members, ten of whom sat in the House of Commons.

The advantages of a seat in the House of Commons as compared with those of a seat in the Upper Chamber have been much discussed. Since the House of Commons is the storm centre of English politics it is desirable for various reasons that many of the heads of departments should sit in that chamber; on the other hand, however, the burdens of continuous and prolonged attendance upon the sessions of the Commons on the part of Cabinet members have proved in many instances to be wellnigh intolerable. The sessions of the Lords are usually brief and comparatively uneventful, while those of the Commons often extend far into the night and not infrequently last until the morning sun tips the spires of Westminster. It will be generally true that the minister, attending the short and soothing sessions of the Lords, will have more of time and vitality to bestow upon the policy of the Cabinet and the problems of his department than he who sits through the longer and more exacting sessions of the Commons.

It was provided in the reign of Queen Anne, by a statute previously referred to, that when a member of the House of Commons accepted an office of profit under the Crown he thereby vacated his seat in Parliament. The statute also provided, however, that in certain cases he might offer himself to his constituents for re-election. This statute, in substance, is now in force; and when a member of the Lower House accepts a Cabinet position he must, with a few exceptions, stand for re-election. This process has been considered unnecessary by many, and various attempts have been made from time to time to relieve the Cabinet member from the necessity of running the gauntlet of election for a second time. The movement has failed in every instance, however; the principal argument against it being that the member was elected while free to devote his time to the interests of his constituents, but that after accepting a place in the Cabinet he must of necessity devote the major portion of his time to the general duties of the Cabinet rather than to the specific interests of his constituency. It is evident that Mr. Arthur J. Balfour, when First Lord of the Treasury and Leader of the House of Commons, was not able to give the same attention to his Manchester constituency that he would have been in case he held no Cabinet position. It sometimes occurs that a candidate for a seat in the House of Commons makes ante-election promises, the fulfil-

Cabinet Members re-elected.

ment of which is impossible in case he holds a place in the Cabinet. In view of these facts it has been held that the constituents should have an opportunity of withdrawing their election, in case they choose to do so. This line of argument has prevailed to the present day and has defeated all attempts to make re-election unnecessary. The law does provide, however, that a man may change from one Cabinet office to another without going before his constituents for another re-election. For example, when Mr. Chamberlain was selected for the Colonial Office, he was re-elected to his seat in the House of Commons. There was a rumour at a later time that he was being urged to take charge of the War Office instead. Had he done this it would not have been necessary for him to ask his Birmingham constituents to re-elect him again. In case it had been, they would probably have done so, as he has represented the same constituency since 1876. It does sometimes happen, however, that re-election is no easy process. Mr. Gladstone was once defeated under these circumstances. He was selected for a Cabinet position by Sir Robert Peel in 1845 and defeated when he stood for re-election. A special effort is sometimes made by the opposite party to defeat a conspicuous candidate for re-election. In case of such defeat, however, an obscure man of the same party, representing a safe parliamentary division, may be induced to vacate his seat in order that the conspicuous leader may stand as a candidate in his division. The man making the sacrifice is then suitably rewarded by office or title.

Parliament is not in session on Saturday, as a rule, hence this is used as the meeting day for the Cabinet.

Meetings. Meetings are, however, often held on other days, when necessity or convenience seems to require it. After the prorogation of Parliament, which usually occurs not later than August 11, it is customary for Cabinet meetings to be suspended until October, or even later. The ministers take their vacations at this time; and as the English grouse law expires on August 12, scores of dignified and learned law-makers may be seen at this season of the year tramping through the forests and fields of Merrie England in search of game.

There is no fixed place of meeting, but as a matter of convenience the Cabinet often assembles at the Foreign Office. It frequently meets at the residence of the Premier, or at any other convenient place. As the body is unknown to the law, so also it has no fixed place of meeting, no definite number of members, no record of proceedings, and no fixed time for assembling. There is no specified quorum, and the body may convene even in the absence of the Prime Minister. On the other hand, the Premier may in an emergency take the reins in his own hands and act without consulting his colleagues.

The questions to be discussed at the meetings are usually not announced beforehand, but the observant minister generally knows what is likely to come up. Departmental details are not discussed at the Cabinet meetings. The head of each department is supposed to manage, and actually does manage, the details of his own department. Only matters of general policy occupy the attention of the Cabinet as a body.

The decision of the Cabinet is binding upon the individual members. After a matter has been discussed and decided, it is looked upon as settled. It is then the action of the entire body and not of the majority merely. If a member feels that he cannot support and defend the position taken by the Cabinet, he should resign at once. There should be no symptoms of discord in the official family of the Premier.

The deliberations of the Cabinet are carried on with the utmost secrecy. This element constitutes an essential part of the oath of the privy councillor, and in the case of the Cabinet minister it is all-important. There is no clerk present who might divulge the proceedings, no records are kept, and even private memoranda are frowned upon. It is, however, sometimes necessary to make a minute of the decisions to be transmitted to the Crown; but not infrequently the Crown is advised of such decisions by the Prime Minister in person. Comparatively little in connection with the meeting is reduced to writing. The Duke of Wellington and Sir Robert Peel were accustomed to bring memoranda to the Cabinet meeting in order to facilitate and systematise business. Other Prime Ministers, and even subordinate ministers, have from time to time adopted the same plan.

While Cabinet meetings are, as a rule, exceedingly exclusive gatherings, it does sometimes happen that a man not a member is invited to advise with that body. In 1848 the Duke of Wellington, then Commander-in-

Chief of the army, was invited to meet the Cabinet to consider the Chartist disturbance then imminent in London. Such cases as this, however, are quite exceptional, and the meetings of the Cabinet are, as a rule, confined exclusively to the members of the body.

The Prime Minister is, of course, the guiding force of the meeting, although questions are sometimes decided by a majority vote of the Cabinet contrary to his wishes. He may, and sometimes does, whip his colleagues into line and compel them to adopt his views.

The Premier is the official link between the Crown and the Cabinet. When a decision has been reached, but not before, it becomes the duty of the Premier to acquaint the Sovereign with the facts. The Prime Minister is also the proper person through whom despatches and other important documents should be placed before the Crown. This is done nominally for the purpose of obtaining the royal pleasure regarding the matters discussed, but as a matter of fact the Crown must ultimately yield to the wishes of the Prime Minister. In case the policy of the Premier were not agreeable to the Sovereign and the latter should insist upon his resignation, it would be found impossible, under ordinary circumstances, to find another to take his place who could command the confidence of the House of Commons.

It is also the duty of the Prime Minister to submit to the Crown a synopsis of each day's debates in Parliament. When the Premier is a peer the Leader of the House of Commons prepares the abstract of the debates in the Lower House.

In bringing our discussion of the Cabinet meeting to a close, it might be well to refer in passing to the final meeting of the Cabinet. When the members are about to retire from office voluntarily, they meet at the royal palace and surrender the keys, wands, seals, and other official insignia to the Crown, or to some one designated by the Crown to receive them. The things thus surrendered are in turn handed over to their successors in office.

It is an old saying that republics are ungrateful. This seems comparatively true when we consider what England and other European monarchies are accustomed to do for their civil **Residences.** officers by way of residences, salaries, and pensions. We supply the White House for the use of the President, but do little more in the way of providing official residences. In England several of the Cabinet members, the Speaker of the House of Commons, and several other high officials are provided with residences. In addition to this, of course, the Royal Family is well cared for in this respect. The late Queen had four residences, — one at Windsor on the Thames near London, one at Osborne on the Isle of Wight, one at Balmoral in Scotland, and Buckingham Palace in London. Two of these, however, — the ones at Balmoral and Osborne, — were the private and not the official residences of the Queen.

The salaries paid to members of the English Cabinet are much higher than those paid to corresponding officers in America; and it is also true that **Salaries.** ministers' salaries in England were formerly much higher than they are at present, yet even now they seem rather generous when compared with those paid in the United States. Our Cabinet members are paid a uniform salary of $8000 per year. In the English Cabinet the members, aside from the Lord Privy Seal, who is usually unpaid,[1] receive from £2000 to £20,000 per year. The majority of the principal working members — the First Lord of the Treasury, the Chancellor of the Exchequer, and the five Secretaries of State — receive £5000 per year, while the Lord Chancellor of Ireland receives £8000, the Lord High Chancellor, £10,000, and the Lord Lieutenant of Ireland, £20,000, — the highest salary in the Cabinet. The scale of salaries was adjusted in 1831, when the remuneration was reduced upon motion of the Cabinet members themselves. The spirit displayed on that occasion is in striking contrast to that exhibited in our "Salary Grab Act" of 1873. A Committee of the House of Commons investigated the salaries of the ministers in 1850 and reported that they were "at the lowest amount which is consistent with the requirements of the public service." They consequently refused to recommend a reduction. It was urged at the time that these great offices should be sufficiently lucrative to enable men of small property but of marked talents to occupy them. It is a fact that some of England's most noted statesmen have been men of decidedly limited means. Fox, Burke, Canning, and the two Pitts are notable examples of this class of men. To make it possible for such men as these to continue to offer their services

---

[1] The Lord Privy Seal in the last Salisbury Cabinet received a salary of £2000 per year.

to the state, the committee refused to recommend any reduction in salaries. It might be remarked in passing that this same line of argument might be used in favour of the payment of members of Parliament, who at present receive no salary whatever.

As noted in a previous chapter, the principle of the pension is carried much further in England than in America. We are familiar with it as a reward for military service, but in England it is granted to civil officers as well. According to an Act of 1834, amended in 1869, pensions may be granted to retiring Cabinet members varying in amount from £1000 to £2000 per year. The recipient of the pension must have been in the service of the state for at least four years, and must declare that his own private income is insufficient to support him in his customary dignity.

Pensions.

CHAPTER VIII

THE CABINET'S RESPONSIBILITY TO PARLIAMENT

REFERENCES: Dicey's *Law of the Constitution*, 303-305; Bagehot's *English Constitution*, 244-286; Todd's *Parliamentary Government in England*, ii. 113-137; Anson's *Law and Custom of the Constitution*, ii. 136-140; Syme's *Representative Government in England*, 195-220; Whates's *Third Salisbury Administration*, 1-17.

IT is now a maxim of the English government that the Cabinet is responsible to Parliament. This at present practically means responsibility to the House of Commons. An adverse vote in the Commons terminates the existence of the Ministry, but a similar vote in the House of Lords does not. It is always essential, then, that the existing Ministry should have the confidence and support of a majority of the members of the House of Commons. Should the latter body vote a want of confidence, or pass a motion of censure upon the existing Ministry, or defeat a measure advocated by the Cabinet and declared to be of "vital importance," or pass any measure contrary to the advice and consent of the ministers of the Crown, — in such cases as these the Ministry would be compelled to resign or to appeal to the country.

The present method of voting a want of confidence in the existing Ministry dates from about 1841. It simply declares a lack of confidence but states no reasons therefor. It is exceedingly direct and expeditious in its operation, is a powerful weapon, and should be used sparingly. Those who vote a want of confidence in an existing Ministry should be ready, if called upon, to form a new Cabinet and carry on the government. Putting a Ministry out of existence is a serious matter, and carries with it grave responsibilities; hence it should not be done hastily or for partisan purposes.

A vote of censure also usually terminates the existence of the Ministry. When passed by the House of Lords, it is not fatal but will set the ministers to thinking. When passed by the Commons, however, the Ministry must retire or dissolve Parliament and order a new election. It may happen, however, that the disavowal of the obnoxious act and the resignation of the member most responsible for it may satisfy the House and thus allow the Ministry to continue in office. These matters are considered to be of such vital importance that a motion to censure or to declare a want of confidence is given the right of way, and settled in advance of other business. This priority is not given, however, to a motion which might terminate the existence of the Ministry indirectly.

There are other indirect ways in which the Commons may express their confidence or the lack of it in the existing Ministry. Should the ministers declare in the course of the debate that the motion pending was of "vital importance," and should the matter be decided against them, then this action must be looked upon as a vote of want of confidence.

The English Government

The ministers may declare themselves to this effect upon any motion whatever, even upon a motion to adjourn. In case the wishes of the Ministry are not respected when they have "taken their stand," the vote must be considered one of a lack of confidence. Ordinarily, however, if the Government majority is not large, the Ministry will not hazard its existence upon any but an important matter. In some cases, however, there is no alternative. The Cabinet must not allow its financial estimates to be defeated or materially changed. This is always a "vital question." When the Cabinet goes before the House of Commons and states that a certain expenditure is necessary for the year, it must stand by the guns. Mr. Gladstone expressed himself forcibly in this matter when he said, "No Government could be worthy of its place if it permitted its estimates to be seriously resisted by the Opposition; and important changes can be made therein only in circumstances which permit of the raising of the question of a change of Government."

If the Ministry, when defeated upon a "vital question," does not resign at once, it must appeal to the country for support; and when such an appeal is decided upon, Parliament should be dissolved with the least possible delay. There is usually some urgent business which cannot be deferred but which must be transacted at once. In attending to this the Ministry has the assistance of the Opposition. The battle on the floor of the House is over, and the opposing party will now turn in and lend a helping hand in preparing for the obsequies.

It is not in case of every defeat, however, that an appeal to the country is allowable. The Cabinet would not be justified in dissolving Parliament out of mere stubbornness. Unless there is good reason to believe that the House of Commons does not at the time represent the will of the people, the Cabinet must submit to the inevitable and resign without dissolution of Parliament. To appeal to the country without a reasonable prospect of success would bring the reproach of the people upon the heads of the offending ministers. In such a case the Opposition would have all the advantage in the campaign and could keep the Government party on the defensive throughout.

When an appeal is made to the country, a new House of Commons is elected and the fate of the Cabinet is then definitely decided. If a majority be returned who will support the present ministers in the Commons, they are vindicated and continue in office. If the opposite is true, there is no alternative but resignation. After an appeal to the country has been made and a general election held, Parliament immediately assembles; and unless the Cabinet has resigned in the mean time, a test vote is taken to determine the status of a Ministry which is apparently in a minority. Such a test vote, however, is usually not necessary. A Prime Minister will now usually resign at once when a general election goes against him. In 1886, Mr. Gladstone, when thus defeated, did not wait for a test vote but resigned before Parliament assembled. In 1892, Lord Salisbury, though defeated by a majority of forty in the general election, did not resign but waited for the adverse vote in the House of Commons, which was speedily passed a short time after Parliament convened. This delay on the part of the Prime Minister was quite unusual, and brought upon him the censure of the press and the general public.

After the defeat and resignation of one Ministry, the leader of the rival party is summoned by the Crown and intrusted with the formation of a new Government. He then becomes Prime Minister and appoints his colleagues subject to the nominal approval of the Crown. All of this takes time. In the past century the interval between the resignation of one Ministry and the appointment of its successor has lasted from one to thirty-seven days. Again, those members of the Commons accepting seats in the Cabinet must be re-elected by their constituents, and this also takes time. During this period of transition no important business is undertaken. Some routine matters are disposed of, but nothing is taken up concerning which there would be a serious difference of opinion.

Upon vacating their offices it is customary for the retiring members to meet their successors personally, and to explain to them the general condition of affairs. Official books, documents, and insignia of office are surrendered by those going out of office and assumed by the new Ministry, the hand of the Sovereign is kissed by the newly appointed ministers, and the change is completed. In the new Parliament the party which was formerly in opposition now sits at the Speaker's right, and the former Government party becomes the party of the Opposition and sits on the opposite side of the chamber.

In order to illustrate the responsibility of the Cabinet to the House of Commons, by concrete examples, it may be well to review some of the recent political history of England, and to note the steps by which changes in Ministries were effected. The resignations of the Salisbury and Gladstone Cabinets in 1886 will serve to illustrate this important matter in a concrete way.

The Resignations of Lord Salisbury and Mr. Gladstone in 1886.

When the House of Commons elected in December, 1885, assembled on Jan. 12, 1886, it was found that the Conservatives, then in power, had elected two hundred and fifty members, the Liberals, three hundred and thirty-four, and the Parnellites eighty-six. This placed the Salisbury Ministry in a very precarious position. The Liberals outnumbered them by eighty-four votes, and had only two votes less than the Conservatives and Parnellites combined. Inasmuch as the Parnellites were in hearty accord with the Liberals in their efforts to obtain Home Rule for Ireland, there was small prospect that the Conservatives could get any aid from that quarter. Whenever the Parnellites and the Liberals saw fit to unite upon any proposition the Conservatives must, of necessity, be placed in a hopeless minority. Such an event was not long delayed. Exactly two weeks after the assembling of Parliament an amendment to the Address was passed, in spite of the opposition of the Ministry, by a vote of three hundred and twenty-nine to two hundred and fifty, the Parnellites voting with the Liberals. Lord Salisbury, being defeated by a majority of seventy-nine, resigned at once. An appeal to the country would not have been in order in this case, as the House of Commons which defeated the Conservative Government was elected only the previous month. This being the case, it was fair to presume that it represented the will of the people, and there was no alternative but resignation.

Mr. Gladstone, as the leader of the Liberals, was summoned by the Queen and asked to form a Ministry. This he did, and at once pressed his scheme of Home Rule for Ireland. When the majority of the Cabinet approved the scheme, Mr. Joseph Chamberlain and Mr. George Trevelyan resigned their positions in that body, as they were opposed to the measure. There were many in Mr. Gladstone's party who did not favour his Home Rule scheme, but he pressed the matter, nevertheless, and on the 7th of June the bill on its second reading was rejected by a vote of three hundred and forty-one to three hundred and eleven, in a scene of the wildest excitement. Mr. Gladstone was thus defeated by a majority of thirty, but did not resign. He dissolved Parliament and made an appeal to the country, hoping that a majority might be returned which would enable him to defeat the combined forces of the Conservatives and those Liberals who opposed Irish Home Rule. In this expectation he was sadly disappointed. The country was evidently not ready to adopt his Home Rule scheme and returned three hundred and eighteen Conservatives, seventy-three Liberal Unionists, one hundred and ninety-three Liberals, and eighty-five

Parnellites. The Conservatives and their allies thus outnumbered the Gladstonians and the Parnellites combined by one hundred and thirteen votes. Mr. Gladstone resigned at once, and Lord Salisbury was appointed Prime Minister by the Queen and constructed a new Ministry which remained in power for six years.

To illustrate still further the precise method by which one Ministry retires and another assumes the leadership, it may be well to note the transition of power from the Liberal Ministry of Lord Rosebery to the Conservative one of Lord Salisbury in 1895. Since this change took place so recently, the facts are quite familiar. It will be remembered that on March 3, 1894, Mr. Gladstone, then Prime Minister, resigned his office because of failing eyesight and other physical infirmities of advanced age. There was some speculation as to his successor, Lord Rosebery and Sir William Vernon-Harcourt being most frequently spoken of in this connection, with incidental mention of Lord Kimberly, Lord Spencer, and Mr. John Morley. Mr. Gladstone favoured Lord Rosebery, and it was soon found that he was also the choice of a majority of the recognised leaders of the Liberal party. As a consequence, Rosebery was recommended to the Queen and was duly appointed Prime Minister on March 3, the same day upon which Mr. Gladstone had resigned.

The Fall of the Rosebery Ministry, 1895.

When Parliament assembled in new session nine days later there was a nominal Liberal majority of thirty-five. This under some circumstances would have been a fairly good working majority, but in this case it was a decidedly precarious one. The Irish Nationalists with seventy-two votes held the balance of power, and they were a very uncertain quantity. They had supported the Liberal party under the leadership of Mr. Gladstone; but it was a well-known fact that the new Premier would take up some other pressing legislation in preference to the Home Rule matter to which Mr. Gladstone had devoted himself so aggressively. This change might affect the attitude of the Irish party towards the new Ministry. On the other hand, there was a possibility that forty-nine Liberal Unionists, then acting with the Conservatives because of opposition to the Home Rule measure, might return to their former allegiance in case the new Premier put the Irish Question sufficiently far into the background. Things were thus in a very unsettled condition. Lord Rosebery assumed the duties of the Premiership at once, making but few changes in the Cabinet as constructed by Mr. Gladstone in 1892. Affairs did not run smoothly. There was no end of trouble in store for the young Premier. The policy of the party invited criticism. Too many reforms were attempted at the same time, thus antagonising many different classes of people. The leaders were not content to finish one reform before attempting another. The Cabinet insisted on driving its legislation abreast instead of tandem, and the public became surfeited with reform movements. The Irish party was, in one sense, an element of weakness. Enthusiasm for Home Rule had somewhat abated, a bill to control the liquor traffic had aroused the antagonism of the "personal liberty" theorists and the brewers, and Mr. Gladstone in his retirement was giving the party only a half-hearted support. Then, too, there was some opposition to Lord Rosebery in the ranks of his own party. Sir William Vernon-Harcourt was Chancellor of the Exchequer, and since the retirement of Mr. Gladstone had been the Leader of the House of Commons. That veteran statesman was unqualifiedly loyal to his young chief, but some of his friends felt, nevertheless, that his great services, long experience, and surpassing abilities should have given him the first place in the Cabinet. Then, too, the non-conformists of the nation soon became alienated from the new Premier. They had rendered the Liberal party under Mr. Gladstone a very substantial support, but their inflexible conscience gave a twinge when Lord Rosebery's horse won the Derby, and rebelled outright when the Premier won a second time. That somewhat inconvenient conscience of Puritan lineage began to draw a deadly parallel between the dignified morality of the Grand Old Man and what seemed to them to be the flippant and sporting proclivities of the young Premier. They were not slow to say that the Premier of England should not hobnob with horse jockeys and be tainted by the atmosphere of the betting ring. These same non-conformists looked upon the Ministry as blundering and timid when the Irish members compelled it to abandon its own proposition to erect a statue to Oliver Cromwell, their greatest apostle of liberty. The "London Times" scornfully remarked at the time that "the Government were compelled to obey their Irish masters." The Parnellite wing of the Irish contingent seceded soon after the session began, and the Liberal majority was reduced to sixteen. The bye-elections of that spring showed gains for the Conservatives, and soon the Liberal majority was reduced theoretically to eight and practically to five, owing to absences and other causes. Thus were the sorrows of the Premier multiplied. The Ministry struggled on until the fatal stroke came on the evening of June 21. At that time Mr. Brodrick, a Conservative, made an inquiry of Sir Henry Campbell-Bannerman, Secretary of State for War in the Rosebery Cabinet, with regard to the supply of arms and ammunition. The War Secretary made a reply which was not considered satisfactory, and after consulting with Mr. Balfour and Mr. Chamberlain, Mr. Brodrick moved that the salary of the War Secretary be reduced £100 per year. After a debate, not as spirited as a proposition to censure would seem to warrant, the motion was carried by a vote of one hundred and thirty-two to one hundred and twenty-five, and Lord Rosebery resigned on the following day, June 22. His resignation was not inevitable, as the vote was somewhat accidental. Had the absent members been present, it is figured that there would have been a majority in favour of sustaining the Ministry. An appeal to the country was out of the question, however, as it seemed evident that the electors would not indorse the Liberal party at that time. Lord Salisbury was immediately intrusted with the formation of a Government and accepted the responsibility on June

25, three days after Lord Rosebery's resignation. It is said that " the outgoing ministers wore an aspect of cheerfulness and even gaiety at their relief from a situation in which they had been at once burdened and hampered."

Lord Salisbury immediately formed a Cabinet from the wealth of material offered by the Conservative and Liberal Unionist parties, then acting together, and on June 29, the new ministers received the seals of office from the Queen, and the entire change of Ministry was effected in eight days.

A dissolution of Parliament may occur and a general election follow without the defeat of the Cabinet. **Voluntary Dissolution.** According to the Septennial Act, the duration of a Parliament is limited to seven years, and in case a defeated Cabinet does not appeal to the country within that period the Prime Minister will dissolve Parliament at some opportune time before the expiration of the term of office. As a matter of fact no Parliament serves out the entire term. In America we elect our senators, representatives, and other officers for a definite term and expect them to serve the entire time to a day, but the English Premier takes advantage of some favourable time to dissolve Parliament before the expiration of the term of seven years. A Parliament rarely lasts longer than six years. The Prime Minister manages affairs in such a way that important matters are disposed of, and popular legislation enacted, about a year before the expiration of the term of office. His party can then go before the country with a good record and make an aggressive campaign. Of the last twenty-seven Parliaments, beginning in 1796, only three have exceeded six years in duration and the longest was six years, one month, and ten days. Thus the average duration of the last twenty-seven Parliaments has been less than four years. The present[1] Parliament was elected in October, 1900. Its predecessor assembled August 12, 1895, and was dissolved by Lord Salisbury after a duration of a little more than five years. For some time before the dissolution actually took place it was evident that the Parliament was approaching its end. A special cable to the "New York Tribune," under date of August 4, 1900, brought the following information from London: "The signs and portents of dissolution are multiplied as the wearisome session of Parliament draws to a close. The general elections have not been ordered, and the party whips do not know when the Government will go to the country, but nobody in the Commons expects that the present Parliament will meet again after it rises next week." The prophecy was correct, and the Parliament was dissolved Sept. 25, 1900.

After having noted the general principles regarding a voluntary dissolution of Parliament, it may be well to consider the dissolution of 1892 and thus illustrate in a concrete way the method of voting a want of confidence. The Parliament which assembled in August, 1886, had a Conservative majority, and under the guidance of Lord Salisbury the Conservative Cabinet continued in office until the Premier decided upon dissolution in

Lord Salisbury's Resignation, 1892.

[1] October, 1902.

1892. On June 28 of that year the Parliament was dissolved after a duration of about five years and eleven months. A general election followed which returned a Gladstonian majority of forty-two. The voting was finished by the 23rd of July, and it was evident to every one that the Salisbury Ministry was in the minority. Yet the Prime Minister did not resign, but continued in office until a vote of want of confidence, on August 12, eight days after the opening of the session, compelled him to retire. When Parliament assembled on the 4th of August, every one knew that the Salisbury Ministry could not survive. As Mr. H. H. Asquith, soon to be appointed Home Secretary by Mr. Gladstone, put it, the members had convened "to perform the obsequies of a dead majority." Mr. Gladstone was received with great enthusiasm and given an ovation when he appeared at the opening of the session. The crisis came on August 11, or more accurately on the early morning of August 12. An amendment to the Address was offered declaring a want of confidence in the existing Ministry. Intense excitement prevailed both within and without the House. Out of a possible six hundred and seventy votes, six hundred and sixty were cast, and shortly after midnight on the morning of August 12 the Salisbury Ministry fell by a vote of three hundred and fifty to three hundred and ten. Lord Salisbury resigned on the same day, and Mr. Gladstone at once set about the formation of a new Cabinet. His work was completed, and the new members had assumed their duties in less than a week. It is generally conceded that

The English Government

Lord Salisbury should have resigned after the result of the elections became known in July, instead of waiting for the inevitable vote of want of confidence after the assembling of Parliament in August. In 1886 Mr. Gladstone handed in his resignation before the meeting of Parliament, after it became evident that he could not command a majority in the new Parliament, and Lord Salisbury was roundly censured for not doing likewise under similar circumstances in 1892. His action was due to the fact that the Conservatives considered the Opposition to be "faction rent," as they said, and did not think that it could hold together.

CHAPTER IX

THE CABINET IN PARLIAMENT

REFERENCES: Todd's *Parliamentary Government in England*, ii. 52–92, and 104–113; F. V. Fisher's article, *Party Government*, in *Westminster Review*, October, 1893.

IN order to witness the manœuvres of the Cabinet as a body it will be necessary to note the actions of the ministers on the parliamentary battle-ground. The members of the Cabinet are in practical command in both Houses, and at the opening of each session the Speech from the Throne demands their attention.

The King's Speech.

The King's Speech corresponds in a general way to the message of the President of the United States. At the opening of a session and on some other occasions the President transmits to Congress such information as he thinks necessary for the guidance of the legislative body. He also recommends the enactment of such laws as he may deem advisable. In like manner the English Sovereign addresses the Parliament at the opening and also at the close of every session. Formerly the Speech was actually prepared and delivered by the Sovereign, but in recent years it has been prepared by the Cabinet, principally by the Prime Minister, and is now looked upon as the official utterance of the Government ministers. It had always been customary for the Sovereign, until a comparatively recent period, to be present in person at the opening of Parliament, and to deliver his own address. In fact, such seems to have been the custom until the reign of Queen Victoria. In 1837, when William IV. expressed his intention of absenting himself from the opening of Parliament, Lord Melbourne expressed his surprise in a letter to Lord John Russell, saying, "No king had ever stayed away before except on account of some personal infirmity of his own." It was not the custom of the late Queen during the latter years of her reign to open Parliament and to deliver her Speech in person.[1] These duties were intrusted to others, as we shall presently see.

Before the Revolution of 1688 it was customary for both the King and the Lord Chancellor to address the Parliament at the opening of the session on different subjects, but since that time there has been but one address. This address is delivered by the Sovereign when present or in the absence of the Sovereign by the Lord Chancellor as a member of a Commission appointed for the purpose by the Crown. It is also customary to treat this Speech, regardless of its authorship, as the official platform of the Government leaders. They are responsible for its utterances, and as a consequence must have charge of its preparation. As a matter of fact, it is written by the Prime Minister or by some one delegated by him to

[1] During the earlier years of her reign Queen Victoria was accustomed to read her Speech in person, and her excellent voice and effective delivery were much admired.

do the work. Before being delivered it is presented to the ministers, and is discussed and approved by them. It then becomes their official proclamation, and they are held responsible by Parliament for its contents. An attack upon the Speech from the Throne is not looked upon as an attack upon the Crown. It is frequently criticised with great freedom and condemned with the utmost severity. On Feb. 5, 1833, Daniel O'Connell went so far as to characterise the Royal Speech as "brutal and bloody." Such freedom would probably not be indulged in, were the Speech looked upon as the personal utterance of the Crown. The shoulders of the Cabinet are broad, however, and its official skin is thick, hence there is lashing without stint and the bounds of legislative courtesy are not transgressed.

The custom of having the Speech from the Throne written by some one besides the Sovereign was of gradual formation. William III. would not consent to such an arrangement, although he had Somers put the finishing touches on the Speech and "clothe his own high thoughts and purposes in dignified and judicious language." In later years, although Somers had retired from the Ministry, he continued to aid in the preparation of the royal address, in thought as well as in language. During a part of the reign of Queen Anne, the Speeches delivered from the throne by that monarch were framed by Robert Walpole. The first Speech of George III., delivered in 1760, was written by two members of a "kitchen Cabinet," and not by the regularly constituted body. The King himself added in his own handwriting the famous paragraph in which he gloried "in the name of Britain." At the present time, however, the Speech is uniformly prepared by the Premier, or under his special direction, and is submitted to the party leaders of both Houses on the evening before its delivery in Parliament. Before 1795 it was customary for the Prime Minister to read the Speech to all the supporters of the Government, on the day preceding its delivery, in the "cockpit," or treasury chambers. It is now submitted only to the chosen few, but all may know its contents, as the newspapers publish accurate forecasts of it on the morning of the day of its delivery.

The Speech at the opening of the session usually contains a summary of the important affairs of state which have occurred since the last meeting of Parliament; and, what is more important, sets forth in a general way the character of the legislation which it is the intention of the Government to initiate. A good part of the Speech is pompously dignified and conventional and means practically nothing; but all are interested in knowing the legislative programme of the Ministry. The Speech at the close of a session will refer to the general condition of the country, give a summary of the laws enacted during the session, but will not take notice of any unsettled question, or of any vote taken or speech made in Parliament. The Speech made at the close of the session in the summer of 1900 referred, among other things, to the hostile attitude which China had assumed at that time.

After the Royal Speech comes the parliamentary reply. It is customary for the two Houses to frame an Address in answer to the Royal Speech on the same day on which the latter is delivered. In the Commons, the Leader of that body selects some representative of the landed interests of the kingdom to move the Address, and a member particularly interested in mercantile affairs to second it. In the House of Lords there is no fixed custom in this respect. In each case the Address is discussed and passed in the regular way, either with or without amendment.

The Address in Reply to the Speech from Throne.

The more serious business of the Cabinet, however, has to do with the enacting of laws. It is now an established principle that the ministers of the Crown are responsible for the introduction and passage of all needful legislation. Private members may introduce measures, as in the United States, but if these are not adopted by the Cabinet, their prospects for success are not bright. It is estimated that about eighty-three per cent of the bills introduced by the ministers become laws, while only about five per cent of those introduced by private members are passed. It is the duty of the Ministry to prevent the passage of objectionable bills such as are sometimes introduced by members of Parliament not in the Cabinet. This can easily be done. While in theory the private member has the right to introduce any measure whatever, as a matter of fact he cannot obtain a suitable hearing for his project without the aid of the ministers. The difficulties are practical rather than theoretical. There are some measures, money bills, for example, which must, for obvious reasons, originate with the ministers.

Cabinet Control of Legislation.

The ministers too, must succeed, if time permits, in the passage through the Commons of all the important measures which they undertake. The fact that the Cabinet has the support of the majority of the Commons makes success in all important matters almost certain, in case the ministers insist. In America the efforts of the two Houses may be frustrated by the veto of the President, but such a hindrance is now impossible in England, and the objection of the Lords to any bill is by no means final. Mr. Gladstone, writing in 1878, said that for only fifteen years out of the last fifty had the existing Ministry possessed the confidence of the House of Lords. This fact shows conclusively that the Lords do not ultimately thwart the efforts of the ministers in the matter of legislation, in case the latter insist. The Cabinet in England has a comparatively free hand, and is expected to achieve results. In America a legislative majority may be sufficiently large, but so unmanageable as to be almost useless from the standpoint of practical legislation. In the English Parliament the discipline is usually good, and something definite is accomplished. Failing in this, the Cabinet is likely to go out of power and the opposing party to come in.

In the debates it is customary for the Speaker to recognise the ministers first and to allow the Premier or the Leader of the Commons to close the discussion. Every fair advantage is thus accorded the Ministry, yet the Opposition also are granted opportunity to express their views. The Speaker usually recognises a member from each side of the House in turn.

A list or programme of debaters is sometimes agreed upon by the Government and the Opposition, which the Speaker generally follows, if requested to do so. Some such arrangement now seems necessary. It becomes constantly more and more difficult to provide for time for the debaters, as the latter are rapidly increasing in number. Before the present reign there were about one hundred and fifty active members in the Commons, — members who did the bulk of the business and of the debating. In 1841 this number was increased to two hundred and thirty-one; in 1861, to three hundred; and in 1876, to three hundred and eighty-five. The increasing number of participants in the debates makes necessary the introduction of certain regulations. This fact, together with the increasing amount of business to be done, makes ministerial control of legislation indispensable.

In order that the Cabinet may exercise an adequate control over legislation, it is necessary to have a recognised Government Leader in each House. Leadership is an important feature of the English Parliament, but Mr. Bryce in his "American Commonwealth" repeatedly notices its comparative absence in America. In the English Parliament, there is one man in each House charged with the management of affairs. In case the Prime Minister is a peer, he will assume the leadership of the Lords and represent the Government of the day in all matters in that chamber. In case the Premier has a seat in the House of Commons he will designate a peer possessing the qualities of leadership to represent the Government in the House of Lords. The

Leader of the House of Lords.

position of a Conservative Leader in the House of Lords is not an arduous one, as the majority usually agree with him in politics; but the duties of a Liberal Leader are by no means so simple and easy. In neither case, however, do the difficulties compare with those encountered by the Leader of the House of Commons.

Leadership in the House of Commons is, for obvious reasons, of vastly more importance than leadership in the House of Lords. The supreme political power of the nation is lodged in the Commons, hence the Leader of that body, if not actually the Premier, ranks next to him in governmental authority. If the Premier be a commoner, as was Mr. Gladstone, he will also assume the leadership of the House of Commons. He could hardly intrust that duty to another. The Prime Minister must be in reality the "First Minister," and cannot consistently or safely confer the leadership upon another in his own presence. The combination of the Premiership and the leadership of the Commons is all powerful. The present [1] Leader of the House of Commons is the Prime Minister, Mr. Arthur J. Balfour.

The Leader of the Commons.

Leadership in the Commons necessarily began with the introduction of parliamentary government. The first Leader of the House of Commons was Charles Montague, who held the position for four years in the reign of William III.

The leadership of the Commons is always held in connection with some important office in the Cabinet, generally with that of First Lord of the Treasury or

[1] October, 1902.

Chancellor of the Exchequer. The office was formerly combined at times with that of a Secretary of State, but the feeling now widely prevails that it can no longer be advantageously combined with a department whose duties are laborious and exacting. The arrangement under the last Salisbury administration seemed a happy one, as the duties of Mr. Balfour as the First Lord of the Treasury were merely nominal, and ample time was left for the duties of leadership, which are numerous and complex. The Leader of the House of Commons is the commander-in-chief of the forces of the majority in that chamber, he is their official spokesman, and in him the greatest of authority and responsibility is centralised.

In order that the Prime Minister and his colleagues may hold complete sway over Parliament, it is necessary that they have subordinate officers to aid in marshalling the forces. The "Whips" render very valuable services in this respect. They are members of Parliament, and the chief Whip is a very important personage. He is usually a teller, and it is his duty to see that the members of his party are in their places in the House when needed. He must "make a house" and see that no "count-out" occurs, when the Cabinet wishes to transact business. He must also placate any dissatisfied members of his party and make himself generally useful in the management of the House.

The Whips.

The Whips of the Opposition have a similar though perhaps not such an important work to perform. In the House of Lords we find the same officials with similar duties.

The ministers are also the authoritative sources of information regarding public affairs. It is customary in both Houses of Parliament for members to address questions to the Ministry concerning matters of public importance. This is a very convenient arrangement, as it supplies the House and the public with authoritative information upon vital matters, and at the same time enables the heads of departments to make statements explanatory of their official acts. Notice is given beforehand of the nature of the question to be propounded, so that the minister has time to investigate, if necessary. These questions are usually printed in the "Order of the Day," but it sometimes happens that important questions are asked without previous notice. Certain restrictions must, of course, be adhered to in the asking of these questions. No argument should be made or opinion stated in making the inquiry. Facts should be sought in the most direct manner, and hypothetical questions are out of order for obvious reasons.

Answers to Questions.

Questions are also sometimes addressed to the law officers of the Crown and to private members of the House of Commons, but the most important questions are usually those addressed to the Ministry.

In answering these questions it is generally understood that the speaker should "stick to his text," but a Cabinet member is not held within such rigid bounds. The minister, too, may use his judgment as to the form and extent of his reply. In some cases he declines to give any reply whatever, and at times even ignores the question entirely.

In the House of Lords the restrictions are not so

severe. The press of business is not so great, and despatch not so essential. The lords are accustomed to wander off into debate while asking and answering questions, and previous notice, in the printed "Order of the Day," is not deemed essential.

The range of these questions is almost unlimited. Sir Robert Peel once caused a list to be made of those propounded to him in a single evening. An analysis showed that information was sought concerning fifty subjects, and the possibilities were not even approached. The process is graphically described by the late Walter Bagehot in his own peculiarly candid and incisive way. "As soon as bore A ends, bore B begins. Some inquire from genuine love of knowledge, or from a real wish to improve what they ask about, — others to see their name in the papers, — others to show a watchful constituency that they are alert, — others to get on and to get a place in the government, — others from an accumulation of little motives they could not themselves analyse, or because it is their habit to ask things."[1]

The Cabinet and their supporters, however, do not constitute all of Parliament, although they are the most important part of it. The supporters of the existing Government sit on the Speaker's right in the House of Commons, and the members of the opposing party or parties on the left. The leaders of the parties occupy the front benches on their respective sides. At the present time [2] the Premier, Mr. Chamberlain, Mr. Ritchie, and other Government leaders are conspicuously placed on the

The Opposition.

[1] "English Constitution," p. 249.   [2] October, 1902.

Speaker's right, while Mr. James Bryce, Sir Henry Campbell-Bannerman, Mr. John Morley, Sir William Vernon-Harcourt, and others occupy a corresponding position on the other side. The presence of a well-organised Opposition is a potent factor in good government. It compels the Government party to be cautious, alert, prompt, and vigilant. Should the Ministry relax its efforts, every advantage would be taken of that fact by the Opposition. The one party is a salutary check on the other. The members of the Opposition stand ready to criticise every act of the Government. It used to be said that the simple duty of the Opposition was "to oppose everything, and propose nothing." There is danger, of course, that this opposition may be carried so far as to be senseless and even harmful. It has sometimes served "factious and unpatriotic" and selfish uses. There are some checks, however, which tend to keep the Opposition within bounds. They must look to public opinion among their constituents; their acts are reviewed and commented upon by the press, and the fact that they may be called upon at any time to assume the reins of government tends to make them conservative. Even the prospect of responsibility has a sobering effect. The Opposition have a chosen leader, and he will not, if he is wise, permit his followers to block the wheels of progress unduly. He must see to it, however, that the opponents of the governmental measures have a fair and impartial hearing. He will also co-operate with the leader of the majority in granting votes of thanks and in extending the courtesies of the House in a non-partisan way.

He will sometimes aid the leader of the Government party to defeat legislation obnoxious alike to both parties, by giving him the benefit of his wisdom and his experience. It is true of the leaders as it is of opposing lawyers in a case, after they leave the forum of debate all bitterness usually disappears. In their social relations the Cabinet ministers and their opponents meet on the most friendly terms. Outside of the House itself the flag of truce prevails. Even while at Westminster Hall the conferences between the leaders on the two sides of the House are not as sanguinary as the threatening attitude and finger of scorn, sometimes so prominent in debate, might imply. Amicable agreements are usually made by the leaders regarding questions of a non-partisan character, and even regarding those which involve party issues, when a compromise or mutual agreement seems necessary.

In the House of Lords there are also the Government party and the Opposition, but the contentions between them are not, as a rule, so strenuous as in the popular body.

The Cabinet is accorded every facility for effective and speedy legislation. The law officers of the Crown render very valuable services in this respect. The Attorney-General and the Solicitor-General always have seats in the House of Commons, and an important part of their duty is to give advice in regard to the framing of bills. This is an excellent provision and one which the United States might well copy. In our Congress, bills are framed by members or outsiders who have had little

The Law Officers.

or no experience in the matter, and the result is that the work is often done in a crude and unscientific way. The wonder is that we do not have more legislative monstrosities, when we consider the manner in which our bills are drafted. The English idea could be carried out by giving the Attorney-General or one of his subordinates a seat in Congress and by assigning to him the duty of framing bills on scientific lines. There might be a better way of reaching the desired end, but the above method would be in harmony with the successful experience of England.[1]

No institution so well illustrates the difference between the theory and the practice of the English government as does the Cabinet. Should the student read the pages of an author who confines himself to the theory of the English Constitution, as does Blackstone, making no mention whatever of the Cabinet, and then visit the mother country and behold the machinery of the government in actual operation, he would surely come to the conclusion that here was a case of mistaken identity.

Theory versus Practice.

According to the theory of the English law there is a complete separation of the executive and legislative departments. As a matter of fact, however, the two

---

[1] The actual drafting of a large part of the bills presented to the English Parliament is done by expert parliamentary draftsmen. In 1869 the "Parliamentary Counsel's Office" was established to do this important work. Mr. Henry Thring (now Lord Thring) was the first incumbent. This whole subject is ably discussed in Sir Courtenay Ilbert's "Legislative Methods and Forms," pp. 75–97 and 237–270. The author of this book is now Clerk of the House of Commons, and was at one time a parliamentary draftsman. He thus speaks with authority on this subject.

departments are very closely united,—even fused. In theory the Prime Minister is appointed by the Crown; in practice the House of Commons governs the choice. In theory the Crown also appoints the colleagues of the Premier in the Cabinet; in practice the Prime Minister dictates these appointments. In theory the Crown makes appointments to office in the nation at large, and dispenses patronage generally; in practice the Cabinet, principally the Prime Minister, performs those duties. In theory the Crown dissolves Parliament; in practice the Prime Minister dictates the time. In theory laws are enacted by the Crown by the advice and consent of Parliament; in practice laws are enacted by Parliament under the guidance of the Cabinet without the advice or consent of the Crown. Such royal advice or consent as is granted is merely formal and could not affect the result. Should the King be rash enough to advise contrary to the wishes of the ministers, his ideas could not prevail. In short, no phase of the English government exemplifies so well as does the Cabinet that which Professor Freeman has well called the "Englishman's love of precedent."

CHAPTER X

THE ORIGIN, COMPOSITION, AND FUNCTIONS OF THE HOUSE OF LORDS

REFERENCES: Pike's *Constitutional History of the House of Lords*; Ewald's *Crown and its Advisers*, Lecture on the *Lords*; Courtney's *Working Constitution of the United Kingdom*, 107-122; Bagehot's *English Constitution*, 157-197; Freeman's *Growth of the English Constitution*, 56-110; Walpole's *Electorate and the Legislature*, 25-46; Anson's *Law and Custom of the Constitution*, i. 185-231; Macpherson's *Baronage and the Senate*, 3-56; Taswell-Langmead's *English Constitutional History*, 742-750; Syme's *Representative Government in England*, 1-36; May's *Parliamentary Practice*, 540-553; Spalding's *House of Lords*, 1-130; Dickinson's *Development of Parliament during the Nineteenth Century*, 98-124; *Subjects of the Day*, No. 4, 1-42; Dod's *Parliamentary Companion* and English political and statistical almanacs.

AMERICANS, and even the English people themselves, are wont to make a good deal of fun of the House of Lords and of the nobility in general; but the fact is that in their more serious moods most persons, either consciously or unconsciously, have much respect, if not admiration, for these venerable institutions. That body which Ewald denominates a "patrician assembly, the members of which constitute the most brilliant aristocracy in Christendom," has a peculiar fascination for most persons reared on British soil. It is true that the harshest critics of the Lords, and it might be added, the most unreasonable, are to be found among the Radicals in England; but the English

Its Importance.

people, for the most part, delight in the contemplation of the nobility. Thackeray said "that there was not a man in England who would not be proud to walk down Pall Mall arm-in-arm between two Dukes." The familiar anecdote of Dr. Oldfield, as related in Boswell's "Life of Johnson," illustrates the same point. The devoted Doctor was given to talking incessantly about the Duke of Marlborough and his doings, in such a way as to produce much weariness of spirit among those of his friends compelled to listen to his adulatory remarks. One day the Doctor came into a coffee-house and announced in an excited manner that his noble Duke had spoken for half an hour in the House of Lords. "And what did he say of Dr. Oldfield?" asked a surgeon to whom the remark was addressed. "Nothing," was the reply of the good Doctor, somewhat astonished. "Why, then, Sir, he was very ungrateful, for Dr. Oldfield could not have spoken for a quarter of an hour without saying something of him." The Dr. Oldfields are not all dead yet. There is a magic spell which nobility casts around itself and which holds in awe those not within the charmed circle. This is especially true of that nobility which had its origin in the distant past. The newer nobility does not fare so well. As Selden once put it: "The Lords that are ancient we honour, because we know not whence they come; but the new ones we slight, because we know their beginning." The nobility of the former brewer of ale and stout does not appeal to the popular fancy until antiquity clouds the origin of his fortune. Defoe was particularly emphatic in

The English Government

expressing his contempt for the new nobility based on wealth.

> "Wealth, howsoever got, in England makes
> Lords of mechanics, gentlemen of rakes.
> Antiquity and birth are needless here:
> 'T is impudence and money make the peer.
>
> . . . .
>
> Great families of yesterday we show;
> And lords whose parents were the Lord knows who."

It matters little, however, what we as individuals may think of the House of Lords or of the peerage; the fact remains that the Upper Chamber of the English Parliament is a body of great power and greater influence, — an object of a reverence which is partly logical and partly sentimental on the part of a large proportion of the English people; hence a consideration of its functions and characteristics can scarcely be amiss.

Forms of government in all ages have maintained a striking outward similarity. Whether we turn to ancient Greece and Rome, to the countries of mediæval Europe, or to those of modern times, we find the governments conforming to a certain set model. *Its Origin.* There is an executive head, — a king, consul, emperor, president, or czar, — and something which corresponds more or less closely to the modern bicameral legislature. There are the Senate and the popular Assembly in Greece and Rome, the House of Lords and the House of Commons in England, and the Senate and House of Representatives in the United States. There is, then, generally speaking, the executive head, his advisory council or the upper house, and the popular assembly. The government of England has in the main conformed to this model.

There never was a time in English history when a national assembly did not exist. The germs of such an assembly were brought to the shores of Britain in the piratical crafts of the Angles, Saxons, and Jutes. The Teutonic ancestors of the present English people knew the national assembly long before the prows of Hengist and Horsa were turned toward Britain. Our authority upon this point is the Roman historian Tacitus, who writes about 98 A. D. and describes in some detail the form of government then in vogue among the Germans. In this government the national assembly occupies a prominent position. When the Angles, Saxons, and Jutes came to Britain, it was but natural that they should bring their governmental ideas with them, as the English colonists did at a later time when they came to America. The national assembly described by Tacitus, wherein all important affairs of state were discussed and decided, became the essential part of the Anglo-Saxon government in England after the conquest. The Witan of Anglo-Saxon times is the lineal descendant of the old national assembly which met in the forests of Germany, and from the Witan the present English Parliament, or more correctly, the present House of Lords, is derived. We may trace the House of Commons back to a very definite date, — 1265, — but in seeking the origin of the House of Lords we go back through the Witan of the Anglo-Saxon period and the national assembly which Tacitus found among the

The English Government

Germans of his day, until finally we find ourselves groping helplessly about in the dark recesses of the German forests. To trace the genesis of a governmental institution like the House of Lords is a very subtle and intangible process, and to attempt to do so in detail would be aside from our present purpose. Certain fundamental facts, however, should be grasped at the outset. In the first place we should not lose sight of the fact that there never was a time when a national assembly of some kind did not exist among the English people. The late Professor Freeman states this fact emphatically when he says: "I will now only call you to bear in mind that England has never been left at any time without a National Assembly of some kind or other. Be it Witenagemot, Great Council, or Parliament, there has always been some body of men claiming, with more or less of right, to speak in the name of the nation."[1] Before Britain was converted into England, the national assembly was that body which, according to Tacitus, managed the affairs of the Germans on the banks of the Elbe and the Weser. After the Anglo-Saxon conquest the national assembly of the Continent was continued in the Witan, or the meeting of the wise men. From this latter body the present House of Lords is descended. Professor Freeman is equally emphatic and explicit on this point. "The House of Lords," he says, "not only springs out of, it actually is, the ancient Witenagemot. I can see no break between the two."[2] If the antiquity of an institution is a

[1] "Growth of the English Constitution," p. 54.
[2] *Ibid.* p. 62.

source of prestige, the influence of the House of Lords must be extensive.

A brief consideration of the Witan or Witenagemot will facilitate our subsequent investigations. The composition of the body is still a matter of doubt. Professor Freeman maintained that every freeman had the right to attend its meetings, but that as a matter of fact comparatively few did so for various reasons. In his opinion only men of means and of political inclinations were in the habit of attending. The Witan is thus looked upon by Freeman and some others as being "democratic in ancient theory, aristocratic in ordinary practice." Bishop Stubbs and others contend, on the contrary, that all of the freemen never had the right of attending the Witan and that the privilege was extended only to certain persons. Whatever may have been the theory of the matter, the fact is that only a comparatively few did actually attend. Kemble was not able to find a record of an attendance of more than one hundred and six. These were the leading and the learned men of the country. The term Witenagemot means an assembly of wise men, and indicates in a general way the composition of the body. The King, ealdormen, governors of shires, thegns, abbots, bishops, and some others prominent in church or state were in attendance. The assembly was certainly aristocratic in practice, whatever may have been the theory of its composition.

The powers of the Witan correspond in a general way to those of the modern Parliament. It had the power to depose a king and exercised this power on at least two occasions; it could also elect a king and was called upon to do so repeatedly; it was the highest court of appeal, as the House of Lords is at the present time; and it participated directly in every governmental act. These vast powers were not uniformly exercised, but might have been at any time. A strong king would sometimes dominate the Witan and assume powers belonging to that body, but the latter assembly might assert its legal right on any occasion. Such, then, were the general characteristics and functions of the Witan from which the present House of Lords is descended.

The House of Lords, at the present time (1902), is composed of five hundred and seventy-nine **Composition.** members distributed as follows: —

Dukes	22
Marquises	22
Earls	123
Viscounts	27
Barons	308
Irish Representative Peers	28
Scotch " "	16
Bishops	24
Archbishops	2
Lords of Appeal in Ordinary (also Barons)	4
Princes of the Royal Blood	3
Total Membership	579

There are also two disputed successions at the present time, and twelve minors entitled to seats when twenty-one years of age.

The membership of the House of Lords is, then,

largely hereditary, the elective principle being introduced only in a subordinate way. Of the five hundred and seventy-nine members, five hundred and two [1] hold their seats by virtue of heredity, and their titles and seats will in turn be inherited by their eldest sons or other heirs. These sons or heirs are entitled to seats in the House of Lords immediately after the death of those whose seats and titles they inherit, provided they are twenty-one years of age at the time. If not, they must wait until they become of legal age before assuming the seats in the House of Lords. Three members of the House of Lords, including the Prince of Wales, sit as Princes of the Royal Blood; twenty-eight Irish peers are chosen from and by the entire body of the Irish peers and hold their seats for life; sixteen Scotch peers are chosen in a similar manner and hold seats for one Parliament; twenty-four bishops and two archbishops (Canterbury and York) hold seats by virtue of their offices, but do not transmit the right to sit to their heirs; the remaining four are Lords of Appeal, appointed to try important cases and to sit in the House of Lords for life with the dignity of Baron. Their seats are not descendible. It is evident, then, that the House of Lords is not the same as the peerage. There are many peers, the Scotch and Irish, for example, who do not sit in the House of Lords unless elected to do so; and there are some members of the House of Lords, such as the bishops, who do not belong to the peerage. Neither does the principle of heredity prevail exclusively; for, as we have seen, the

[1] The Dukes, Marquises, Earls, Viscounts, and Barons.

The English Government

Lords of Appeal, bishops, archbishops, and Scotch and Irish peers do not transmit the right to sit to their heirs. There are, then, three classes of members in the House of Lords at the present time, — (1) the hereditary peers of the United Kingdom; (2) the peers who are not hereditary members of the House of Lords, such as the sixteen representative peers of Scotland chosen for each Parliament, and the twenty-eight Irish representative peers chosen for life; and (3) those who are members for life but who do not transmit to their heirs the right to sit, such as the twenty-six spiritual members [1] and the Lords of Appeal.

A comprehension of these details is essential to a right understanding of the composition and functions of the House of Lords.

In theory peers are created by the Crown, but in practice the power lies in the hands of the Premier. A man is frequently elevated to the peerage as a recognition of illustrious services rendered in some particular line. Thus Sir William Thomson was made Baron Kelvin in 1892 in recognition of his eminent services as a physicist, and Frederick Sleigh Roberts, of South African fame, was made Baron Roberts in the same year, and was later made an Earl as a reward for conspicuous military services. The famous Duke of Marlborough obtained his title, pension, and estate at Woodstock in recognition of services of a similar character; and in May,

Creation of Peers.

---

[1] Should a bishop resign his office, he would, *ipso facto*, vacate his seat in the House of Lords. A Lord of Appeal might resign and still retain his seat in the House.

1901, Sir Alfred Milner, Governor of the Transvaal and Orange River Colony, became Lord Milner of Cape Town as a result of the gratitude of King Edward and Lord Salisbury. It is also customary to elevate the Speaker of the House of Commons to the peerage when vacating his office. This was done in the case of Arthur Wellesley Peel, who was made Viscount Peel upon retiring from the Speakership in 1895. When a commoner is made Lord Chancellor, it is likewise customary to make him a peer. Sir Julian Pauncefote, Ambassador to the United States, was made a Baron in 1899 in recognition of his eminent services in diplomatic and other lines. The theory, then, is that the peerage is conferred in recognition of eminent services in some particular line, but in scores of cases it is quite difficult to see in just what way the services were eminent. In fact, in a large number of cases the peerage seems to have been granted as a reward for party service rendered by way of contributions to campaign expenses.

Peerages may be conferred at any time, but royal birthdays, jubilees, changes of Ministries, and the beginning of the new year are looked upon as particularly auspicious occasions for the bestowal of honours. The obtaining of a peerage in Great Britain is looked upon as a fitting climax for a successful career, and is prized more highly by the average Englishman than it is possible for us to appreciate. It is true that some English statesmen prefer to be "great commoners" rather than be translated to the Upper Chamber and have the "doors of the House of Lords close upon them like the gates of obli-

The English Government

vion." These, however, are the exceptions and not the rule.

The right of the Crown to confer the peerage of the United Kingdom is unlimited, but the Acts of Union with Scotland (1707) and Ireland (1801) impose some restrictions upon the creation of Scotch and Irish peers. The Act of Union with Scotland made no provision for the creation of additional Scotch peers, while the Act of Union with Ireland provided for the creation of a peer of Ireland for every three peerages that became extinct, until the whole number of Irish peers should be reduced to one hundred. Although it was the evident intent of the Act that the number should not fall below one hundred, very few creations have been made in recent years, and the number now stands at ninety;[1] it would appear, then, from the provisions of the two Acts of Union that the Crown has no power to create additional Scottish peers, and can create a peer of Ireland only under certain circumstances. This power has been exercised so rarely in recent years that it was thought by some to have fallen into abeyance, and that no further additions would ever be made to the number of Irish peers. The conferring of an Irish peerage upon Mr. G. N. Curzon in 1898, however, upset these calculations, and other creations may follow.[2]

It is, perhaps, needless to repeat in this connection that the power of the Crown in this as in many

[1] For complete list see "Constitutional Year Book" for 1902, pp. 104-105.
[2] No Irish peerage was conferred for thirty years prior to 1898.

other instances means the power of the Prime Minister, since this prerogative is exercised only on his advice.

When a man is elevated to the peerage he receives a "patent of peerage," and a writ of summons to the House of Lords. When introduced to the House for the first time, he appears between two peers of his own rank, all clad in their robes, and preceded by the Gentleman-Usher of the Black Rod and other high dignitaries. He then falls upon one knee before the Lord Chancellor, and presents to him his patent, which being read is entered with the writ of summons upon the records of the House. At the conclusion of the ceremony the new peer is conducted to his seat. The introduction of a distinguished peer is a notable event. The first appearance of Lord Kitchener of Khartoum attracted no little attention.

Introduction of New Peers.

In case a man inherits a peerage, he is entitled, if he be of full age, to assume his seat at once after some few formalities. The new peer must present a certificate of his father's marriage and of his own baptism, as well as the evidence of his father's death. In case there is no contest for the title and seat, he is allowed to sit at once. In case of a disputed succession, the matter is decided by the House after an investigation and report by a committee.

There are at the present time (1902) three Royal Dukes or Princes of the Royal Blood who sit in the House of Lords. These are the Prince of Wales, the eldest son of the King, and heir apparent to the throne; the Duke of Cam-

Princes of the Royal Blood.

The English Government

bridge, first cousin to the late Queen; and the Duke of Connaught, third son of Queen Victoria. All of these have the title of Duke, but sit as Princes of the Royal Blood, and take precedence of the other nobility. The Princes of the Royal House very seldom now either speak or vote in the House of Lords, and never on party questions. The present King when Prince of Wales voted for the Deceased Wife's Sister Bill, but such instances are very rare. There is, of course, no legal restriction upon them in this respect. They possess the constitutional right to speak and vote like other peers, but choose not to do so. They very seldom attend the sessions.

According to statute the peers of Scotland are summoned to meet at Edinburgh or some other convenient place, when a new Parliament is summoned, to elect sixteen of their number to sit in the House of Lords during the existence of that one Parliament. *Scotch Representative Peers.* By custom the peers meet at Holyrood Palace in the city of Edinburgh and, seated at a long table, proceed to the election, the result of which is, in due time, transmitted to the Clerk of the House of Lords. In case a peerage of the United Kingdom is conferred upon a representative peer of Scotland, his seat at once becomes vacant, and a new election is held.

As noted above, not all of the peers of Ireland are allowed to sit in the House of Lords, but only those — twenty-eight in number — who are chosen to do so by the whole body of Irish peers. *Irish Representative Peers.* As the Irish representative peers hold their seats in the House of Lords for life, an election takes place only upon the death of one of their number. The mode of procedure is quite unlike that used in the election of Scottish peers. When an Irish representative peer dies, two other representative peers send a certificate of his death to the Lord Chancellor, who directs that an election be held to fill the vacancy. "Voting papers" are then sent to all of the peers of Ireland. These papers are filled out and forwarded to the Clerk of the Crown. The polls are closed fifty-two days after the issuance of the writ of election, the votes are counted, and the result proclaimed. The peer thus chosen is then entitled to a seat in the House of Lords for life, but this right is not transmitted to the son upon the death of the father, as in the case of a peerage of the United Kingdom.

In case an Irish representative peer is made a peer of the United Kingdom no vacancy is caused in the Irish representation. The Irish peer also has some privileges not accorded to those of England or Scotland. Seats in the House of Commons are denied to peers of England and Scotland, but an Irish peer, if not chosen to sit in the House of Lords as a representative peer, may sit in the Lower House for any constituency outside of Ireland. While a member of the House of Commons, however, he is not eligible to election to the Upper House and cannot vote for the representative peers. The presence of an English peer is not tolerated on the floor of the Commons. As soon as a member of the latter House succeeds to a peerage, or has one conferred upon him, he must vacate his seat. Mr. William W. Palmer, now Lord

Selborne and First Lord of the Admiralty, was a member of the House of Commons when he inherited a peerage upon the death of his father in 1895. He was interested in the passage of certain legislation at the time, and desired to remain for a short period in the Lower House after he became a peer, but upon his first appearance in the Commons after the death of his father "a hundred fingers were pointed at him and a dozen men called attention to the presence of a stranger in the House, whereupon the Speaker ordered the Sergeant-at-arms to eject him." Special privileges in this respect were accorded the Irish peers by the Act of Union of 1801.

The spiritual and temporal lords sit together in the Upper House. The spiritual members are lords of Parliament, but not peers; that is, they are not of noble blood. There are at present twenty-six spiritual lords in the Upper House, —two archbishops and twenty-four bishops. They hold seats during their continuance in ecclesiastical office, but do not transmit the right to sit to their heirs. This number, twenty-six, does not include all of the bishops of the English Church, but only those entitled by statute to seats in the House of Lords.

The Spiritual Lords.

The Crown as the head of the Church has the power to appoint the bishops and archbishops. This means, of course, that the prerogative is exercised only on the advice of the Prime Minister.

After the appointment of a bishop he is confirmed in his office, and is required to do homage to the King and to take an oath of fealty to him. The confirmation ceremony is described by Anson as "solemn, elaborate, and idle." Those who oppose the confirmation are called upon to show cause why the bishop-elect should not be confirmed in his office. Should these opponents appear, however, they would not be listened to. In the case of Dr. Hampden there were those present who were prepared to argue against his confirmation, but the Vicar-General refused to hear them after the formal call for such opposition had been made. After these ceremonies of confirmation, homage, and fealty have been performed, the bishop is entitled to take his seat in the House of Lords; or if his bishopric does not entitle him to sit at once, he waits his turn.

The Archbishops of Canterbury and York, the Bishops of London, Durham, and Winchester, are entitled to seats in the House of Lords immediately upon their appointment; but the other bishops obtain the right to sit in the order of their seniority, not more than twenty-one of them being entitled to seats at any one time. This is a matter of statute regulation. There are now (1902) eight bishops who do not sit in the House of Lords, but who will succeed in the order of the seniority of their appointments on the occurrence of vacancies. The Bishop of Sodor and Man is a sort of territorial delegate; he has a seat in the House, but no voice in its proceedings. After the union with Ireland in 1801, four Irish bishops were given seats in the House of Lords to represent the Church of that island, but these bishops were excluded after the disestablishment of the Irish Church in 1869.

When a bishop acquires the right to sit in the

The English Government

House of Lords he is introduced to that assembly by two other bishops, and after presenting his writ while kneeling before the Lord Chancellor, he is conducted to a seat with the other spiritual lords.

The bishops sit in a section of the Lords' chamber by themselves, in the upper part of the house on the right of the presiding officer. Being clad in their ecclesiastical robes, they are easily distinguished from the other members of the body. They participate in nearly all of the regular business of the House. They have the legal right to try cases when the House sits as a court of appeal, but as a matter of custom do not do so. In fact, very few members exercise their legal right in this respect. The bishops are often prominent in the debates, and not infrequently prove formidable antagonists in the give-and-take of an animated discussion.

The House of Lords in its judicial capacity corresponds to the Supreme Court of the United States. It is the highest court of appeal in Great Britain, and this jurisdiction is vested according to legal theory in the entire House or in such members as choose to attend; but since O'Connell's famous appeal in 1844 the judicial power has, in practice, been delegated to the law lords, or to the Lord Chancellor and other peers who hold or have held high legal or judicial positions. There were very good reasons for this change. A court consisting of five hundred and seventy-nine judges would be unwieldy, to say the least; and many of these five hundred and seventy-nine would have no knowledge of the law nor interest in the proceedings. The result has been that by a sort of a survival of the fittest these judicial functions have been delegated to those most competent to exercise them.

In 1876 and in 1887 Acts were passed providing for the appointment of "Lords of Appeal in Ordinary," in order to strengthen the judicial capacity of the House. The Lords of Appeal now, then, consist of the Lord Chancellor, who presides, and four Lords of Appeal in Ordinary, three of whom constitute a quorum. Other peers, holding or having held high judicial positions, may also be included; and, as remarked above, there is nothing in the theory of the law to prevent the attendance of any member of the House.

A few words in regard to the Lords of Appeal in Ordinary may not be amiss. They have a salary of £6000 per year, and have the dignity of Baron for life, but do not transmit their seats or titles to their heirs. They are life peers. Before appointment as a necessary qualification, the candidate must have held some important judicial position for two years at least, or have practised at the British bar for fifteen years. Should a Lord of Appeal in Ordinary resign his judgeship, he would still retain the dignity of Baron for life, and could continue to sit and vote in the House of Lords, but could transmit no such privilege to his heirs.

The method of conducting a case before the Lords of Appeal is such as to give the observer confidence in the equity and stability of Anglo-Saxon institutions. The proceedings are characterised by thought, seriousness, and dignity, and are devoid of any semblance of bombast. It might be remarked in passing that the proceedings of our own Supreme Court are not less dignified and reassuring.

The above sketch, then, comprises all of those entitled to sit in the House of Lords. In most respects the various classes of members are of equal standing, but in social and ceremonial matters there are marked differences in rank. *Precedence.* The question of rank, now rapidly becoming an important one in Washington, has always been important in England. In the House of Lords there is a fixed order of precedence of long standing. The Prince of Wales stands first on the roll, and is followed by the other royal Dukes or Princes of the Royal Blood. These are followed by the Archbishop of Canterbury, the Lord Chancellor, the Archbishop of York, the Lord President of the Council, the Lord Privy Seal, the Dukes, Marquises, Earls, Viscounts, Bishops, and Barons, in the order named.

In practice the members are not seated in the House according to their rank. While the bishops sit by themselves, the other members do not observe the prescribed order. To do so would conflict with the business of the House. The Government peers sit on the right of the woolsack and the Opposition on the left, while those who wish to remain neutral occupy the cross benches between the table and the bar.

There are certain disqualifications which prevent a peer from sitting and voting in the House of Lords. Infancy is one of these. In the *Disqualifications.* eye of the law a peer is an infant until twenty-one years of age. There are twelve such peers now waiting until they attain their majority before taking their places in the Upper Chamber.

Conviction of felony also operates as a disqualification in case the peer be sentenced to "penal servitude, or imprisonment with hard labour for any term, or without hard labour for a term of twelve months." The peer thus convicted must either serve his term or receive a pardon before being eligible to sit and vote in the accustomed way.

A sentence of the House sitting as a court of justice also disqualifies a peer from participating in the business of the House. The Crown, however, may remove the disqualifications and restore the peer to his former privileges in case it sees fit to do so.

The House of Lords now has nearly six hundred members and is frequently spoken of being as unwieldy. It is nearly seven times the size of the United States Senate, but its expansion is a matter of comparatively recent times. Although an institution of great antiquity, it was comparatively insignificant in numbers until the accession of the House of Hanover. During the reign of Henry VII. (1485-1509) the House contained from fifty to eighty members, and the majority of these were spiritual lords. In this reign the number of temporal peers was only twenty-eight. Prior to 1509 only twenty-seven peerages had been conferred, and in the two hundred and five years between this date and the accession of the present house in 1714, only fifty-six additional peers were created, making a total of eighty-three Welsh and English peers at that time.

Growth of the House of Lords.

After that date creations were more rapid, and in the one hundred and seventy-seven years from 1714 to 1891 we find that peerages were conferred upon four hundred and seven persons. In the nineteenth century creations were made more rapidly than at any previous time. From 1830 to 1898 there were three hundred and sixty-four peerages conferred, two hundred and twenty-two of which were conferred under Liberal Ministries, and one hundred and forty-two under Conservative auspices. During this period the Liberals were in office forty-two years, and the Conservatives twenty-seven.[1] More than one-third of the present peerages were created within the last half-century. Two centuries ago (1702) the House of Lords contained one hundred and eighty-eight members; it now has five hundred and seventy-nine. Its growth in recent years has been exceedingly rapid; some think it excessive, and would reduce the membership by at least one-half. Some of the irreverent are wont to say that the House of Lords is as full as Westminster Abbey and with material quite as inert. The joke, however, is a poor one in point of fact, as the present membership of the House contains the names of many illustrious, active, and able men. The average ability of the individual peers is remarkably high; but it must be confessed that collectively the peers do not constitute a very effective organisation. The material, however, has stood the test of practical experience. A recent poll of the House (1898) shows that the peers individually have rendered very valuable services in various lines of public

[1] See "Constitutional Year Book," 1899, p. 73.

activity.[1] It must be borne in mind constantly that the peers have much power and influence aside from their membership in the House of Lords.

The officers and clerks of the House of Lords are numerous, but a glance at the duties of the more important of these will suffice for our present purpose. The Lord Chancellor, of course, demands our first attention. He is by virtue of his office a member of the Cabinet and the presiding officer of the House of Lords. If not a peer when chosen, he is usually elevated to the peerage immediately after his appointment, and thus becomes a member of the body over which he presides. He need not, however, be of necessity a peer, as the woolsack, or the famous historic seat of the Chancellor, is not technically within the limits of the House of Lords. In case he were not a peer and hence not a member of the House of Lords, his position would be analogous in this respect to that of the Vice-

The Lord Chancellor.

---

[1] Public Services of the peers:

"Service in the House of Commons 169
Services in offices of State (exclusive of Royal Household) . 147
Army Service 182
Navy   "   17
Militia "   114
Yeomanry Service 113
Volunteer " 99
Judges and Eminent Lawyers 23
Colonial Governors and Ministers 32
Diplomatic Service 25
Civil Service 24
Church (exclusive of Bishops) 4
Mayors and County Councillors . . . . 151."[1]

[1] "Constitutional Year Book," 1899, p. 72.

President of the United States, who presides over a body of which he is not a member.

The famous woolsack which constitutes the seat of the Lord Chancellor originated in the reign of Elizabeth. At that time an Act of Parliament was passed prohibiting the exportation of wool, and in order that the importance of the new industry might not be lost sight of, it was directed that the judges in the House of Lords should sit upon woolsacks. These were originally sacks filled with wool, but the woolsack now is a large couch or ottoman, upholstered in red and having a back-rest in the centre. Its present appearance does not suggest its historic origin.

The authority of the Lord Chancellor is slight as compared to that of the Speaker of the House of Commons. The latter official is in absolute control over the Lower House, but all matters of importance in the Upper House are passed upon by the lords themselves.

In addition to the Lord Chancellor, there are the Sergeant-at-Arms, who is the personal attendant of the presiding officer and the custodian of the mace; the Clerk of the Parliaments who keeps the records; the Reading Clerk, and the Gentleman-Usher of the Black Rod, a curiously antiquated and ridiculously pompous official who corresponds in a general way to the Sergeant-at-Arms in other assemblies. The duties of this rigid and picturesque official are neither onerous nor numerous, and consist for the most part of obtaining the presence of the Commons in the Lords' chamber, when for any purpose, a joint session may be required; of executing orders for commitment of persons guilty of contempt; of assisting in the introduction of peers, and of taking a dignified but apparently useless part in other ceremonies. The Yeoman-Usher is his deputy.

The House of Lords assembled for legislative purposes prior to 1882 at five o'clock in the afternoon; but on March 24th of that year the time was changed to a quarter past four. The House still continues to meet at this hour, except on Tuesdays, on which days the sessions begin at half-past five o'clock in order to accommodate those lords who are members of the standing committees. The House very rarely meets on Wednesdays or Saturdays. There is no fixed hour for the adjournment, but the sessions are usually very short as compared with those of the Commons. This is easily possible as "they frequently have literally nothing to do."[1]

Time of Meeting.

Three lords constitute a quorum to do business, one of whom may be in attendance for the purpose of taking the oath of office, and hence not actually a member at the opening of the session. If, however, a division be taken upon a bill and it appears that thirty lords are not present, the presiding officer declares the question not decided. The number constituting a quorum seems ridiculously small when compared with the membership of the House, but it is probably true that a much larger quorum would at times be difficult to obtain. The lords are sometimes compelled to adjourn because three members are not present.

Quorum.

[1] Spencer Walpole's "Electorate and the Legislature," p. 150.

The sessions of the lords are always opened with prayer. The prayer now in use is the same for both Houses and was devised in 1660 by the lords. It was subsequently adopted by the Commons, and is generally read in that body by the Chaplain and in the Lords by one of the bishops.

Prayer.

As noted above, the Speaker of the House of Commons has absolute control of the debates in the Lower House, but the Lord Chancellor has no such authority in the House of Lords. The House itself decides whether a speaker be heard or not. When two members, desiring to speak, rise simultaneously, unless one gives way to the other, the members will call upon the favoured one to proceed. In case of a difference of opinion a division must decide. In case the Lord Chancellor rises in his place to speak at the same time that other peers rise, it is customary to give precedence to the presiding officer. In the Commons the member who has the floor addresses his remarks to the Speaker, but in the Lords the member speaking addresses the House. By a standing order "the lords are directed to keep their dignity and order in sitting, and not to move out of their places without just cause; and that when they cross the house, they are to make obeisance to the cloth of estate."[1] It is perhaps needless to say that the lords do not always keep their order, and sometimes not their dignity. They would be unique among legislators if they did.

Rules of Debate.

Important matters in either House are usually decided by a "division." Divisions in the House of

[1] May's "Parliamentary Practice," p. 325.

Lords are conducted in practically the same way that they are in the House of Commons. The "contents,"

Divisions. or those voting in the affirmative, go to the lobby at the right of the woolsack and the "not-contents" to the lobby at the left. Tellers appointed by the chairman do the counting. A peer may be excused because of infirmity from going into the lobby and his vote recorded while he remains in his seat. The vote of the presiding officer is taken first, and in case of a tie he has no casting vote and the "not-contents" prevail. In case a peer does not wish to vote he may withdraw to "the steps of the throne," and being then outside of the House, he is not counted in the division. Voting by "proxy" was discontinued in 1868 and will probably not be revived. The absurdity of the practice must have been evident long before that time. A noble lord campaigning with the army in a distant continent could scarcely be expected to have an intelligent opinion upon the various matters coming up for decision in the House of Lords.

There are certain privileges enjoyed by the lords which deserve a passing notice. The House of Lords

Privileges. possesses those ancient privileges common to all Anglo-Saxon law-making bodies,— freedom from arrest during the sessions except for serious crimes, freedom of speech in debate, and the right to pass upon the qualifications of those claiming seats in the Upper Chamber. The lords also possess the privilege of freedom of access to the person of the Crown, which right does not exist in the case of commoners. The House of Commons collectively has access to the Sovereign, but this same privilege exists for the lords individually. Socially this is a matter of some importance, but politically it is now of no consequence, since the power of the Crown is nominal rather than real. The House of Lords also possesses the right to regulate its own proceedings, and even to commit to prison for contempt.

The powers and functions of the lords have been referred to incidentally, but a more definite mention of them may not be amiss at this time. **Powers and Functions.** In the first place the lords as individuals have titles of honour which give them precedence on certain occasions; secondly, they are individually, according to legal theory, the hereditary advisers of the King; thirdly, they are, as a body, together with the lords spiritual, when not sitting as a House of Parliament, the permanent council of the Crown; fourthly, they are, collectively, in conjunction with the lords spiritual, the highest court of appeal in Great Britain; and fifthly, they are, in connection with the bishops, the Commons, and the Crown, the legislative assembly of the nation.[1] It might be well to remark in this connection, however, that the House of Lords is not co-ordinate as a legislative body with the House of Commons. Since 1832, in case of a conflict between the two Houses, the Lords must give way if the Commons persist. Mr. Bonamy Price has well said in the "Contemporary Review"[2] that it was the province of the Lords " to test,

[1] See May's "Parliamentary Practice," p. 48.
[2] Vol. 38, p. 947.

by temporary resistance, the sincerity and strength of the will which demands a change." The House of Lords now confines itself for the most part to the revision and emendation of bills coming from the Commons, and rejects proposed legislation only on very rare occasions when it feels that the measures of the Commons do not represent the will of the nation. The lords rejected the Home Rule bills of Mr. Gladstone on this basis, and were undoubtedly correct in their interpretation of public opinion.

Not all of the importance of the peers, however, is due to their official positions. They exert a social and industrial influence which is no small factor in English life. A large part of this influence is due to their ownership of land. The possession of a landed estate in England has always carried with it a peculiar distinction, and the peers are, of course, the largest land-owners in the kingdom. The area of the United Kingdom is in round numbers 78,000,000 acres. Of this area 48,000,000 are cultivated land. Mr. Arthur Arnold, making use of Lord Derby's investigations of 1874-75, found that 15,303,165 acres of the cultivated land, or nearly one third of the whole, were in the hands of the peers, 525 in number. Mr. Arnold estimated that in addition to this amount not less than 5,000,000 acres of the uncultivated land were in the hands of this same class, making a total of 20,303,165 acres, or an average of 38,672 acres for each peer. The influence of such vast landed estates as these is almost incalculable, and their number and extent have doubtless increased by the additions made to the peerage

The Landed Influence of the Peers.

in recent years. It is evident that the peers in England exert a wide and strong influence entirely aside from their powers as legislators, and it is a peculiar fact that the landed possessions of the peers accord nicely with their rank. The Dukes have on an average 142,564 acres each; the Marquises, 47,500; the Earls, 30,217; the Viscounts, 15,324; and the Barons, 14,152 acres. These broad acres have given the peers a sort of feudal suzerainty over legions of their fellow-citizens. In many notable instances the influence thus acquired has been used with beneficent results.

Such, then, are the principal functions and characteristics of the House of Lords as it exists in England at the present time. It is a body of great antiquity, has been an undoubted power in the state, and is now a body of great influence. Times have changed, however, and the House of Lords has not kept pace with them; for this reason there has been in recent years an agitation looking towards the reform or abolition of the Upper Chamber. To the essentials of this agitation we must now address ourselves.

CHAPTER XI

THE PROPOSED REFORM OF THE HOUSE OF LORDS

REFERENCES: Spalding's *House of Lords*, 133-255; Pike's *Constitutional History of the House of Lords*; Macpherson's *Baronage and the Senate*, 59-370; Dickinson's *Development of Parliament during the Nineteenth Century*, 1-97, and 125-183; Courtney's *Working Constitution of the United Kingdom*, 118-120; *Subjects of the Day*, No. 4, 74-117; Houfe's *Question of the Houses*; Rose's *Rise of Democracy*; Bagehot's *English Constitution*, 157-197; *Drifting towards the Breakers*, by *A Sussex Peer*.

See also pamphlets and magazine articles mentioned in bibliographical note at the close of this volume.

THE abolition or reconstruction of the House of Lords is a live question at the present time in England.[1] There are some who see no reason for the existence of what seems to them a superfluous and antiquated body and would abolish it entirely; while others, recognising the necessity of a second chamber and appreciating the past services of the lords and realising the possibility of future usefulness, would retain the Upper House, but would reconstruct it in such a way as to make it conform more nearly to modern ideas of representation. The reformers seek

[1] Perhaps it might be well to remark that since 1895 the agitation in favour of the reform of the House of Lords has subsided, owing to the predominance of the Conservative party. But, as a prominent member of the House of Commons recently remarked, "it might revive as a burning question if the Liberal party came in and the House of Lords began again to throw out or spoil bills passed by the House of Commons."

generally to restrict the hereditary principle, and to extend the elective in the composition of the body. There are also those in England conservative enough to believe that the House of Lords as at present constituted is a satisfactory legislative body, and that no material change should be made in its composition. The fact of the matter undoubtedly is that the House of Lords has not adapted itself to the growing democratic spirit in England to the same degree that the Crown and the Commons have. The result is that there now exists a broad chasm between that body and the masses of the English people. The sympathy of the lords has been turned in the direction of the few and not of the many. It is this fact that has caused Spalding to characterise the Upper Chamber in his forcible way as "the one stagnant and unprogressive branch of the legislature."[1]

The prophecy of Walter Bagehot made a generation ago has been fulfilled in large part. Speaking of the possibility of the reform of the House of Lords, Mr. Bagehot remarked: "The danger of the House of Commons is, perhaps, that it will be reformed too rashly; the danger of the House of Lords certainly is, that it may never be reformed. Nobody asks that it should be so; it is quite safe against rough destruction, but it is not safe against inward decay. It may lose its veto as the Crown has lost its veto. If most of its members neglect their duties, if all its members continue to be of one class, and that not quite the best; if its doors are shut against genius that cannot found a family, and ability which has not five thousand a

[1] "House of Lords," p. 5.

year, its power will be less year by year, and at last be gone, as so much kingly power is gone — no one knows how. Its danger is not in assassination, but atrophy; not abolition, but decline."[1]

The cry for the reform of the House of Lords became more distinct after 1832. In 1834 it was proposed to relieve "the archbishops and bishops of the Established Church from their legislative and judicial duties." This suggestion came from the ranks of the dissenters, however, and was aimed at the Established Church rather than at the House of Lords. In 1835 the peers opposed measures passed by the Commons and a storm of popular indignation arose forthwith. The peers themselves were fearful as to the existence of their legislative chamber. Many of them thought that it would be swept away by the rising tide of democracy. The Duke of Richmond declared that he "thought the House of Lords was nearly done for;" Lord Lyndhurst saw "no chance of their surviving ten years;" and Lord Abercromby thought it impossible that "any body of men should recover from the state of contempt into which they have fallen."

In 1867 their opposition to the Act to extend the franchise again aroused the ire of the democracy; and again in 1884, when the lords refused to pass the Franchise Bill, Mr. Gladstone became indignant enough to quote Shakespeare, and John Morley declared that the time had come to "mend or end" the Upper Chamber.

In 1870,[2] an attempt was made to provide for the

[1] "English Constitution," pp. 196-197.
[2] Pike, "House of Lords," p. 382.

gradual elimination of the bishops from the House of Lords. It was proposed that those bishops then in the House should remain, but that none consecrated in the future should sit in the Upper Chamber. Such a reform will doubtless come about in the fulness of time, and will allow the bishops to attend to diocesan rather than legislative duties.

These expressions of opinion are by no means isolated. The most striking fact in connection with the present agitation is the unanimity with which some form of reconstruction is advocated. We are not surprised to find that many members of the Radical wing of the Liberal party are in favor of reconstructing or, in some cases, of abolishing the House of Lords; but the fact that so many members of the House itself advocate some sort of reform comes in the nature of a surprise to those who have not followed with some care the drift of current English politics. That Henry Labouchere and Sir Charles Dilke should not be satisfied with the present status of the Upper Chamber is not strange; but the American who takes only a casual interest in English politics will be surprised to find that Lord Rosebery has evolved an elaborate and somewhat radical plan for the reconstruction of the House of which he is a member, and his surprise will be the greater when he knows that even Lord Salisbury, a leader of the Conservative party, has taken steps — short ones, it is true — looking to the same end. Nor are these two great leaders alone in their position on the reform question. The House of Lords has debated the matter with earnestness and fervour on more

Reform advocated by Lords themselves.

than one occasion. There is undoubtedly a very strong reform sentiment within the Chamber itself. As long ago as 1891 a writer in "Subjects of the Day" gave it as his opinion that the discussions in the House of Lords on this subject pointed definitely to the three following conclusions: "First, that with few exceptions, the peers themselves feel the necessity for some kind of reform and for the strengthening of their chamber. Secondly, that many are of opinion that the hereditary principle is not consistent with the democratic tendencies of the age, and they are prepared to supply an alternative in the form of a greater or less infusion of life-peers; and, Thirdly, that a considerable minority would add to the introduction of life-peerages, the elective element, in deference to what they believe to be the views of the constituencies."[1]

Among the most notable utterances of discontent with the present status of the lords are those of Lord Rosebery, made in 1888, when he moved the appointment of a select committee to inquire into the constitution of the House. Lord Rosebery took occasion to remark at that time what had been obvious for a considerable period that "that incompatibility of temper between the two yoke-fellows, the House of Lords and the House of Commons, is daily increasing, and is not unlikely to increase." He declared himself opposed to the "indiscriminate and untempered application of the hereditary principle." "A House based solely upon the hereditary principle," he declared, "is a House based upon the sand. It

[1] "Subjects of the Day," No. 4, p. 46.

makes legislators of men who do not wish to be legislators, and peers of men who do not wish to be peers." The only hereditary peers that he would allow to sit "by right as such" would be the Princes of the Royal Blood. He would exclude all others unless elected to sit as representative peers by some suitable method of selection.

The Earl of Kimberly, another Liberal peer, expressed himself in this discussion to the same effect when he said: "I have come to the conclusion that the time has come for reconstructing the House on a new and different basis.... We cannot any longer rest on the hereditary principle alone on which the House is based."

Lord Salisbury, then Prime Minister, met these views by advocating "a very weak infusion" of life peers into the House. His bill looking to this end was withdrawn, however, after the second reading. It was evident that the great leader of the Conservative party was not ready to go to the stake in order to bring about a reconstruction of the Upper Chamber.

In an article in "Subjects of the Day"[1] the Earl of Pembroke, an advanced Conservative peer, declared himself in favour of strengthening the House of Lords by the introduction of life and ex-officio peers. He declared against the hereditary principle as "distasteful to the democratic spirit of our time," and expressed himself against abolition, believing that "a second chamber is an obvious and undeniable necessity." He expressed himself as opposed to all schemes of reform which involved the admission of

[1] No. 4, p. 47.

peers to the House of Commons. "The result would inevitably be," he said, "as a general rule, that the strong men would enter and stay in the Lower House, and the weak and worn out ones go to the Upper." He would not make any appreciable reduction in the number of members, neither would he introduce the elective principle. He believed that its large numbers were a source of strength and influence, and that the peers should represent the entire nation and not particular constituencies. The substance of his scheme is that the present predominance of the hereditary element should be "qualified by a strong infusion of life and ex-officio peers."[1] He would have the House of Lords "an assembly of all the great men in the country" instead of a body of "land-owners and plutocrats."[2]

It might be well to examine somewhat more in detail the objections which are urged against the House of Lords as it now exists. In other words, we should ask the attorneys for the prosecution to furnish us a "bill of particulars." The objections to the present constitution of the House are both theoretical and practical, abstract and concrete. It is urged that its present organisation is not in harmony with accepted political theory, and that practical experience has repeatedly shown its shortcomings.

Theoretical Objections.

The hereditary principle has been the centre of attack. It has been looked upon as illogical and incompatible with free institutions. Thousands nodded their assent when John Bright declared that "a he-

[1] No. 4, p. 52.   [2] *Ibid.* p. 53.

reditary House of Lords is not and cannot be perpetual in a free country." It is urged that appointments to the peerage represent political, judicial, military, and naval service and wealth, and that the favoured ones are not always the most eminent in their respective classes. Then, too, it is urged that a man may be a brilliant success as a warrior but a failure as a legislator; and that an individual might be a good law-maker while his son might have no ability whatever in this line. "We allow babies to be ear-marked in their cradles as future law-makers, utterly regardless as to whether they turn out to be statesmen, or fools, or rogues." It is urged that peerages are conferred in a haphazard way, without reference to any general rule, and that the attendant honours rather than the duties are emphasised. It is held, and rightly so, by those who object to the present organisation of the House of Lords, that a title of honour should not carry with it a title to legislate. It is obviously true that many who are entitled to the honour thus conferred are by no means qualified to discharge the legislative duties which at the same time devolve upon them; and it is true in many instances that the peerage is prized for the social distinction which it carries with it, and that the legislative duties are not taken seriously. Many men who have striven most zealously to obtain the coveted prize of a peerage have looked upon the seat in the Upper Chamber as a matter of minor importance. This is shown by the way in which the peers have persistently neglected their legislative duties. The peers themselves are to blame to a great extent for the decadence of their

Chamber. The public will not highly prize any legislative body composed of six hundred men, many of whose sessions are attended by not more than a dozen members, and whose quorum for the transaction of business is three. A stranger not conversant with the facts, visiting the lords' chamber during an ordinary session, would form but a faint conception of the actual membership. Lord Rosebery, while speaking in favour of reforming the lords in 1884, referred to an instance when a noble Earl spoke in the House for four long hours before an audience consisting of the presiding officer and one other peer. On another occasion Lord Lyndhurst, the presiding officer, after being bored by a long and tiresome speech and having given numerous indications of his weariness of body and mind, arose and expressed his determination to "count out" the speaker; "and," Lord Rosebery adds, "it was well within the province of the late Lord Lyndhurst to do it, because he and the noble Lord who was addressing the House were the only peers present." The generally light attendance and the apathy of those present lead us to think that that critic was not far wrong who remarked that "the cure for admiring the House of Lords is to go and look at it." It is true that the attendance in the Upper Chamber is large on some occasions of unusual importance, but it can hardly be denied that the vast majority of those whose attendance is spasmodic are not sufficiently conversant with legislative affairs to act intelligently. All of these facts have caused many to conclude that titles of honour and titles to legislate should be kept separate and distinct. There is no logical connection between the two.

The concrete arraignment of the lords is more tangible. The attitude of the peers toward the Reform Bill of 1832[1] is well known. Their hostility was uncompromising and they held out until virtually forced to submit.

The Peers and the Reform Bill of 1832.

After the rejection of the bill by the House of Lords on several different occasions, the Prime Minister, Earl Grey, obtained the written consent of the King to the creation of a number of peers sufficient to carry the measure. It was provided, however, that in the new creations the eldest sons of peers should be preferred to others. After this step was taken the lords submitted to the inevitable and allowed the bill to pass by absenting themselves in large numbers, and making only a formal protest. They preferred to allow the passage of the measure rather than to submit to the permanent enlargement of their membership, and the new peers were not created. The fears of the lords in regard to the measure were unfounded. The results of the bill have been good, and the principle which it involved was just. This fact is now admitted on all sides, and it is difficult at this time to see how the Duke of Wellington and other equally intelligent men could justify themselves in holding out against it so strenuously; yet this is always the way in which the succeeding century looks upon any great reform. English conservatism is a powerful force and slow to change, and in the light of this fact, it is not per-

[1] For a discussion of the measure, see Chapter XII.

haps to be wondered at that the reforms proposed by the Bill of 1832 were not eagerly embraced. Yet the peers were mistaken in their attitude toward this measure, and in any concrete arraignment of the House of Lords their opposition to reform in 1832 must always be an important count.

The significance of this contest was appreciated at the time. Thomas Babington Macaulay remarked in 1832: "The Lords are hastening the day of reckoning. . . . I am quite certain that in a few years the House of Lords must go after Old Sarum and Gatton." However, Macaulay did not live to see the abolition of the House of Lords, and twenty-five years after his prophecy was made, he was himself a member of that body.

The reform, culminating in 1832, gave rise to some very memorable discussions. Sydney Smith, in a speech at Taunton upon the rejection by the lords of the Reform Bill in 1831, made a very effective comparison between the efforts of the lords and those of good Dame Partington. "The attempt of the lords," he said, "to stop the progress of reform reminds me very forcibly of the great storm at Sidmouth, and of the conduct of the excellent Mrs. Partington on that occasion. In the winter of 1824 there set in a great flood upon that town: the tide rose to an incredible height, the waves rushed in upon the houses, and everything was threatened with destruction. In the midst of this sublime and terrible storm, Dame Partington, who lived upon the beach, was seen at the door of her house, with mop and pattens, trundling her mop, squeezing out the sea water, and vigorously pushing away the Atlantic Ocean. The Atlantic was aroused. Mrs. Partington's spirit was up. But I need not tell you that the contest was unequal. The Atlantic Ocean beat Mrs. Partington. She was excellent at a slop or puddle, but she should not have meddled with a tempest."[1]

The year 1832 marks an important turning-point in the history of the House of Lords. Since that time the Upper Chamber has had no right to be classed as a co-ordinate legislative body. The lords saw at that time that they could not oppose the will of people indefinitely, and "their subsequent policy has therefore been as far as possible to avoid meeting the advancing forces of democracy in set battle;" as Bagehot put it, the House of Lords has been conspicuous for its timidity in recent years, and has not, as a body, always been sincere in the expression of its opposition to reform measures. The alleged ground of opposition was often a mere pretext rather than an expression of sincere conviction. "Just as the lapwing pretends to be wounded to attract the observer from the neighbourhood of its nest, the House of Lords, in order to defeat a measure which it detests, but dares not reject upon its merits, assigns some reason other than its detestation for opposing it."[2]

The Record since 1832.

Thomas Alfred Spalding, a barrister-at-law and an avowed advocate of the reconstruction of the House

[1] Jennings' "Anecdotal History of the English Parliament," pp. 56-57.
[2] Spalding's "House of Lords," p. 173.

of Lords, charges the peers with "dilatory and evasive" tactics since their Waterloo in 1832. The consideration of bills, he says, is evaded on the ground, incorrectly, as he thinks, that time is wanting for their proper discussion. Again the peers are accused of "mangling" bills which are obnoxious to them by appending amendments intended to paralyse "the efficiency of the bills" and to make them unacceptable to their framers. In the third place Mr. Spalding charges that the peers have been unmindful and even hostile in respect to the rights of small minorities, and instances their opposition to the removal of Jewish disabilities as a case in point. Mr. Spalding illustrates each count in his indictment with concrete cases, and makes out a very strong case against the lords. The reader is impressed, however, with the fact that the concrete illustrations were excellently chosen for the particular purpose which they were intended to serve, and that Mr. Spalding has marshalled his evidence with effect. The careful reader, however, will not lose sight of the fact that these cases were chosen from a very large number, and that Mr. Spalding has omitted as well as selected his cases with rare judgment. It must be evident that in some few instances, at least, the lords were not at fault. In rejecting the various Home Rule proposals of Mr. Gladstone the lords were undoubtedly more in accord with British public opinion than the Commons were in approving them. Yet with all that can be said in favour of the legislative record of the lords since 1832, it must be confessed that that record is far from satisfactory from the progressive standpoint.

In 1880 there appeared a small pamphlet containing articles reprinted from the "Pall Mall Gazette" and entitled "Fifty Years of the House of Lords." The name of the writer of the articles does not appear, but Mr. Gladstone once remarked that they were published, as he understood, "under the auspices of a member of this House [the Commons] of great authority in a matter of this sort." The aim of the writer is to show that the lords have rejected, mutilated, or delayed nearly all progressive legislation sent up to them from the Commons during the fifty years from 1830 to 1880. The lords are charged with being obstructive and destructive, and hence a stumbling-block to all progress in legislative matters. The writer makes his study a concrete one by reviewing the attitude of the lords toward reform measures along various lines.

Fifty Years of the House of Lords.

Many of the English periodicals have made earnest endeavours to ascertain and to record the opinions of the various classes in England respecting the reform of the House of Lords.

The Lords and the Labourers.

In 1891 Mr. James Samuelson, editor of "Subjects of the Day," devoted an entire issue of that review to a discussion of the House of Lords. The editor himself investigated the attitude of the labouring classes toward the peers, by conferences with labour leaders and others, and came to the conclusion that the majority of the skilled artisans would favour either the reform or the abolition of the House of Lords, in case a plank looking to either result were placed in the platform of a responsible political party; that among the miners there was a feeling of indifference regarding the matter; that the town and dock labourers "disapprove emphatically" of the House and applaud methods of "ending" or "mending" it; that the majority of agricultural labourers would vote for abolition; and that in general the labourers, both skilled and unskilled, applaud all utterances of political orators advocating the abolition of the Upper Chamber.[1] These conclusions are significant inasmuch as the labourer is a factor of increasing importance in English politics.

The case against the House of Lords is stated very emphatically in the "Financial Reform Almanac" for 1899. The argument in part is as follows: "That ancient institutions die hard and receive a veneration they do not always merit, is a well-known fact; and the House of Lords is no exception to the rule — for surely its age is the only reason for its being allowed to exist, with all its present powers and privileges. If ever there was a time when it was an institution of value, that time is long past. Let it, for a moment, be supposed that we had no second Chamber, but it was thought advisable to create one, does any one suppose that a suggestion to have one constituted like our House of Lords would meet with anything but scorn and derision? Yet, because we have it, there are men dull enough to endure it without complaint, and others even stupid enough to defend it. What is a Lord that he and his fellow Lords should have a legislative Chamber all to themselves? A Lord is only a more or less ordinary — sometimes

[1] Pages 104-108.

very ordinary— individual, who is possessed of a
'patent of nobility;' that is to say, either he or an
ancestor of his has, for some reason, been granted by
the Crown the exclusive right to call himself Baron
This or Earl of That, as the case may be. For this
patent fees have to be paid, just as for the patent of
a machine, the difference being that, while the patent
for the machine lasts for a few years only, the patent
of nobility lasts as long as there are heirs to inherit it;
but it does not make the patentee or his descendants
wiser or better men. The reasons for granting the
patent may be good or bad. Wealth is essential, and
has sometimes been the only qualification. Were
nobility limited to the noble in character, there would
be some justification in a Legislative Chamber restricted to Peers. But, even if a man 'be raised to
the Peerage' because he has proved himself excep-
tionally wise, his son may be a veritable booby; and,
though the father may be eminently fitted to legislate,
his son may be very much the reverse. It is not the
inheritance of *title*, but the inheritance of the right to
legislate, with which we quarrel; and we object to
that right being, without any other qualification, a necessary accompaniment to the title. To have a legislative body composed of men who are members solely
by reason of their titles, is about as foolish and imprac-
tical an arrangement as it is possible to conceive. A
man may be made a Duke because he has been a
successful soldier, but it does not follow he will be
a successful legislator. Peerages have been bought
before now, and may be again; but, though there is
no harm in a man buying a title, if he thinks it worth

the money, there is a very great harm in his buying with it a perpetual right for himself and his heirs in tail to legislate for the country."[1]

Having glanced at the charges against the House of Lords, it now remains for us to consider the proposed remedies. There is no dearth of reform plans. Political pathologists of every persuasion have diagnosed the case and agree only in the conclusion that the patient should "take something." Even those writers who defend the House of Lords as it now exists, generally conclude their remarks by making some concessions to the reform party. *(The Proposed Changes.)*

Conspicuous among the would-be reformers are Lord Rosebery and Lord Salisbury, — if indeed the latter may be called a reformer, acting as he was in this instance largely in self-defence. On the 20th of June, 1884, Lord Rosebery moved in the House of Lords, "that a select committee be appointed to consider the best means of promoting the efficiency of this House." The motion thus couched in general terms looked very inoffensive on its face, but every one knew what was in Lord Rosebery's mind, and his subsequent explanation made the matter doubly clear. He showed that the House of Lords had not adapted itself to the changing conditions of the times, and hence was not in harmony with the present will of the English people. "Of course," he continued, "it may be said that this is due to its inherent and original perfection, but I do not believe that there is any institution that can afford to remain motionless and seal

[1] Page 291.

itself against the varying influences of the time." He asserted that the inefficiency of the House was due largely to the fact that it contained members of one class only. One set of interests and one class of people were represented, while other interests and classes were either inadequately represented or not at all. He argued that new or additional representation should be given to the dissenters, to the professions of medicine and literature, to commercial interests, to the colonists, to the labouring classes, and to the arts and sciences. He would also accord representation to the tenant as well as to the landlord. He did not at this time formulate any definite scheme of reform, but he indicated quite clearly the lines along which, in his opinion, the changes should be made. It was quite characteristic of the openmindedness of Lord Rosebery that he should include the labouring classes in the outline of his proposed plan. There must have been looks of consternation upon the faces of many of his hearers when he remarked frankly and with truth: "I believe one reason of our relative weakness, when compared with the House of Commons, is that we have no representatives of the labouring classes." The presence of the representatives of the labouring classes in the House of Lords would seem to many of England's aristocracy not unlike the presence of Attila and the Huns within the sacred precincts of Rome. The fate of Rosebery's motion was identical with that of the various proposals made in our state legislatures to constitute the acceptance of a railroad pass by a public official a misdemeanour. The motion was defeated as promptly and as overwhelmingly as the United States Senate defeats every proposal looking to the election of its members by popular vote.

In 1888 Lord Rosebery again moved that "a select committee be appointed to inquire into the constitution of this House." Again he made a plea for "the broad basis of popular support" and pronounced against "indiscriminate and untempered heredity." The proposals for reform now made were more definite and more radical than those made in 1884. His scheme involved the extension of the elective principle for the purpose of introducing new blood into the old organism. Without going further into the details of his plan, let us glance at the two bills introduced by Lord Salisbury, then Prime Minister.

Lord Salisbury had previously advocated the introduction of a limited number of life peers into the House, but could not tolerate the idea of substituting election for heredity on such an extensive scale as that proposed by Lord Rosebery. "No second chamber," he contended, "is likely to answer so well in the long run as a second chamber based upon the hereditary principle." His characteristic conservatism also asserted itself when he said to the House: "You are treading upon very dangerous ground, you are touching weapons of a terribly keen edge when you undertake to reconstruct the ancient assemblage to which we belong." Lord Salisbury was, however, forced at a subsequent time to grapple with the problem. While opposing a bill introduced by Lord Dunraven, looking to the reconstruction of the Upper Chamber, he pledged his Government to take up the matter. In accordance with this pledge the Premier introduced two bills on the 18th of June, 1888, one providing for the introduction of fifty life peers, and the other for the exclusion of "black sheep." Not more than five of those fifty peers were to be created in any one year, and these were to be chosen, for the most part, from the ranks of the judges, ambassadors, privy councillors, high colonial officials, naval and military officers. "Black sheep" were to be excluded by an address from the House to the Crown, praying that the writs of the members be not issued. This plan of the Premier was very limited in scope, and had more of the characteristics of temporising than of statesmanship. From the standpoint of the Premier, however, such a step was justified by the fact that it would probably defeat the more radical proposals of Lord Rosebery and others, which seemed to him disastrous. The two bills, having doubtless served the purpose for which they were intended, were withdrawn after the second reading. This step removed the matter from the House of Lords for the time being, and many breathed easier.

There are other members of the Upper Chamber who have from time to time offered suggestions for **Spalding's Plan.** the reform of the House of Lords; and there are those among the members of the Lower House who, like Mr. Bryce, have gone on record as being in favour of a more or less radical reconstruction of the Upper Chamber; but even if time permitted, it would probably not be profitable for us to pass these various schemes and suggestions in review. There is one other scheme of reconstruction, however, which is worthy of our attention. Mr. Thomas Alfred Spalding, in his book entitled "The House of Lords: A Retrospect and Forecast," has made a very careful study of the entire situation, and has presented a comprehensive plan of reform. Whether the proposed changes seem advisable or not a review of them cannot be amiss.

Although an enthusiastic opponent of the House of Lords in its present form, Mr. Spalding takes the very sensible view that "the abolition of the House of Lords is outside the range of practical politics," and proceeds to suggest a plan for its reconstruction. He would have the second chamber not one of co-ordinate jurisdiction "but primarily a court of review and suggestion." He would have political partisanship reduced to a minimum, and would have the members "cast off the political bias as effectively as the majority of judges cast it off when they ascend the Bench." He would reduce the membership to three hundred, and raise the quorum to one hundred, and even to one hundred and fifty, in rejecting a bill sent up from the Commons. He would allow the Upper House to reject any given bill twice but not oftener; when sent up a third time by the Commons it should become a law without further objection on the part of the Lords. He would not have the second chamber purely elective, as the House of Commons is, for the reason that, among other considerations, it would involve "too complete a divorce between the old and the new." Whatever we may finally think of the scheme of reconstruction which Mr. Spalding offers, we must admit that his view in respect to the evolution of governmental institutions is in harmony with that which has always characterised the Anglo-Saxon race. Mr. Spalding[1] would have the entire body of hereditary peers now having seats in the House of Lords, elect one hundred from their number to have seats in the new or reformed chamber. He would have the Scotch and Irish peers elected in much the same way that they are now, except that the former should be chosen for life instead of for one Parliament as at present. In order to eliminate the hereditary element by a gradual process, he would have one new member chosen for every three vacancies which occur in the case of peers of the United Kingdom, and one for every two vacancies in the case of the Scotch and Irish peers. His plan would then provide for one hundred peers of the United Kingdom, twenty-eight Irish and sixteen Scotch peers, or one hundred and forty-four representative peers for the beginning of the new upper chamber. This number would, of course, be automatically reduced by the process just described, until the hereditary element should entirely disappear. Mr. Spalding, then, after providing for about one-half the membership of his new or reconstructed upper chamber in the manner above indicated, would supply the remaining membership by "some system of indirect selection." He would have these additional members "represent all the larger interests of the empire," instead of creating, as Lord Rosebery once put it, "a mere zoölogical collection of abstract celebrities." He would accord three members to

[1] Page 240.

each self-governing colony representing the *law*, the *statesmanship*, and the *general interests* of the colony, respectively. This provision is intended to advance the growing idea of British imperialism. He would also provide for "some form of representation for India." The remaining vacancies he would have filled by men representing the following classes or "categories": (a) politicians; (b) law; (c) the army; (d) the navy; (e) foreign relations; (f) the civil service; (g) colonial officials; (h) the Church; (i) education; (j) local government; (k) finance: (l) trade; (m) shipping; (n) railways and canals; (o) engineering; (p) medicine; (q) science; (r) land, including the landlord and the tenant; (s) labour, and (t) philanthropic effort. Mr. Spalding makes no attempt to go into the details of the method of selection, inasmuch as his object is "not to draw a Bill for the reform of the House of Lords, but to furnish a rough sketch of the manner in which such a reform might be effected..."[1] Mr. Spalding omits from his list two categories, the "dissenters" and the "literary men and artists," which are usually included in the schemes for the reform of the House of Lords. The dissenters, he says, are not a homogeneous body, and it would be impracticable to represent them equitably and to their own satisfaction. No man could be found who would make an acceptable spokesman for the Baptists, the Roman Catholics, the Salvation Army, and the various branches of this great body known as the dissenters. In the case of the "literary men and artists" he believes it possible for them to

[1] Pages 246-247.

qualify under one or other of the recognised categories, and further, that a seat in the upper chamber should not "be conferred as an honour, but on account of a qualification which makes the senator an efficient exponent of some large question of national importance."[1] It is of course intended by the author of this proposed plan of reform that the members chosen from these various classes or categories, should eventually constitute the entire upper chamber after the disappearance of the hereditary element.

It is not our purpose at this time to pass upon the relative merits of the various plans proposed for the reformation of the House of Lords. It should be said, however, that the plan above outlined has much to recommend it, and is vastly more sane than the majority of the more radical plans proposed, especially those which involve the entire abolition of the Upper Chamber. These latter plans are not in harmony with the conservative and evolutionary processes of reform which have been used with such conspicuous success by the Anglo-Saxon race, and their adoption would involve the abandonment of the bicameral principle which is now an axiom in political science.

One of the most novel and, to some, amazing suggestions, comes from a Conservative member of the **Indian Princes.** House of Lords. The Earl of Meath contributed an article to the May number of the "Nineteenth Century," 1894, entitled, "Shall Indian Princes sit in the House of Lords?" His reply is in the affirmative. He believes that the result of the experiment would be good. He would

[1] Page 252.

not only admit representatives from India but those from other parts of the empire as well. By this process he would advance the idea of imperial unity, or of federation. He would make the House of Lords an "Imperial Council" consisting of men "from every part of the empire." This suggestion, although made in good faith, will hardly be taken seriously by those who look upon the Indians as an inferior race, and will not be welcomed by those who decry the further advance of the imperial idea.

Another phase of opinion regarding the reform of the House of Lords remains to be noticed. There are those in England who are opposed to the bicameral principle. They believe *One Chamber.* with Sieyès that " if a second chamber dissents from the first, it is mischievous; if it agrees, it is superfluous." The views of Sir Charles Dilke, "an advanced Liberal" and well-known writer on political affairs, are interesting in this connection. Dilke, like Benjamin Franklin, is opposed on principle to the existence of upper chambers, and would consequently prefer to see the House of Lords abolished. He looks upon it as "an institution of doubtful utility," by which he means that it is an institution of positive evil, since it thwarts the will of the people as expressed by the House of Commons, by rejecting or "mangling" bills which come up from that body. He conceives it, too, little less than a national calamity that membership in the House of Lords should be forced upon men of first-rate ability, and that they should be denied membership in the Lower House, where their abilities would count for so much more.

The services of such men as Lords Salisbury, Kimberly, and others are much less effective under present conditions than they would be if those men were members of the House of Commons. Lord Rosebery, too, he conceives, if he had his choice in the matter, would not "prefer the red benches to the green." He has no faith in the various schemes for the reorganisation of the Upper Chamber. He is hostile to the House of Lords in its present form, but conceives it to be impossible to constitute another which would not be "plutocratic" in instinct and subservient to the landed interests. If he had his way about it he would abolish the House entirely, but he would prefer to have it remain in its present form rather than have it remodelled after any one of the various plans which have been proposed.

Other writers would abolish the House of Lords, not because of any opposition to the bicameral principle, but because of the hatred they bear towards its hereditary and aristocratic characteristics.

It must not be supposed, however, that the House of Lords is without its staunch defenders. Mr. Macpherson, in his able book "The Baronage and the Senate," wards off, in a rather effective way, the various attacks which have recently been made upon the Upper Chamber. Lord Wemyss thinks that the House of Lords " is the best assembly for deliberation as at present constituted in the world, and that to make it elective would destroy its independence and value, and I say this," he continues, " after having had forty-two years' experience in the House of Commons."

Defenders of the Lords.

In 1895 Mr. G. Lowes Dickinson, Fellow of King's College, Cambridge, published a work entitled "The Development of Parliament during the Nineteenth Century," in which he defends the House of Lords as it now exists, although he would not be averse to the making of some slight changes in its constitution. After a careful historical review of parliamentary legislation during the nineteenth century, Mr. Dickinson comes to the following conclusion: "On the whole, then, a survey of the action of the Lords, from 1832 onwards, does not appear to have borne out the popular impression that they have been dominated by the narrow spirit of a caste."[1] He defends the hereditary principle on the ground that the people respect it, and that it makes the legislator more independent than popular election would do. Against the charge that the Upper Chamber is a House of landlords he does not argue so strenuously. He admits the truth of the charge and concedes the fact that such a composition is a drawback, although he believes "the landed aristocracy to be far more generous and public-spirited than the commercial plutocracy which is thrusting them aside."[2] He has faith in the saving grace of the aristocratic element, and contends that the House of Commons is becoming too democratic for the welfare of the nation. His opinion of the current agitation against the House of Lords is emphatically expressed in the closing lines of his book when he says: ". . . The present agitation against the House of Lords, on the lines on which it is being conducted, is as frivolous and short-sighted a piece of

[1] Page 123.   [2] Page 177.

rhetorical folly as is to be found in the annals of modern politics."[1]

Another defender of the present constitution of the House of Lords is Mr. T. E. Kebbel. Writing in the "Subjects of the Day,"[2] in 1891, he pictures the House of Lords as a "perfectly independent" body "under no temptation to stoop either to flattery or dissimulation." He sees that "every peer is a man of business from his youth," and does not know "how we could hope to find another assembly or another such combination of qualities so exactly suited to our wants." He appeals to sentiment as well as to utility in his discussion, and maintains "that with all educated Englishmen the splendid history of the House of Lords counts for much: that its Parliamentary privileges, stretching back into the blue distance of immemorial antiquity, commend themselves to the 'study of imagination' even when they fail to satisfy the pure reason. . . ." In case it should become necessary to make changes in the constitution of the Upper Chamber, — he does not think that it is necessary at the present time, — he has his ideas as to the proper method to pursue;[3] but he is reluctant to begin, for the same reason that many Presbyterians are opposed to the revision of the creed, — he is unable to see the stopping-place. "Once make an inroad in that which is now protected by the prestige and prescription of centuries," he says, — "once impair the reverence which is engendered of long usage, custom, and the habit which is second nature, — and we should find it very difficult to stop." Hence

[1] Page 183.   [2] No. 4, pp. 74-95.   [3] *Ibid.* p. 86.

The English Government

he would not allow profane hands to be laid upon the ark.

I beg leave, in conclusion, to quote a few lines from a small book by "A Sussex Peer," entitled "Drifting towards the Breakers," which appeared in 1895. I do this merely as a matter of curiosity, not because of the worth of the volume. It really has none. It is interesting as a bit of freak literature, but its value as a contribution to the present controversy is insignificant. The writer evidently thinks that England is to be deluged by civil war as a result of the agitation against the lords, and urges that forces be organised to meet and repel the attack. "It is no longer," he says, "the Hyde Park orator who leads this seditious movement; it is Mr. Gladstone. It is no longer the petty demagogue who shouts for the downfall of the lords; it is the Prime Minister of England. You may sneer at Mr. Burns and laugh at Mr. Labouchere, but you cannot as reasonable beings pooh-pooh Mr. Gladstone, Lord Rosebery, and the great Liberal meetings at Portsmouth and at Leeds, where at the first the leaders of the Liberal party pledged themselves to the uncompromising policy of total abolition; and where at the second, Leeds, the delegates of the extremer section of the democratic party resolved upon a definite course of action, — a little more temporising outwardly, but in effect as uncompromising and fatal as the policy of the Portsmouth gathering."[1] The book concludes with the following inflammatory remarks: "Combine, then, and organise. It would be folly to fold our arms,

[1] Pages 14-15.

indulging in dreams of a false security which does not exist. . . . As the Secretary for Ireland says, 'The movement must go on,' therefore shut your eyes if you will, close your ears if you like; but it would be a negation of the senses God has given us if we, as intelligent beings, refused any longer to acknowledge the sound of the rising tide of a democratic revolution which is even now rippling against the very steps of the throne. The movement must go on; the conflict must take place. Victory will follow the forces, the readiest, the best equipped; organised wealth and force will prevail over undisciplined numbers, however great. Our cause is our Constitution and our Monarchy. . . . Combine and organise! and then with unflinching hearts, in tones of defiance to our foes which shall not be misunderstood, with a voice which will ring not only throughout England but through the listening nations of the world, we will say to our Sovereign, 'If you call us, we will come.'"

The utterances of the book are of an emotional and alarmist character throughout, and I almost feel like apologising for incorporating the above excerpt in this discussion, as the opinions expressed are not typical of any significant part of the English people. It is sometimes interesting, however, to watch a man fight windmills.

There has been a flood of literature upon this subject in recent years, and we might continue its review almost indefinitely, but enough has been said, perhaps, to indicate the trend of public opinion. In this connection the conclusions of Editor James

The English Government

Samuelson are of interest. After discussing with the aid of experts the problem of the House of Lords in all its phases, Mr. Samuelson expresses himself in his editorial remarks as follows: "Whatever may be the views of individual statesmen or of social or political parties, we believe there can be no doubt that at the present time the great body of the British nation still approves of the existence of a Second Chamber; they wish, however, to see that Chamber a reality, and not a select assemblage of one privileged class, resting its strength and claims on inherited rank, musty precedents, and pompous ceremonial, but a Senate, representative of the whole nation, and fortified by the authority and sanction of the National Will as expressed by the voice of the constituencies." [1]

Impartial observers, viewing the problem in the light of historical perspective, and not fascinated by the charm of aristocracy or intoxicated by excessive democracy, will probably come to the conclusion that the Second Chamber of the English Parliament will continue to exist, but probably in a slightly modified form. The bicameral system, as developed in England, will not be abandoned by the Englishman with his love of precedent, and no revolutionary changes will be made in the Upper House which will cause it to lose its peculiar character. The strength of English institutions has always been their conservatism, and we may logically expect that conservatism to continue.

General Conclusion.

[1] "Subjects of the Day," No. 4, p. 117.

CHAPTER XII

THE ORIGIN, DEVELOPMENT, AND COMPOSITION OF THE HOUSE OF COMMONS

REFERENCES: Anson's *Law and Custom of the Constitution*, i. 75-184; Bagehot's *English Constitution*, 198-243 and 340-359; Walpole's *Electorate and the Legislature*, 47-89; Courtney's *Working Constitution of the United Kingdom*, 3-99; Taswell-Langmead's *English Constitutional History*, 742-750; Syme's *Representative Government in England*, 1-60; Dod's *Parliamentary Companion* and English political and statistical almanacs. See also pamphlets and magazine articles mentioned in the bibliographical note at the close of this volume.

WE come now to a discussion of the House of Commons, — the most important governmental institution in England. For several centuries after the Norman Conquest the Crown was the most important factor in the English government. The power of Parliament was comparatively insignificant. That body made large claims to governmental authority, but was not uniformly able to withstand the encroachments of the King. However, as we trace the development of the English government during the latter part of the middle ages and the early part of the modern period, we notice that the power of the King steadily declines while that of Parliament just as steadily increases. This process continues until the Revolution of 1688, when the power of the Crown becomes merely nominal and that of Parliament becomes absolute. In the mean time, too, relatively speaking, the power of the House of Commons was increasing and that of the House of Lords was decreasing. This process continued until 1832, at which time it became evident that the House of Commons was the real governing power in England, and that the two branches of the legislature were no longer co-ordinate. From 1832, then, until the present day, the will of the House of Commons has prevailed against that of the Crown on the one hand and the Lords on the other, and it is, therefore, no exaggeration to call that body the most important branch of the English government.

The origin of the House of Commons, unlike that of the House of Lords, may be traced to a very definite date. It was founded by Simon de Montfort in 1265. The event is one of the most important in all English history. Henry III. was King of England at the time, and his despotic character was the immediate cause of the establishment of the popular branch of the legislature. He had repeatedly and solemnly confirmed the provisions of Magna Charta only to disregard them persistently. He harboured many unworthy foreign favourites at his court, and was prodigal in the expenditure of money. To supply the necessary revenue he extorted money from the people by various illegal methods. He was also the champion of the Roman as against the National Church. By these means he succeeded, as did King John in 1215, in arraying practically the entire English nation against himself. The barons, taking up the cause of the people, prevailed against Henry as they had previously done against John, and succeeded in gaining his unwilling consent to a set of

Origin.

articles known as the Provisions of Oxford, by which his power was very greatly curtailed. Three years later, in 1261, the King boldly refused to be bound by the Provisions, and civil war ensued. The decisive battle was fought at Lewes near Hastings, where the Norman William had defeated the Saxon Harold in 1066. King Henry was utterly defeated, and the government of England fell, as a result, into the hands of the barons of whom Simon de Montfort was the leader. This patriotic man made good use of the vast power of which he found himself possessed. The governmental authority up to this time had been lodged in the King and the two Estates of the Realm, — the Lords and the Clergy. The common people had been excluded. Simon de Montfort now issued writs for a Parliament to which representatives of the common people or the Third Estate were to be admitted. The sheriffs were directed to return two knights from each shire, two citizens from each city, and two burgesses from each borough to meet in London on the 20th of January, 1265. This assembly, known as the Parliament of Simon de Montfort, met according to call in 1265, and this date marks the birth of the House of Commons. The beginning of the popular chamber was a humble one, and thirty years were destined to elapse before there was a perfect representation in Parliament of the three Estates of the Realm. Even then all of the members of Parliament sat together, constituting one House, and continued to do so until about the middle of the fourteenth century.[1]

[1] 1341. See G. B. Smith's "History of the English Parliament," vol. i. p. 199.

Such, then, was the surpassing service of Simon de Montfort to English liberty. He was not, as Guizot termed him, "the founder of representative government in England," — for the principle of representation was in use long before his time, — but he certainly was the "founder of the House of Commons" and that is honour enough for one man.

The "founder of the House of Commons"[1] well deserves a word in this connection. He was a member of an illustrious French family and was born in France in 1208. In 1230 he came to England, and nine years later became the Earl of Leicester. He became one of the King's councillors and was on intimate terms with the Royal Family. Simon de Montfort was a natural leader, and just the man demanded by the crisis in England. He was possessed of a chivalrous spirit, was a man of political foresight, and was popular among the clergy and the learned classes as well as among the common people. The popular enthusiasm for his name found expression in a song, "The Strong Citadel," "because he loved right and hated wrong." He was killed in the battle of Evesham, but his work lived on, and the light of his noble character still illumines the pages of English history. He was foremost in the political, religious, and military life of his time, and in private life was pure and tolerant in the midst of licentiousness and tyranny. "He stood forth in the midst of an age cursed by the cruelties and oppression of feudalism, the seer and harbinger of the new era." He was the Moses who led the English people out of the

Simon de Montfort.

---

[1] Freeman's "English Constitution," pp. 183-184.

wilderness of oppression into the promised land of liberty; and though great in peace and war, his greatest claim to the undying gratitude of posterity lies in the fact that it was he who first admitted the people to their inheritance, and thus "first struck the keynote of constitutional government."

Quite opportunely, while these lines are being written, the "Atlantic Monthly" for August, 1901, comes to hand with an admirable little poem by William Watson entitled "For England," showing that the services of the noble Earl Simon are deemed worthy of the pen of the poet six centuries after his death.

> "Of all great deaths on English ground, thine most,
>   Simon de Montfort, doth my spirit stir.
>   Thou fought'st for England, and thou died'st for her,
>   Thyself of other race, from outland coast.
>   Law's mandatory and Freedom's, thou thy host
>   Didst hurl against a sceptred lawbreaker;
>   Nor didst thou blench when Fate, in plume and spur,
>   On Evesham field swept like a hungry ghost.
>   Then for their lives thou bad'st thy nobles fly.
>   'Thou dying, we would not live,' they made reply,
>   And dauntless, round thy dauntlessness were mown.
>   And thou, with wrath that hewed its way on high,
>   Fell'st fighting the steep fight of Liberty,
>   In a crashing forest of the foe, alone."

It is not our purpose to trace the development of the House of Commons from its origin in 1265 to the present time. We are concerned with the House as it now exists rather than with its historical development, yet a word in regard to a few turning-points in its history may not be out of place.

Evolution of the House.

We have noticed that it was not until 1295, thirty years after the founding of the House of Commons, that the three Estates of the Realm were perfectly represented in Parliament. At that time there were two hundred and seventy-four members in the Lower House. In the reign of Queen Elizabeth the number had risen to four hundred and sixty-two, and just before the union with Scotland there were five hundred and thirteen members. The Act of Union with Scotland in 1707 added forty-five members from that country to the English Parliament, making a total of five hundred and fifty-eight. The union with Ireland in 1801 caused an addition of one hundred Irish members, making a total membership of six hundred and fifty-eight. By an Act passed in 1885 the membership was increased to six hundred and seventy, where it still remains.

Representation in the Lower House of the American Congress is based upon population, and an effort is made to keep the representation of each state proportional to the number of its inhabitants by providing for a reapportionment of representatives among the states every ten years. The states are also redistricted from time to time for congressional purposes, in order that the representation of localities may be equitable. Representation in England has never been, and is not now, placed upon such a precise mathematical basis; yet there is a feeling at the present time that the representation of any locality in the House of Commons should, in a general way, be proportional to its population. This idea, however, is of comparatively recent origin, and before 1832 the representation of the various localities was adjusted so infrequently that gross inequalities resulted, and these were allowed to continue for centuries.

During the one hundred and sixty years preceding 1832 no change was made in the composition of the House of Commons, aside from the admission of the Scotch and Irish members in 1707 and 1801, respectively.[1] The population of many of the rural districts of England had either not increased, or had actually decreased, during this period; while the great manufacturing centres like Manchester, Birmingham, Leeds, and Sheffield had become the homes of tens of thousands of people. In general it may be said that the representation of rural England was excessive, while the manufacturing towns had almost no representation at all. When the members were apportioned among the various localities these manufacturing towns were either not in existence or were too insignificant to be recognised. "In Plantagenet times . . . Liverpool was a little group of cottages; Manchester was a village; Birmingham a sand-hill; and the wealth and trade of the country were mainly concentrated in London, Norwich, and Bristol. The industrial revolutions of the eighteenth century, the introduction of steam, the invention of machinery, the construction of roads and canals, altered these conditions."[2] The population of the rural districts began to decay, while that of the manufacturing towns increased by leaps and bounds. "Some boroughs had almost literally no inhabitants. Gatton was a park; Old Sarum a mound; Corfe Castle a ruin; the remains of what

[1] Walpole's "Electorate and the Legislature," p. 57. [2] *Idem.*

once was Dunwich were under the waves of the North Sea."[1] Many other boroughs contained only ten or a dozen voters, yet all these sent their members to Parliament, none the less. Thus while the lapse of time was increasing the number and significance of the "rotten boroughs," the great industrial centres of the north and west of England were becoming giant powers in the commercial world while they remained ciphers in the political. During all this transformation little or no change was made in the number or apportionment of members of the House of Commons, and the most glaring inequalities and inconsistencies developed. The difficulty, too, was aggravated by a low state of political morality and by the tenacity with which the owners of "rotten boroughs" clung to their ancient privileges. The suffrage was very much restricted, and bribery and sale were of common occurrence. Horace Walpole tells us in his "Memoirs" that the borough of Sudbury advertised itself for sale to the highest bidder, with no apparent effort to disguise the transaction. The situation in Scotland was no better than in England, — in some respects it was worse. The right of voting was very much restricted. In one county (Cromarty) in 1823 the number of qualified electors was nine. The county of Bute had twenty-one electors, of whom one only was a resident of the county. An election was held at which the resident, the sheriff, and the returning officer were present. The said resident, not being afflicted with overmuch modesty, took the chair, moved his own election, seconded his own

[1] Walpole's "Electorate and the Legislature," p. 56.

motion, put the question to vote, and declared himself duly and unanimously elected. In Ireland also the majority of the seats in Parliament were filled at the dictation of a comparatively few men.

A few figures will serve to summarise and to make definite these general statements. In 1793, three hundred and fifty-four out of the five hundred and fifty-eight members of the House were nominally returned by less than fifteen thousand electors; as a matter of fact these members were elected on the recommendation of the Government, or upon the indorsement of one hundred and ninety-seven private persons of influence. In 1801, when one hundred Irish members were added to the House, seventy-one of them were chosen by the influence of fifty-six individuals. In 1816 the situation was still worse. Dr. Oldfield found at that time that the election of four hundred and eighty-seven of the six hundred and fifty-eight members was dictated by the Government and by two hundred and sixty-seven private patrons, of whom one hundred and forty-four were peers. There was, of course, little of popular representation in such a situation as that. The younger Pitt saw the true inwardness of things when he exclaimed, "This House is not the representative of the people of Great Britain; it is the representative of nominal boroughs, of ruined and exterminated towns, of noble families, of wealthy individuals, of foreign potentates."

These conspicuous defects in the representative system were not unnoticed by English statesmen. As early as 1766 Mr. Pitt (afterwards Lord Chatham) declared for parliamentary reform. His efforts were destined to fail for the time, but the agitation was continued and finally crowned with success by the passage of the famous Reform Act of June 7, 1832. The contest was a memorable one. The reform measure was violently opposed by all of the conservatism of England and by those borough owners and patrons of influence whose power would be curtailed by its passage. The Duke of Wellington while Prime Minister set his face as firmly against the reform measure as he did against Napoleon at Waterloo. It seems strange that a measure which commends itself so fully to our ideas of fairness and justice should have been opposed so strenuously, but conservative England would not easily admit untried new-comers within the charmed circle of legislation. "The first minister of the Crown," said Macaulay, "declared that he would consent to no reform; that he thought our representative system, just as it stood, the masterpiece of human wisdom; that if he had to make it anew, he would make it just as it was, with all its represented ruins and all its unrepresented cities." However, the wheels of progress were not to be blocked indefinitely, and a Whig Ministry under the premiership of Lord Grey, who had advocated the reform of the representative system for forty years, took up the matter with an earnestness not to be denied. After repeated defeats the Prime Minister secured the permission of the King for the creation of a sufficient number of peers to take seats in the House of Lords to insure the passage of the measure. The lords recognised the logic of the situation and allowed the bill to become a law "amidst the greatest popular excitement," on the 7th of June, 1832. The passage of this bill was one of the most notable triumphs in the history of constitutional government in England. It marks an epoch in the history of the House of Commons. It decided that representation in the Lower House should be equitable, and that the two branches of the legislature were no longer co-ordinate in power. Since 1832 the House of Lords has been compelled to give way to the House of Commons whenever the latter body insisted upon the passage of its measure.

The Reform Act of 1832 went straight to the heart of the matter. It disfranchised fifty-six "rotten boroughs," which returned one hundred and eleven members, and reduced the representation in thirty others. The seats thus obtained were distributed among the more populous localities in such a way as to make the representation more equitable. During the same session Reform Acts were passed for Ireland and Scotland. These Acts were by no means perfect, but they were giant strides in the right direction. The good work was continued in the Reform Acts of 1867, and by the Franchise Act of 1884. In 1885 a Redistribution Act was passed by which the membership of the House of Commons was increased from six hundred and fifty-eight to six hundred and seventy. According to this Act, which is in force at the present time, England and Wales have four hundred and ninety-five members, Ireland has one hundred and three, and Scotland seventy-two. By these various reform movements culminating in 1832,

1867, 1884, and 1885, representation in the House of Commons was made more equitable, and the franchise was extended. On the whole it may be said that the tendency in England during the last century has been toward representation on the basis of population and toward manhood suffrage. It has been estimated that five hundred thousand voters were added to the polling lists by the Act of 1832, one million by the Act of 1867, and two million by the Act of 1885.[1]

The members of the House of Commons are divided into three classes according to the constituencies **The Present Situation.** which they represent. These classes represent the counties, the boroughs or towns, and the universities. There are at present three hundred and seventy-seven county members, two hundred and eighty-four borough members, and nine university members. According to the redistribution scheme of 1885, all towns with a population less than fifteen thousand were disfranchised and merged in the county districts. All towns having a population between fifteen thousand and fifty thousand were entitled to one member, and those having populations between fifty thousand and one hundred and sixty-five thousand were to be represented by two members, and one additional member was allowed for every fifty thousand people. The system of "single member districts" was to prevail in all large cities except London. At the present time London returns sixty-one members to the House of Commons,

[1] G. B. Smith's "History of the English Parliament," vol. ii. p. 547.

Liverpool nine, Birmingham seven, Manchester six, Sheffield and Leeds five each, Bristol four, Glasgow seven, Edinburgh four, Dublin four, Belfast four, and the smaller cities a less number in proportion to their populations. Seventy-three out of one hundred and five towns in England return only one member each. Eight of the nine boroughs in Wales return one member each, and the ninth, Merther Tydvil, returns two members. Of the Scottish boroughs only Glasgow, Edinburgh, Dundee, and Aberdeen return more than one member each. Of the Irish boroughs only Belfast, Dublin, and Cork have more than one representative each in the House of Commons. The representation of the English counties varies from one to twenty-six. The tiny county of Rutland, with a little less than one hundred and seventy[1] square miles of territory, has one representative. All other counties return more than one member, York returning the largest number, twenty-six, while Lancashire has twenty-three. Each county is divided into districts corresponding to the number of members to which it is entitled. In Wales, where the population is more sparse, eight of the twelve counties return one member, while Glamorgan returns the largest number, five. In Scotland in five instances two counties were united to form one parliamentary division, and eighteen others return one member each. Only six counties out of thirty-four return more than one member each, Lanark returning the largest number, six. All of the thirty-two Irish counties except

[1] This is less than one-half the area of an average county in the state of Indiana.

Carlow return more than one member each, and Cork returns the largest number, seven.

The above distribution of members made in 1885 is no longer equitable. The population of the United Kingdom is now (1901) 41,454,621. According to the present membership, six hundred and seventy, each member should represent 61,866 people. Upon this basis England should have four hundred and ninety-eight members instead of four hundred and sixty-five; Wales should have twenty-eight instead of thirty; Scotland should have seventy-two, as at present; and Ireland should have seventy-two, instead of one hundred and three as at present. This inequality has arisen largely from the increase of population in England and from the phenomenal decrease in Ireland. The population of Ireland has decreased nearly fifty per cent since 1841, due largely to emigration. The matter of a redistribution of seats has been discussed in Parliament from time to time, and there is good reason to expect a readjustment in the near future.

In addition to the county and borough members, there are nine members representing the universities **The University Members.** of the United Kingdom. At the present time Oxford has two representatives; Cambridge, two; the University of London, one; Dublin University, two; the Universities of Edinburgh and St. Andrews, one joint representative, and the Universities of Glasgow and Aberdeen, one joint representative. The representation of the universities began in the reign of James I. (1603–1625), when they were accorded four members. The graduates of each university are entitled to vote for the member or members representing their *Alma Mater*. The number of such graduates entitled to vote at the last general election (1900) was as follows:

Cambridge	6886
Oxford	6221
London	4403
Glasgow and Aberdeen	9397
Edinburgh and St. Andrews	9987
Dublin	4669

These university graduates may also vote in the various localities where they reside or have property. In England it is possible for a man to have several votes, but there is now an agitation in favour of giving to "one man one vote." A man may vote in the several localities where he possesses property. A merchant like Sir Thomas Lipton may have numerous votes; and since the parliamentary elections are not all held on the same day, but extend over a month or more, there is an opportunity to cast these various votes. The alumnus in voting for a university member may deliver his vote orally or by means of a "voting paper" sent from his place of residence.

Six of the present university members are Conservatives, the remaining three being Liberal Unionists. Some of the university members have rendered illustrious services to their universities and to the government. Prof. Sir R. C. Jebb has represented Cambridge University for the past ten years. He is well known as an author and is one of the greatest Greek scholars of the time. His works are of a sterling rather than brilliant character, as thousands of American college students will testify who have pored over the rigid dignity of the pages of his "Primer of Greek Literature." Sir Michael Foster, Professor of Physiology at Cambridge, and the well-known author of treatises on Physiology, is the present representative of London University. Rt. Hon. James A. Campbell, a retired merchant of Glasgow, has represented the Universities of Glasgow and Aberdeen for the last twenty-two years. One of the members for Oxford is Sir William R. Anson, Warden of All Souls College and author of the well-known works on "Law of Contract" and "Law and Custom of the Constitution." These books are familiar to law students on both sides of the Atlantic. All Souls College has practically no students[1] and desires none; the members of her faculty are well employed in original research, of which the Warden is a worthy exponent. Rt. Hon. William E. H. Lecky, the famous historian, is now one of the members representing the University of Dublin. His "History of England in the Eighteenth Century," his "History of European Morals," and his "Democracy and Liberty" have made his name familiar to students of history and political philosophy, both in Europe and America.

The university members in England have rendered valuable services to the government, and constitute a peculiar link between the state and the institutions of higher learning, which has never existed in America. There has been, however, a tendency in recent

[1] There were six in 1901.

years in the United States to enlist to a greater extent than ever before the services of university men in the affairs of state. This movement has been encouraged by Seth Low, late President of Columbia University; Daniel C. Gilman, late President of the Johns Hopkins University; James B. Angell, President of the University of Michigan; Jacob G. Schurman, President of Cornell University; Ambassador Andrew D. White and others, and the results must commend themselves to all thinking persons.

The university members in England are now, as a rule, returned without opposition except from Dublin University. In that case there is quite likely to be a contest.

The English Parliament has insisted for centuries upon its three great privileges,—freedom of speech, freedom from arrest, and the right to deter- *Contested* mine contested elections. It is the last of *Seats.* these that concerns us at the present moment. The House of Commons has the power to decide all questions relating to the election of its members. The same power resides in the Senate and the House of Representatives of the American Congress. It was formerly the custom in England, as it is now in the United States, to refer contested elections to a committee for investigation and report. Before 1770 these matters were passed upon by the whole House, and the vote was usually strictly partisan. Efforts were made from time to time to arrange some plan whereby these contests might be decided upon their merits, but no satisfactory solution of the difficulty was reached until 1868, at which time the

House of Commons transferred its jurisdiction in these cases to the law courts. Petitions relating to contested seats are now presented to the courts instead of to the House of Commons, as formerly. "The House has no cognizance of these proceedings until their termination: when the judges certify their determination, in writing, to the Speaker, which is final to all intents and purposes."[1] This method of determining contested elections is more satisfactory than that which obtains in the Congress of the United States. Yet in this latter body the tendency is in the right direction, and the members are more disposed than they formerly were, to decide cases upon their merits rather than upon partisan grounds.

When vacancies occur in the House of Commons writs for new elections are issued by order of the Speaker. A vacancy may occur due to any one of several causes, but never as the result of a resignation. "It is a settled principle of parliamentary law that a member, after he is duly chosen, cannot relinquish his seat;"[2] and in order to evade this principle the member who wishes to resign applies for some office under the Crown, the acceptance of which vacates his seat. The member usually applies for the office of the stewardship of the Chiltern Hundreds, which is granted as a matter of course. The office is merely nominal, having no fixed term, no duties or fees, but is granted "with all the wages, fees, allowances," etc., and thus has the effect in law of an "office of profit." When the office

Vacancies.

[1] May's "Parliamentary Practice," p. 617.   [2] *Ibid.* p. 605.

The English Government

has served its purpose, it is relinquished to be used by another member with similar effect. Of course this method is simply one of indirect resignation, and proposals have been made on various occasions to allow a member to relinquish his seat directly, but English conservatism has invariably said "No."

It frequently happens that a man stands for election in more than one constituency and is elected in more than one. In such a case he must decide within a week after the opening of the session, which of the constituencies he prefers to represent, and must make known his intentions either by a letter addressed to the Speaker or by an oral statement made to the House itself. A bye-election will then be held to fill the vacancy. In the United States no such plural election could occur, since it is an almost invariable rule that the nominee lives within the district which he aspires to represent. In England the choice is restricted neither by law nor by custom, and a resident of London may represent a constituency in York or elsewhere.

There are certain disqualifications which incapacitate a man for sitting as a member of the House of Commons. These should be noted briefly. *Disqualifications.*

Infants or minors are not eligible to seats in the House of Commons, yet the rule has not always been strictly enforced. Charles James Fox was elected, took his seat, and participated in the proceedings of the House before becoming of age. Lord John Russell was elected to the House when he lacked a month of being twenty-one. These men, like Henry

Clay, when he was elected to the United States Senate before attaining the age of thirty, maintained a discreet silence and performed the functions of their office unmolested. There has been no instance of such violation of law in England in recent years.

Lunacy or idiocy also operates as a disqualification for obvious reasons.

Aliens are not eligible to sit in Parliament, but may become naturalised and thus qualify themselves for seats. An Act was passed about 1870 enabling them to do this.

English and Scotch peers are not eligible under any circumstances to seats in the House of Commons. An Irish peer, however, may sit for any constituency in the United Kingdom outside of Ireland, provided he be not one of the twenty-eight Irish representative peers chosen to sit in the House of Lords. The sons of peers are, of course, commoners and are eligible to sit in the House of Commons. They must vacate their seats at once, however, when they inherit seats in the Upper Chamber. There are always a few members of the House of Commons to whom the title "Lord" is commonly accorded. The sons of peers bear the second titles of their fathers by courtesy, if there be second titles. For example, the son of the Duke of Devonshire is, by courtesy, the Marquis of Hartington. He is a commoner, however, and eligible to sit in the House of Commons, but not in the House of Lords. Lord John Russell was a "Lord" only by courtesy, and in a legal document would be the Honourable John Russell. He was a younger son of the Duke of Bedford. Lord Palmerston was an Irish peer, not one of the twenty-eight representative peers of Ireland, and was elected to sit in the House of Commons. Lord Randolph Churchill was also a member of the House of Commons, and Lord George Hamilton, the third son of the first Duke of Abercorn and brother of the present Duke, is a member of the House of Commons and Secretary of State for India. These titles by courtesy are sometimes confusing to an American, and are apparent exceptions to the rule that a peer is not eligible to a seat in the House of Commons.

Clergymen of the English Church and ministers of the Church of Scotland were disqualified by statute in 1801, and the Roman Catholic clergy were similarly dealt with in 1829. An Act passed in 1870 makes it possible for clergymen of the English Church to divest themselves of their orders and thus qualify for Parliament. This has been done in several instances.

The holders of certain offices are disqualified for sitting in the House of Commons; for example, certain of the offices held under the Crown disqualify the incumbents. Certain pensioners are also disqualified by statute for sitting in the Commons. The statutes, however, specifically exempt civil service and diplomatic pensioners from the operation of the rule.

Contractors for public works are also disqualified, and a penalty of £500 per day is imposed for the time which such contractor continues to sit and vote. Contractors for government loans are exempt from the operation of this rule.

Convicted felons and bankrupts are disqualified, under certain conditions, from sitting in the House of Commons.

Persons found guilty of "corrupt practices" in elections are disqualified for certain periods of time. Perhaps a more extended comment upon this matter might not be amiss, since it would serve to illustrate the general stringency of election laws in England. The Corrupt Practices Act of 1883, which is now in force, serves to eliminate undue influences from parliamentary elections. By this Act the briber or the person bribed is imprisoned for a term not exceeding twelve months, with or without hard labour, or he is fined to an amount not exceeding £200. If the bribery be committed by the candidate personally, he loses his seat, if elected, and becomes ineligible for ever representing the particular constituency. If the bribery be the unauthorised act of an agent, the election is void and the candidate is disqualified for seven years for sitting for the constituency in which the offence was committed. This penalty is a very severe one when we consider the inclusive definition that the Act gives to bribery. It is bribery, for example, to pay the day's wages of any voter, or to give him money for railway fare or loss of time. Should the voter be "treated" for the purpose of influencing his vote or inducing him not to vote at all, the penalty is the same as for bribery. The treating of wives and other relatives of the voters for the purpose of influencing votes is punishable in the same way that bribery is. The regulation cuts both ways, as those who accept food or drink in this way are liable to the same penalty which is inflicted upon those who give it. The withdrawing of one's custom or employment and the threat to evict a tenant are punishable in the same way that bribery is. The paying or receiving of money for the conveying of voters to the polls is prohibited under heavy penalty, so is the paying of a voter for posting or distributing bills or notices. The person receiving the payment is also liable to punishment. A regularly authorised advertising agent, however, is exempted by the Act. It is also an offence against the Act to "pay for bands, torches, flags, banners, cockades, ribbons, or other marks of distinction." The Act further provides that election placards, posters, and bills of various kinds shall contain the name and address of the printer and publisher. Failure to comply with this specification may render the election of the candidate void, and subject him to a fine not exceeding £100.

The amount of the legitimate expenses of the campaign is also strictly limited. There is a maximum expenditure beyond which the candidate may not go without entailing the loss of his seat, if elected, and incurring the penalty for "illegal practice" in any case. The scale of expenditure is based upon the number of electors in the constituencies, and the maximum is £350 for the boroughs where the number of electors does not exceed 2,000, and an additional £30 for every additional 1000 voters. The maximum expenditure allowed is sometimes as high as £1500, with additional fees for the returning officer. Serving in Parliament is evidently not a paying occupation from the financial standpoint, since the office carries with it no salary. The maximum for a county division is nearly twice as great as for a borough division of the same population. The personal expenses of the candidate are not included in the scale, and are not limited to any particular sum; yet if they exceed £100 they must be paid through the election agent. The fees of the returning officer are also outside the maximum prescribed in the scale. The number of persons whom the candidate may employ in the campaign is limited, so also is the number of committee rooms which he may engage. The law prescribes the various ways in which money may be legitimately expended in the campaign, and the agent of the candidate is required to make a detailed return of the amount expended under each head. The return must be certified to upon oath before a justice of the peace by the agent and by the candidate; and a false declaration renders them liable to prosecution for perjury, and, if convicted, to seven years' penal servitude.

Since the above Act is rigidly enforced it is needless to say that elections in England are comparatively honest. The chief difficulty in this connection arises from the tendency of judges to take different views of the provisions of the Act of 1883.

It might be well to note in this connection that there were many other disqualifications which are now extinct. The disabilities were removed from Catholics by the Act of 1829. Jews were admitted to Parliament in 1858. The Oaths Act of 1888 made it possible for persons having no religious belief to make an affirmation instead of taking an oath. This was the result of the famous Bradlaugh case. The property qualification for members of Parliament was done away with in 1858. Residence in the district was required by an Act passed in the reign of Henry V. By the time of Elizabeth this requirement had fallen into disuse and was repealed in 1774.

It is also within the power of the House of Commons to expel a member. This expedient is resorted to only in cases where the retention of the member would serve to bring discredit upon Parliament. **Expulsion of Members.** The offences for which a member may be expelled are usually serious. Members have been expelled for participating in rebellion against the government; for forgery, perjury, and fraud of various kinds; for breaches of trust, misappropriation of public funds, conspiracy to defraud, corruption in the administration of justice, or in public office; for "conduct unbecoming the character of an officer and a gentleman;" for contempts, libels, and other offences against the House itself.[1] The jurisdiction which Parliament exercises over its members is extensive, but by no means excessive. Such jurisdiction is essential to the proper performance of its functions. The Houses of the American Congress exercise practically the same absolute sway, and neither in England nor in America has there been an abuse of power in recent years.

It is convenient at this point to note the classes of persons who possess the right to vote for members

[1] May's "Parliamentary Practice," p. 55.

of the House of Commons. Although the suffrage has been greatly extended in England in recent years, it is still much more restricted than in the United States. This is due in the main to the property qualification, which, though reduced in amount, still obtains in England. The Acts of 1832, 1867, and 1884–85, extended the right to vote in the direction of manhood suffrage, but did not abolish the property qualification entirely. This qualification tends to restrict the number of electors. The population of the United Kingdom, according to the census of 1901, is 41,454,621. Of this number 6,517,719,[1] or fifteen and seven-tenths per cent of the whole number, are entitled to vote for members of the House of Commons. The census figures for 1900 show quite a contrast in the United States. The population is 76,000,000, and of these 14,000,000, or about twenty per cent of the whole number, are entitled to vote for members of the House of Representatives. These figures indicate a more extended suffrage in the United States. In general, it may be said that in the United States all male citizens of full age and of sound mind and not dependent are entitled to vote. Even aliens are granted the franchise in some States. There is no property qualification. In England, however, the right to vote depends for the most part upon "property," "occupation," or "residence." It might seem that the two latter terms were synonymous, but they are not so, according to the construction of the English law, as a man might "occupy" a piece of property, such as a warehouse

The Franchise.

---

[1] This number would be reduced if deductions were made for plural voting.

or a shop, without making it his residence. The English franchise is now based for the most part upon an Act passed in 1868 and extended in 1884. The Act of 1832 is still effective in some constituencies. The provisions of the various Acts are greatly complicated and contain a thousand details upon the discussion of which it would not be profitable to enter at this time. Let it suffice to say that in general in England a man bases his right to vote upon the *ownership, occupation,* or *inhabitancy* of a certain amount of property specified by law. For example, a man possessed of a freehold estate in lands or tenements to the annual value of forty shillings is entitled to vote; so also is the occupier of any land or tenement of a yearly value of not less than £10. As explained above, " occupation " does not of necessity mean " residence." Also the man who occupies lodgings of a yearly value, if let unfurnished, of £10 or upwards, is entitled, with some few restrictions, to vote for members of the House of Commons. It might be remarked in passing that the qualifications for electors for county members are now practically the same as those for electors for borough members, yet some few minor differences yet remain. It might also be well to call attention to the fact that these property qualifications do not apply to electors for a university constituency.

It is evident from the above regulations that one man may have several votes. Each one of several pieces of property, for example, may entitle him to a vote. This is quite contrary to American practice, and a determined crusade has been inaugurated against it in England. In 1887 Mr. Gladstone placed the plank, "One man, one vote," in the Gladstonian Liberal platform, and any one who has followed the recent trend of events in England will probably agree with Justin McCarthy when he says: ... "The time must come when that principle will have to be established in our legislation, and a man will no longer be allowed to have one vote for his house in the West End, a second for his office in the City, a third for his country house in one of the shires, a fourth for his shooting-place in Scotland, and so on."[1]

It is evident that, in case restrictions were not placed upon the matter, it would be possible for a man of wealth to obtain for himself a large number of votes by the possession of a number of small freeholds, each of an annual value of forty shillings. Early in the eighteenth century an Act was passed, by which the splitting of interest and temporary conveyance of property for election purposes were expressly forbidden.

The above constitute the general rules governing the franchise. To make the matter more definite it may be well to note those classes of persons to whom the right to vote is specifically denied.

Disqualifications.

Women are not entitled to vote. The courts have uniformly held that the parliamentary franchise in England was restricted to males. An "infant" is also disqualified; but as the law does not recognise fractions of days a man may vote on the day preced-

[1] "History of our own Times," vol. iii. p. 151.

ing his twenty-first birthday. Peers are also disqualified. They have their adequate representation in the House of Lords. "No Peer other than a Peer of Ireland who has been actually elected and is serving as a member of the House of Commons has a right to vote."[1] Returning officers are disqualified except in the case of a tie vote. In such a case the returning officer may cast his vote and thus break the tie. Agents, canvassers, clerks, messengers, and others employed in any capacity in an election are not entitled to vote. Aliens, idiots, and lunatics are disqualified, and so are persons convicted of treason or felony, unless a pardon has been obtained or the term of imprisonment has been served. Persons who have, within a year, received "parochial relief or other alms" are thereby disqualified. Relief, however, in the form of medical or surgical attendance does not now disqualify. The elector must also register before being qualified to vote. The method of making up the registration rolls is so elaborate and thorough that frauds are not easily perpetrated.

There is nothing in England exactly like our caucus or convention for the nomination of candidates for office. A committee of voters, chosen from the parliamentary division, selects **Nominations.** some one to stand for election in the constituency as the candidate of some particular party. The matter of nomination is usually cared for by the local party association or its committee. It often occurs, however, that the central party office is asked by a particular constituency to send a candidate. The proc-

[1] Anson, "Law and Custom of the Constitution," part i. p. 118.

ess is much simpler and less formal than in the United States, and contests for nominations are not so vigorous, as a rule. The plan works fairly well. Other nominations are then made in the same way by opposing parties, and the campaign is on. It is short but decidedly vigorous while it lasts. A large number of public meetings are held, quite similar to political meetings in America, at which addresses are made by the candidate and his political and personal friends. Several meetings may be in progress on the same evening and may be addressed by practically the same speakers. When a man has finished his address at one meeting, he hurries off to address the voters assembled in another part of the division, and another man is ready to take his place. Women are quite prominent at these meetings, and the candidate is usually accompanied by his wife and other ladies. In most instances the addresses are short business-like talks instead of long and laboured " efforts." The candidate, of course, is the object of most interest, and his views upon current politics are matters of great concern to the voters. He is frequently submitted to an ordeal of questioning by the audience or "heckling," as it is called, and may make or mar his future according to the way in which he conducts himself. Judging from somewhat limited observations it would seem that there was less attempt upon the part of the speakers to play upon the emotions of the audience than with us, yet the demagogic element is by no means absent. Cards and circulars of various kinds are distributed in and about the places of meeting, and these often contain the well-known arguments of the demagogue. Some of these have simply a straightforward and dignified request for the vote of the reader, as the following: —

"EAST ST. PANCRAS BYE-ELECTION,

1899.

Your vote is earnestly requested

for

JOHN DOE,

the

Liberal, Radical, and Progressive Candidate."

Some of the more elaborate circulars may contain an arraignment of the one party or a defence of the other, particularly along financial lines. The politician knows well that the pocket-nerve of the voter is very sensitive, and prefers to make his attack in that locality. The campaigning is very carefully and systematically done, particularly in those divisions where the two great parties are quite evenly balanced. Some members are so fortunate as to be elected without opposition. In the last general election of October, 1900, two hundred and forty-four members were returned unopposed. This number, however, is unprecedentedly large. A general election in England is an interesting spectacle to an American. He is impressed, as he compares it with a congressional election, by the fundamental similarities and the minor differences. Richard Harding Davis, in his book "Our English Cousins," gives an interesting popular sketch of a general election in England.

The American observer is usually surprised to note the extent to which the women of England partici-

Women in English Politics.

pate in politics. They enter zealously into almost every phase of the work of the campaign. They do clerical work in the committee rooms; they aid in planning the campaign; they make personal canvasses among the voters, and not infrequently "take the stump" for their favourite candidates. On one occasion a woman drove a carriage to carry voters to the polls when it was suddenly discovered that there was no man available to perform that service. The candidate who is soliciting votes at political gatherings may be accompanied by his wife, sister, and other women who wish to aid him in his canvass. The women thus not only add to the picturesqueness of the campaign, but are effective forces in determining the result.

All of the political parties have encouraged the women to organise in order to further the interests of the respective parties. The Primrose League was the first organisation of women in England for active participation in politics. It was founded in 1883 by Sir Henry Drummond Wolf, Lord Randolph Churchill, and others, in honour of the memory of Lord Beaconsfield, who for many years was Prime Minister of England. The League is thus an organisation to further the interests of the Conservative party. It is frequently thought of as being a woman's organisation exclusively, but as a matter of fact, it is mixed, there being "Primrose Knights" as well as "Primrose Dames." However, the activity of the "Dames" has given the organisation its peculiar individuality. The

"Knights" seem to be silent partners. The League was a very effective organisation and grew rapidly from the start. It now occupies palatial headquarters in London and has more than a million members. The grand festival of the League, held annually, is an event of great political significance. The Conservative leaders often make notable declarations of policy at these meetings, and their utterances are always watched with interest. The League is active and not merely ornamental. It enters into every phase of the work of the campaign, and charges of corruption have been repeatedly made against it. Evidences of its success appear in the abuse and imitation of rival political parties. Its origin was hailed with ridicule and sarcasm and its success met with angry abuse. Sir Robert Peel must have been goaded to desperation by the effectiveness of the League when he spoke of its members as "the filthy wenches of the Primrose League." However, as soon as the first volleys of abuse had died away, rival organisations began to spring into existence. "The Women's Liberal Federation" was founded in 1886 with Mrs. Gladstone as president, and two years later the women's Liberal Unionist organisation was launched. The two latter societies seem to have been founded in self-defence, and were ushered into the political arena almost apologetically.

This active participation of women in political affairs naturally led to a more vigorous agitation in favour of woman suffrage. Here many of the political leaders drew the line. They were pleased, apparently, to avail themselves of the services of the women during the campaign, but could not think of allowing them to deposit ballots on their own account. The leaders of the woman suffrage movement were not slow to resent this. They charged Mr. Gladstone with inconsistency and ingratitude because he said, in 1879, when urging the women to aid the Liberal cause, that participation in politics "would gild their future years with sweet remembrances," and later declared that the right to vote would invite them to "trespass upon their delicacy, their purity, their refinement, the elevation of their own nature." Mr. Balfour was rather more consistent, and supported the suffrage measure which Mr. Gladstone opposed. He declared it to be absurd to encourage women to participate in politics and then to deny them the suffrage.

Before entering upon their duties the members must take the oath of office or make a solemn affirma-

Oath of office. tion in its stead. The affirmation is used in case the member has religious scruples against taking an oath, or has no religious belief whatever. The matter of the oath has been the subject of many long and angry debates. Before 1858 Jews were prevented from sitting in Parliament because they could not subscribe to the oath of office ending with the words "upon the true faith of a Christian." This objectionable phrase was abolished for Jewish members in 1858, after a struggle lasting over many years, and was later abolished for all members of the House of Commons. Before its abolition, however, Baron Lionel Nathan de Rothschild and other noted Jews were prevented from sitting in the House of Commons after having been duly elected by their constituents. These men could not take the oath of office in the form in which it then existed, and of course could not omit the oath entirely. They were therefore excluded until the oath was modified. The Quakers were permitted at an early date to make affirmation instead of taking the oath, and the same privilege was given to the Moravians and others. Finally, in 1888, as a result of the Bradlaugh case, the Oaths Act was passed, which provided that any person might substitute the affirmation for the oath either because the taking of an oath was contrary to his religious belief, or because he had no religious belief whatever. Mr. Bradlaugh asserted at a meeting of Parliament in 1880 that he had no religious belief and hence should be permitted to make affirmation in lieu of taking the oath. The court decided that he was not entitled to this privilege, but he was relieved by the Oaths Act of 1888.[1]

The House of Commons has on numerous occasions presented an animated scene when the members were being sworn in at the opening of a new Parliament. These stormy scenes have passed, however, and the matter is now one of dull routine. Justin McCarthy, who has been present on many such occasions, describes the present process as follows: "As a general rule, nothing can be less dignified or less interesting than the proceedings of the House of Commons during these few days. The new mem-

[1] See "The Bradlaugh Episode," McCarthy's "History of our own Times," vol. iii. ch. ii.

bers come in whenever they like, and in what order they can, to be sworn in or to affirm. At the opening of a new Parliament no member is introduced. There is no one to introduce him. He is of the same date as all the rest. The great anxiety of each member is to get sworn in as fast as he can, and be done with the whole formality. Members are usually sworn in in groups or batches of four or five. One copy of the New Testament does service for each little cluster. There is at times a somewhat unseemly scramble for a copy of the Testament, and when some little group has got hold of one, and an opportunity offers, the swearing-in of that group takes place. Some words are muttered. The words of late years are: 'I do swear that I will be faithful and bear true allegiance to her Majesty Queen Victoria, her heirs and successors, according to law; so help me God.' Each member mutters over the same words, each puts his lips to the Testament, and the ceremony is complete. This performance goes on for the whole day until the time fixed for adjournment has arrived; and it goes on day after day. No one takes any interest in it except the members who are still waiting to be sworn in; and even their interest is only represented by their personal anxiety to get through the ordeal at the first possible moment and go away. Such a time is, as a general rule, almost the only time in the House of Commons when nothing exciting could possibly be expected."[1] Such tranquillity as is here described, however, has not always prevailed. When Jew, Infidel, or Quaker, for

[1] " History of our own Times," vol. iii. pp. 20-21.

example, stood at the bar of the House, either demanding the right to take the oath or to have it modified in such a way as to make it palatable, there was excitement enough.

After taking the oath of office the member signs the " Test Roll," is introduced to the Speaker by the Clerk, and is then ready to enter upon his duties as a full-fledged member of the House of Commons.

CHAPTER XIII

THE REGULATIONS, PROCEDURE, AND PERSONNEL OF THE HOUSE OF COMMONS

REFERENCES: Palgrave's *House of Commons*; Ewald's *Crown and its Advisers*, Lecture on the *Commons*; Courtney's *Working Constitution of the United Kingdom*, 156-162; Tyler's *Glimpses of England*, 92-121; Dod's *Parliamentary Companion*, and English political and statistical almanacs.

AS the House of Commons, unlike the House of Lords, is homogeneous in composition, it is not necessary to consider rank or order in assigning places or seats. In fact, no such assignments are made. The simple rule is that those members supporting the Government of the day occupy the benches at the Speaker's right, while the Opposition members sit at his left. As a matter of custom the ministers sit on the Treasury Bench — the front seat at the Speaker's right — and the leaders of the Opposition are similarly placed at the left. The rank and file of the parties occupy the benches behind their leaders. The members from the city of London have generally claimed and exercised the right of sitting on the Treasury Bench at the opening of a new Parliament. Some of the older members have retained the same seats so long that they have obtained a sort of right by possession which others respect. There are always some independent members who do not wish to ally themselves

Places and Seats.

unreservedly with either party. These members sit "below the gangway," — a narrow aisle cutting the long benches into two parts at right angles to the broad aisle in the centre of the chamber. John Bright and John Stuart Mill sat for years on the Liberal side of the chamber below the gangway. They were in accord with the principles of the Liberal party on most matters, but wished to reserve for themselves the right to act independently when they saw fit to do so. The remaining members sit wherever it seems most convenient. As there are not seats enough for all, it is sometimes desirable to make reservations. In order to do this, members must be present at prayers and place cards with the words "at prayers" printed on them in receptacles placed on the backs of the seats for that purpose. Attempts to reserve seats before prayers have been defeated by order of the Speaker. Sometimes members retain seats by placing papers, gloves, or other articles upon them, but do so as a matter of courtesy, not of right. The above provisions are important when a significant debate is in progress, and the attendance exceeds the accommodations.

It was formerly customary for the House of Commons to meet at eight o'clock in the morning, and **Time of Meeting.** frequently as early as six or seven. It then adjourned at eleven, leaving the afternoon for committee work. The hour of meeting gradually became later until it was placed at fifteen minutes before four in the afternoon. This was the time of meeting for about twenty-five years prior to 1888. At that time it was ordered that on Mondays,

Tuesdays, Thursdays, and Fridays, the House should assemble at three o'clock in the afternoon, and on Wednesdays at twelve o'clock, noon. This schedule is now in force.[1] The House does not usually sit on Saturday or Sunday. On the former day the Houses of Parliament are open for the inspection of the public.

The arrangement of hours above mentioned leaves the members free for committee work during the forenoon. The House does sometimes hold "morning sittings," but these do not interfere with the business of the committees as they begin at two o'clock in the afternoon. They are usually held on Tuesdays and Fridays. It does sometimes happen that the House will sit in protracted session through the entire night and during the next day as well, and thus conflict with the sittings of the committees. In 1877 the House sat in continuous session for twenty-six and one-half hours. This was the longest sitting on record up to that date. In 1881, however, the House met at a quarter before four on Monday and continued to sit until half-past nine on Wednesday morning, making a sitting forty-one and three-fourths hours in duration. This is probably the longest sitting on record. On numerous occasions the House has continued in session all night and a good part of the succeeding forenoon. In 1783, when discussing the question of peace with the United States, the sitting lasted until nearly eight o'clock in the morning, and the discussion on the Reform Bill protracted one sitting until seven o'clock of the following morning. These long sittings sometimes

[1] Changed recently. See note at close of chapter.

cause confusion, but a member of the House always knows the time for the next meeting, as the Speaker causes the announcement to be printed at the close of the "Votes and Proceedings," which are delivered at the residences of the members each morning.

It might be well to observe that the House, by a Standing Order passed in 1888, provided that adjournment should take place at one o'clock (except that the Wednesday sitting should terminate at six) if the House did not see fit to adjourn at an earlier hour. This rule, however, has not been rigidly enforced. It would be neither convenient nor dignified for the House to adjourn "with their picks in the air," as some workmen do when the whistle blows. They frequently prefer to finish or to push on business which may not be conveniently left in an unfinished state. Then, too, certain kinds of business, such as proceedings on a ways and means bill, are "exempted" from the operation of the rule, and the House often sits far beyond the limit imposed by the order of 1888. The business, may, however, be brought to an issue at any time by the application of the closure rule. Since 1882 the House has been able to vote on the motion, "Shall the question be now put?" If carried, the debate must close and the question be decided at once.

Forty members of the House of Commons now constitute a quorum for the transaction of business.

Quorum. This number was fixed by a resolution of Jan. 5, 1640. The attendance at that time was apparently lax, and it was resolved, "That Mr. Speaker is not to go to his chair till there be at least forty in the House." This resolution is still in force, although efforts have been made from time to time to modify it. The rule was either not rigidly enforced during the first century of its existence, or the attendance was uniformly good, as the records show that the House adjourned for the first time because of a lack of a quorum on April 26, 1729. In 1801, when Parliament met for the first time after the union with Ireland, an attempt was made to raise the quorum to sixty. It failed.

If the Speaker finds a quorum present at the time for meeting, he takes the chair; if not, he sits in the Clerk's chair or retires from the chamber. At four o'clock he again appears, and, standing upon the upper step of the platform upon which his chair is placed, he counts the House and adjourns it, in the absence of the requisite number, until the time for the next regular sitting. If at any time the Speaker's attention is called to the fact that forty members are not present, he inverts the two-minute sand-glass upon the table and the members are summoned from all parts of the Houses as for a division. After the expiration of the two minutes the Speaker counts the members present, and if the number be below forty a "count out" occurs, and the House adjourns until the time fixed for the next regular sitting. In case a message be received from the King, or from the Lords Commissioners acting in his stead, a "house" is held to be "made," although there be less than forty members present. After the transaction of the royal business the House continues to sit until some member raises the point of "no quorum."

It has sometimes happened that a sitting of the House was brought to an abrupt close in a rather unceremonious and unexpected way. It is recorded that in 1641 "one day's discourse was stopped" because the members flocked to the windows in such large numbers to see the Earl of Strafford in his barge on the Thames, in much the same way that school children are wont to peer out upon the caravan of an overland circus. On another occasion in the early part of the nineteenth century the benches were deserted in favour of a boat race which was visible from the east windows; and it is also recorded that in 1648 so many of the members were in jail that it was necessary at times for the Speaker to send for a sufficient number to attend under guard to make a quorum.

Members of the House are supposed to attend all of the sittings of that body. In 1801 it was resolved,

Attendance. "That no member do presume to go out of town without the leave of the House." Leaves of absence may be obtained for sufficient reason, yet these have been refused in some instances. However, attendance upon the deliberations of the House is not insisted upon so rigidly as the above might seem to imply. Practically, there is nothing to insure the attendance of a member save his devotion to duty and the opinion of his constituents. The attendance, however, is good, and is, of course, remarkably good in comparison with that of the House of Lords. There are some members, notably the ministers and the leaders of the Opposition, who are almost always in their places, and large numbers of others who are fairly regular in attendance. Of course, not all of the members present on any occasion have an absorbing interest in the proceedings of the House. Some look bored while the souls of many others are "far away, sailing in the Vesuvian Bay." Even a pleasant little nap is not entirely unknown. Mr. Palgrave, in his interesting little book entitled "The House of Commons," tells of a case of total mental eclipse on the part of the Commons, which, while exceptional, is probably not without parallel among audiences of a similar character. In January of 1722, according to Mr. Palgrave, the House attended divine service in a body in St. Margaret's, their official church, as was their custom on certain state occasions. The service was carried out according to programme, and a sermon was preached by Rev. Dr. Nowell. The discourse apparently made a very favourable impression upon the auditors, as it was ordered to be printed and a vote of thanks was tendered to the good Doctor. All this was duly entered upon the "Journal" of the House. Sometime later, after the document appeared in print, the Commons found the utterances of Dr. Nowell to be not only political in character, but actually subversive of the Constitution; and they were on the point of ordering the hangman to burn the sermon, when they fortunately discovered that the titlepage of the pamphlet revealed the fact that the tract which they were execrating was printed by their official printer according not only to the express direction but even with the approbation of the House.[1] It was once a

[1] Pages 73–74.

common sight to see stacks of books piled up near the front of Westminster or the Royal Exchange to be burned by the hangman. While they were burning, the city crier proclaimed with a loud voice: "These are seditious books burnt by order of the House of Commons." Mr. Palgrave does not say whether the obnoxious sermon was burned or not, but the presumption is that it was not reduced to ashes, but still continues to "subvert" the English Constitution.

Aside from the Cabinet ministers and a few others the members of Parliament are not paid for their services. In addition to the comparatively few members, who for special reasons are paid by the government, there are some, such as the members of the Home Rule party and labour members, whose salaries are provided for by organisations of various kinds. Were it not for this provision, many of these members would be unable to accept seats in the House of Commons at all. In recent years there has been an agitation in England looking toward the payment of members of Parliament. Mr. Taylor, a member for Leicester, said in the House of Commons in 1870 that such a step was sure to be taken and was only a question of time. The arguments are familiar and obvious, for the most part. It is urged that a man without wealth is not able to take up his residence in London and give his time to the government without compensation. It is also urged that a poor man is unable to bear the necessary expense of a parliamentary campaign, and that his limited means will not allow him to curry popular favour by subscribing to charities. Again it is said that workingmen would

The Payment of Members.

be enabled to hold seats in Parliament in case the members were paid. The payment of members, however, has not so operated in the case of the American Congress. The workingmen are far more numerous in Parliament than in Congress, as our subsequent analysis of the House of Commons will tend to show.

The argument for the payment of members has been elaborately and emphatically expressed in pamphlets published in England for political purposes. One of these campaign documents was written by H. Hawken and published in London in 1892. The views of the writer are vigorously expressed, in part, as follows: "What else, therefore, than a House of Commons consisting for the most part of landed proprietors, with their sons, nephews, and nominees, of successful traders, large contractors, and hungry lawyers? Each of these has what the proposer of a vote of thanks would call 'a pleasing duty to perform,' to wit, the protection of the interests of his own class. The landlord has acres to watch; the trader, prices to maintain; the contractor, wages to keep down; the lawyers, everybody to befool. Do men gather figs of thistles? Would not the sanity be called into question of a man who would expect temperance legislation from a house of brewers, or democratic from a House of Lords?"[1] The writer of the pamphlet estimates that £250,000 would suffice for the annual payment of the members, — an amount, he says, less than one-third of the cost of the Royal Family. Another writer predicted that the first Par-

[1] "Payment of Members of Parliament," p. 4.

liament of paid members would save by business-like and economical methods an amount sufficient to pay the salaries of the members for half a century. The advocates of the system also find that members of legislative bodies are paid in the great majority of European and American countries, and with good results.

In 1870 Mr. Gladstone expressed himself against the payment of members. "When there are numbers of well-qualified men," he said, "ready to give their labour without being paid, why should we go out of our way and insist upon adding to the taxation of the country for the purpose of giving them a payment?" However, it is said that at a later time Mr. Gladstone expressed himself "guardedly in favour of a payment." However that may be, it is certain that the opponents of the system are no less determined and vigorous than its advocates. The argument against the payment of members may be briefly stated. It is urged that the method would give rise to a class of political adventurers and professional politicians such as are said to exist in the United States, and that under such a system there would be an endless amount of corruption. John Stuart Mill said that to pay members of Parliament would be "to offer six hundred and fifty-eight prizes for the most successful flatterers and the most adroit misleaders of their fellow-countrymen."

There would seem to be no immediate prospect of the payment of members of Parliament. Neither is there any urgent necessity for such payment. The labour unions and similar organisations, by providing for the members who represent their interests, have met the exigencies of the case in a satisfactory and practical way. It is well that there should be under every government a large number of offices which are rather honorary than remunerative.[1]

Strangers are present in the galleries of the House only on sufferance and may be excluded at any time. It is interesting to note, however, that an order for the exclusion of strangers is not held to include the occupants of the ladies' gallery, which is not supposed to be within the limits of the House. The gallery which Moses Coit Tyler referred to as a "miserable, dark, Mohammedan cage in which the representatives of the dangerous sex are penned," is really so high and so remote that this is almost literally true. The newspaper reporter has had a hard fight for recognition in the Commons, but is now snugly ensconced in a gallery of his own, although the publication of the proceedings of the House is theoretically forbidden. In 1738 the House condemned the publication of its proceedings as "a high indignity and a notorious breach of privilege." Yet the reporting of the debates still continued and is done at the present time in great detail, the order of the House to the contrary notwithstanding. It is probably a fact that not all of the reporters know that the publication of the debates was prohibited, as the order has not been enforced for years. After the order was made in 1738 it was evaded in numerous and ingenious ways. The reporters secreted themselves in corners of the galleries and behind articles

Strangers in the House.

[1] See Sidgwick's "Elements of Politics," p. 24.

of furniture, and one was writing under his hat when caught in the act and ejected. The reporters were cordially hated. Their reports were not accurate. Sometimes they were purposely inaccurate. Mr. Wilberforce was made by a reporter to lament the fact in the course of a speech, that potatoes in sufficient quantities were not given him when a child to make him grow. "Potatoes, Mr. Speaker, potatoes, Sir, make men healthy; potatoes make men tall. More especially do I feel this, because, being under the common size, I must ever lament that I was not fostered upon that genial vegetable, the potato."[1] This was the reporter's sweet revenge. During these years of persecution the papers were accustomed to refer to the House and the Speaker by feigned names in order to evade the letter of the prohibition. Staunch defenders of the press were not wanting; and on one occasion from five o'clock in the evening to five in the morning Edmund Burke arrayed all his powers of wit, wisdom, jest, and ridicule, in such a way as to bring contempt upon the effort to exterminate the reporter. On March 12, 1771, the reporter's gallery was constructed, and he now sends his "copy" in vast quantities to his paper, although he is violating the order of the House by every word that he writes. The House says in effect to the newspaper man, "You must not publish a word of the proceedings of this body in your scurrilous sheets, yet I will give you every opportunity for doing so."

The office of Speaker of the House of Commons is both ancient and honourable. It dates back to 1377.

[1] Palgrave's "House of Commons," p. 80.

At that time Sir Thomas Hungerford was chosen the first Speaker of the Commons. The Speaker is the official spokesman of the House, and also its presiding officer. He is elected by the House and continues in office, not for the session merely, but for the entire Parliament. It is customary, too, to re-elect the former Speaker at the opening of a new Parliament. Speaker Gully of the last Parliament was re-elected by the new one in 1901. The present[1] Speaker, though formerly a Liberal in politics, has served through Liberal and Conservative administrations alike. This is due to the fact that the presiding officer of the House of Commons leaves partisanship behind him when he assumes the chair. Herein lies a marked difference between the English and the American Speaker. As Miss Follett has shown,[2] the American Speaker has always been a political leader and not a mere moderator, as the English Speaker has been. The American Speaker is partisan, while the English is impartial. The American Speaker expects to go out of office, and actually does go out, with his party, but the English Speaker may, and usually does, continue in office after the defeat of his party and the organisation of the Opposition. Although the English Speaker is elected by a party, he knows no party when in the chair. He is strictly impartial in public and private intercourse with the members. "It makes little difference to any English party in Parliament whether the occupant of the chair has come from their own

The Speaker.

[1] October, 1902.
[2] "The Speaker of the House of Representatives," ch. i.

or from the hostile ranks. . . . A custom as strong as law forbids him to render help to his own side even by private advice. Whatever information as to parliamentary law he may feel free to give must be equally at the disposal of every member."[1]

The authority of the Speaker of the House greatly exceeds that of the Lord Chancellor, the presiding officer of the Upper House. In the House of Lords all important matters are decided by the House itself, while in the Commons the Speaker is the real leader and the master of the situation. He enforces the rules of procedure, puts questions, and declares the results. He is literally the "Speaker" of the House, and represents it on all official occasions. He expresses its thanks and delivers its reprimands. In short, he represents the House "in its powers, its proceedings, and its dignity." When he enters or leaves the House, the mace, the symbol of authority, is carried before him. While he is in the chair the mace rests on the table before him, but when another presides it is said to be "under the table," — in reality, suspended at the side. When the Speaker rises, "he is heard in silence." He may repress irrelevant discussions in debate, and has no mercy upon motions which are obviously dilatory. He may suppress disorder by compelling the members at fault to withdraw, by suspension, or by "naming" members, as Speaker Gully did in July, 1901, in the cases of Redmond and O'Brien. When the Speaker, because of sickness or other reason, is unable to perform the duties of his office for a considerable time, the House

[1] Bryce's "American Commonwealth," vol. i. p. 135.

elects another Speaker in the usual way. When the former Speaker recovers, it is the duty of the second to resign or "fall sick," and the first Speaker is then re-elected in the manner prescribed.

In rank the Speaker precedes all other commoners, and when vacating his office he is granted a pension, and a peerage is conferred upon him. The office has always been held in high esteem. It is one of great dignity and authority. Not every member of the House of Commons is able to measure up to the standard of its requirements. In 1597 Speaker Yelverton apologised for his shortcomings in the following way: "Your Speaker ought to be a man big and comely, stately and well spoken, his voice great, his carriage majestical, his nature haughty, and his purse plentiful. But, contrarily, the stature of my body is small, myself not so well spoken, my voice low, my carriage of the common fashion, my nature soft and bashful, my purse thin, light, and never plentiful."[1] Not all Speakers-elect scrutinise their qualifications so closely, yet many illustrious men have filled the office.

The principal officers of the House aside from the Speaker are the Sergeant-at-arms, the Clerk, and his two Assistants. These perform the duties usually devolving upon such officials. The Sergeant-at-arms, under the direction of the Speaker, preserves order, and the Clerk keeps a careful record of the proceedings of the House. This record is printed for distribution on the day following. Copies of these "Votes and Proceedings" are sent each morning to

[1] Palgrave's "House of Commons," p. 58.

the residences of the members, and the "Journal" is made up from these records under the supervision of the Clerk and the Speaker. The House, however, may make changes in the records at any time. Entries have occasionally been expunged from the "Journal" by a vote of the House. Notices of such alterations have also been sent by the Clerk to the principal librarians of Great Britain with the request that the proper changes be made in the copies of the "Journal" in their libraries.

The wigs and gowns of the officers of the House give them an appearance of mediævalism in the eyes of an American, yet the garb adds to the ceremony and dignity of the office.

The Liberals and the Conservatives are the two most important political parties in England. While there are historical and fundamental differences between these two parties, the Home Rule matter forms at present the most distinct line of demarcation. Since Mr. Gladstone pressed the matter of Home Rule for Ireland and split the Liberal party into two wings, the Liberal Unionists have acted with the Conservatives in opposing the Home Rule scheme, and the Gladstonian Liberals have united with the Irish Nationalists in favour of the Home Rule cause. The last general election was held in October, 1900, and resulted in a decided Unionist majority. Four hundred and two Unionists were returned to the House of Commons and two hundred and sixty-eight Liberals and Nationalists. England returned a strong Unionist majority; Wales and Ireland strong Home Rule majorities; while the rep-

Parties in the House of Commons.

resentation of Scotland is quite evenly divided between the two parties.[1] It will be observed that the Unionist majority is now one hundred and thirty-four, — four more than at the dissolution of the preceding Parliament, and eighteen less than after the general election of 1895.

All of the university members are ranged on the Unionist side.

It has often been said that the House of Commons is not truly representative of the English nation. It has been held that the representation of **The Personnel of the House.** the aristocratic element was excessive, while that of the democratic was scanty. Moses Coit Tyler referred to the House of Commons in 1866 as containing "rows of well-fed fox-hunters and billiard players, lordlings, and parvenus."[2] A study of the membership of the House will disclose the fact that this statement is entirely too sweeping and flippant. There are hundreds of men in the House of Commons to whom such a characterisation as this would not apply. However, it is not impossible for a man to be well fed, to ride after the hounds with ease and grace, to play billiards skilfully, and at the same time to be a practical and clear-headed legislator.

An analysis of the House of Commons elected at

---

[1] The figures are as follows:

	Unionist.	Liberal and National.
England	339	126
Wales	4	26
Scotland	38	34
Ireland	21	82
	402	268

[2] "Glimpses of England," p. 100.

the last general election (October, 1900) discloses some interesting facts in regard to the occupations of the members and the classes from which they come. According to the sketches in Dod's "Parliamentary Companion" for 1901 the present House of Commons is made up as follows: —

Barristers, Advocates, and Solicitors	152
Politicians	120
Merchants	56
Manufacturers (Cotton, Iron, Wool, etc.)	59
Army Officers	45
Journalists and Editors	26
Bankers	15
Farmers (Owners)	11
Ship-owners	11
Physicians and Surgeons	9
Professors and Teachers	12
Mine-owners	8
Stockbrokers	7
Engineers (Civil, Mechanical, Marine, etc.)	8
Brewers	6
Directors and Managers of Railways, Canals, etc.	9
Contractors	5
Distillers	5
Navy Officers	3
Shipbuilders	3
Publishers	2
Tenant Farmers	2
Insurance Men	2
Law Students	2
Warehousemen	2
Mariner	1
Horsebreeder	1

The English Government

Chemist and Druggist	1
Pilot	1
"Average Adjuster"	1
Race-horseman	1
"Refreshment Contractor"	1
Printer	1
Auctioneer	1
Novelist	1
Mechanics and labour leaders:	
(a) Railway Employee	1
(b) Stationary Engineer	1
(c) Mine Labourers	6
(d) Carpenter	1
(e) Stone Mason	1
(f) Labourer	1
Men of Leisure, or Occupation not given	69
Total	670

A mere glance at the above table will suffice to show that the membership of the House of Commons is not derived from any one class. A large variety of interests is represented, and the labouring classes are far more numerously represented than in the American Congress.

Perhaps a few words of comment and explanation in regard to the above analysis may not be amiss. The comparatively small number of lawyers in the House of Commons will be a surprise to many who know that men of that profession constitute two-thirds of our House of Representatives. There are, it is true, many members of the House of Commons who have been called to the bar, but who are devoting themselves to other pursuits, or who, like John Morley, have never practised at all. These are not included in the number, one hundred and fifty-two, given in the table. But it is also true that many of those listed as lawyers do not enjoy a very extensive or lucrative practice. Detailed information is wanting in most cases of this kind; yet there is one member who is said to be "one of the leaders of the Irish bar," and another "a teacher of considerable repute in his district," while a third "has long been a prominent public man in Birmingham." Such details as these, however, are as rare as they are unreliable.

It is, perhaps, needless to say that the term "politician" in the table is used in the better sense. The term "statesman" might be applied appropriately to a large number of those termed politicians. The class includes those who have followed a political career, devoting their energies for the most part to the public service. Politics offers a more continuous and hence more attractive career to young men in England than it does in the United States, and the result is that large numbers prepare themselves for the public service and devote their lives to it. The life of the late William E. Gladstone furnishes an excellent example of such a career.

The number of farmers in the table is much less than it would be if the data were complete. A large part of the sixty-nine members who do not specify any particular occupation are large landowners and gentlemen farmers. Many of the members are not so specific in defining their occupations as the man who says he "is a turkey-red dyer and calico-printer."

The number of directors of corporations would

also be largely increased if it included those directors who devote the major part of their energies to other occupations, and who are, therefore, placed more properly in other classes.

The House of Commons at the present time contains some picturesque characters, and many who have had varied and interesting careers. One member is a native of India, the son of a Parsee merchant of Bombay. He is an author and a barrister, and has had many honours conferred upon him in recognition of his legal and literary attainments, and glories in the name of Sir Mancherjee Merwanjee Bhownaggree. Another member " has travelled three times around the world," while another " has travelled over most of the globe." There is an occasional member who seems afflicted with " the curse of the wandering foot," or who, like Harry Hotspur, says, " Fie upon this quiet life " and starts out to hunt for sensations. One of the Irish members, for example, was educated at the University of Dublin and at the Sorbonne, Paris, was then an officer in the French army, and was later on the staff of the " New York Herald." Next we find him a prisoner of war in Cuba, then a participant in the United States expedition against Sitting Bull in 1876. In 1884 he was in the Soudan, and is now the London editor of the " Irish Daily Independent." He has been in Parliament for the last twenty years, and has managed to write a book in addition. He is now only fifty-six years of age. One of the members for Durham began work in the quarries at the age of ten, and was working in the collieries at thirteen. At nineteen he went to sea, and from twenty-six to thirty he worked in Pennsylvania and Illinois. He was later a founder and an official of various mining associations, and was also "active as an advocate of total abstinence, and as a Primitive Methodist local preacher." He was elected to Parliament at the age of forty-eight and now sits as an "advanced Liberal." Another member entered the royal artillery but retired in 1889 "on succeeding to the property of his cousin." A member from Buckinghamshire lays claim to the honour of having "twice swam across Niagara," and a member for the city of Cork was tried for high treason in 1867 and sentenced to be "hanged, drawn, and quartered," but now dispenses wine and tea in Dublin.

It is not fair, however, to spend too much time on the peculiarities or the eccentricities of either the House or its individual members. These are, of course, the rare exceptions and not the rule. In point of substantial ability the House of Commons is not surpassed by any legislative body in the world. The remark of Moses Coit Tyler, made in 1866 and cited above, is certainly not true at the present time. The average member of the House is conscientious in the performance of his duty and takes a serious view of life. He is sober, earnest, and educated without being dramatically brilliant. To borrow an expression from Charles Reade, it is not necessary "to fly him with a stout string" in order to avoid the reckless aerial escapades common in the Latin countries. His deliberateness inspires confidence.

It would have been desirable in some respects to make a class of "authors" in the above table, but the difficulties involved would be numerous. It would not be easy to know just where to draw the line. A majority of the members of the House have written books or pamphlets, but only a comparatively few of them would be entitled to be called "authors." That term would, however, describe more fittingly than any other such men as Lecky the historian and Gilbert Parker the novelist, and might be applied not inappropriately to John Morley, James Bryce, and other members who have pursuits other than that of letters.

The student of current English politics will miss some very familiar names when he looks over the list of members chosen at the last general election. Justin McCarthy, the journalist, novelist, and historian, after having occupied a seat in the House for more than twenty years, declined a re-election in 1900 because of advanced age. Sir Richard Webster, the famous barrister, who sat for the Isle of Wight for fifteen years, was made Lord Alverston in 1900 and now sits in the House of Lords. Sir George J. Goschen, who sat in the House almost without interruption since 1863, and who was at one time First Lord of the Admiralty, was made a peer in 1901 and thus transferred to the Upper Chamber. He has attained the age of threescore years and ten, and has earned his transfer to the less strenuous life of the House of Lords. Sir Matthew White Ridley, formerly Secretary of State for Home Affairs, who sat in the House continuously since 1868, was recently elevated to the peerage with the title Viscount Ridley. Sir John Lubbock, the noted banker and scientist, who represented London University for twenty years, was made a peer on New Year's day, 1900, and now sits in the House of Lords as Baron Avebury. Each general election witnesses the departure of many familiar figures from the green benches, and the introduction of new men, famous perhaps in other lines, but with their parliamentary spurs yet to win. The general election of 1900 was no exception to the rule in this respect. However, the House of Commons is a comparatively constant body because of the long term of office and the repeated re-elections in the case of a worthy member.[1]

In conclusion, it might be said that the House of Commons, though not perfect either in the theory or the practice of its composition, is a remarkably strong body both individually and collectively. There is need, however, for all the strength which it can master. There is no legislative body in the world with an authority more extensive. Since the power of the Lords has waned and that of the Crown has vanished, the power and the responsibility of the Commons have increased to an unprecedented degree. All of the great reforms in the government of England since the time of Cromwell have served to am-

---

[1] I am indebted to Mr. Alfred Fellows of Birmingham, England, for the following remarkable instance.

At the general election of 1835, Mr. Charles Pelham Villiers came to Wolverhampton, and offered himself for election to Parliament. He was an absolute stranger to the place and had no connection with it either by property, interest, or friends. He was elected and re-elected again and again until his death in 1898 at the age of ninety-six. He thus sat without a break for the same constituency for sixty-three years.

plify the authority of the Commons. The whole tendency of the last century was democratic and the same spirit still pervades English politics. This fact throws an ever-increasing responsibility upon the shoulders of the Commons. However, if we may judge the future by the past — and there is no safer guide — the House of Commons will not be found wanting when called upon to act in supreme emergencies.

NOTE. — In 1902 new rules of procedure were adopted by the House of Commons. The House now meets at two o'clock on Mondays, Tuesdays, Wednesdays, and Thursdays, and at twelve o'clock on Fridays. The rules relating to suspensions for "disregarding the authority of the Chair," breaking the rules of the House, or wilfully obstructing business, have been revised and extended. The rules relating to "Questions to Members" have also been enlarged. A complete copy of the revised rules of procedure may be obtained for twopence from Messrs. Eyre and Spottiswoode, printers to the King, East Harding Street, London.

CHAPTER XIV

THE SOVEREIGNTY, PRIVILEGES, AND PROCEDURE OF PARLIAMENT

REFERENCES: Walpole's *Electorate and the Legislature*, 1-24, and 90-163; May's *Parliamentary Practice*, 36-56, 57-410, and 433-492; Dicey's *Law of the Constitution*, 37-170; Courtney's *Working Constitution of the United Kingdom*, 100-106, and 179-216; Todd's *Parliamentary Government in England*, ii. 138-271; Anson's *Law and Custom of the Constitution*, 1. 42-74, 232-303, and 347-374; Dickinson's *Development of Parliament during the Nineteenth Century;* Rose's *Rise of Democracy*.

THE English Parliament as a whole has certain powers and characteristics not possessed by either House individually. A brief discussion, therefore, of the two Houses acting conjointly is necessary to an adequate understanding of the English government.

The Parliament of the United Kingdom of Great Britain and Ireland is composed of the King and three Estates of the Realm, — the Lords Spiritual, the Lords Temporal, and the Commons. Since the Lords Spiritual and Temporal, however, constitute a single branch of the legislature, it is customary to speak of the King, Lords, and Commons, simply. *Composition.*

The authority of Parliament is bounded only by the limits of the British Empire. It extends to the colonies and other possessions in all parts of the world. Ordinarily, of course, Parliament does not legislate directly for the self- *The Sovereignty of Parliament.*

governing colonies. It exercises only a very general and remote supervision. However, by an Act passed in 1833 Parliament abolished slavery throughout all of the British possessions. In the words of Sir Edward Coke, the power of Parliament "is so transcendent and absolute that it cannot be confined, either for causes or persons, within any bounds." However, it is true that the power of Parliament, like that of all sovereign bodies, is limited by the "willingness of the people to obey, or their power to resist."

It is frequently said that the English Parliament is a sovereign body. Since this is a significant and characteristic attribute of Parliament it may be well to inquire what this sovereignty means. "The principle of parliamentary sovereignty means neither more nor less than this, namely, that Parliament thus defined has, under the English Constitution, the right to make or unmake any law whatever; and, further, that no person or body is recognised by the law of England as having a right to override or set aside the legislation of Parliament."[1] In other words, the Parliament of England is not bound down by a written constitution such as obtains in the United States; neither is there any Supreme Court, such as exists here, with power to declare an Act of Parliament null and void.

It is not difficult to find examples in English history illustrating the absolute sovereignty of Parliament. The Acts of Union whereby Scotland and Ireland became integral parts of the United Kingdom are good examples of an unbounded parliamentary

[1] Dicey's "Law of the Constitution," p. 38.

sovereignty; and the Septennial Act of 1716 illustrates the same principle admirably. The duration of Parliament was limited to three years by a statute passed in 1694. Under this Act the Parliament in session in 1716 would have been compelled to dissolve in 1717 at the latest. The King and Cabinet did not wish to order a general election at that time because they feared that the power of the Jacobites might imperil the peace of the nation. Parliament was, consequently, induced to pass the Septennial Act, whereby the duration of Parliament was extended from three to seven years, thus deferring the necessity for a dissolution until 1721. By this simple act the Parliament then in session prolonged its own existence by four years, and did not exceed its legal powers in so doing. Parliament also has, as Coke has pointed out, adjudged minors to be of full age, attainted a dead man of treason, and transformed an alien into a subject born. The list might be greatly enlarged, but perhaps the above examples will be sufficient to show the absolute sway of Parliament.

It might be well to remark in passing that Blackstone is not a safe guide upon the subject of the sovereignty of Parliament, since he treats of the theory rather than the practice of the English Constitution. He ascribes to the modern constitutional monarchs all of those powers which the most despotic of the English kings possessed. Such a view as this necessarily precludes the recognition of the sovereignty of Parliament.

Parliament is required by statute to meet once in three years, but, as a matter of fact, it is practically obliged to meet annually. Supplies cannot be voted for a longer term than one year. This provision is **Annual Meetings.** a relic of the time when the army and navy were instruments of oppression, and appropriations for the support of these organisations were limited to one year. For this reason, as well as for the despatch of other urgent business, an annual session of Parliament is essential. The session usually begins in midwinter and lasts until the early part or the middle of August.

There are certain privileges which appertain to Parliament as a body, and others which apply to the **Privileges of** individual members. The House of Com-**Parliament.** mons particularly has always striven zealously to maintain and to defend its privileges. When a Speaker is elected at the opening of a new Parliament, it is customary for that official to claim, in behalf of the House, the " ancient and undoubted rights and privileges " of the Commons. He enumerates freedom from arrest, freedom of speech, access to the person of the King, and a " favourable construction " upon the proceedings of the House. These rights and privileges are confirmed, as a matter of course, by the King or by the Lord Chancellor acting in his stead.

Before discussing in detail the privileges of Parliament it may be well to glance at two so-called privileges which are in reality rather matters of courtesy than of privilege. The House of Commons claims and exercises the right of access to the person of the King on certain important occasions. This right is exercised when the House, headed by the Speaker, presents an address or petition to the King. This right appertains to the Commons as a body and not to the individual members, as is the case with the Lords. It is an ancient custom and was formerly significant, but since the introduction of parliamentary government and the reduction of royal authority to its lowest terms, the privilege is not important and is now but rarely exercised. The "favourable construction" of the proceedings of the Commons which is asked for is also a matter of personal courtesy not to be enforced by constitutional methods. This, too, has lost its importance since the introduction of parliamentary government.

It might be well to note in this connection that the term "privilege" has a technical meaning. There are certain rights which are peculiar to each House separately, but a "privilege" in the correct technical sense applies to both Houses equally. Each House may defend these privileges, but is not at liberty to create new ones.

Each House has the right to commit persons for contempt. This right has been questioned in many historical instances, but is now universally conceded and has been for a long term of years. The right is both necessary and just, and is exercised without question by the Congress of the United States and other legislative assemblies. Each House takes cognisance of a breach of privilege and punishes it in its own way. The House of Lords claims to be a court of record, and punishes the offender by imprisonment for a fixed period or by the imposition of a fine. The House of Commons, on the other hand, does not specify any term of imprisonment and imposes no fines. The last fine imposed by the House of Commons was one of £1000 inflicted upon Mr. Thomas White in 1666. It is now customary for the House of Commons to commit persons to Newgate, to the Tower, to the Clock Tower, which forms a part of the Houses of Parliament, or to the custody of the Sergeant-at-arms. There is no fixed term of imprisonment and the prorogation of Parliament releases the prisoner.

Freedom of speech is one of the three great privileges enjoyed by the English Parliament and the American Congress, and is essential to the deliberations of any untrammelled legislative body. Under this privilege members of Parliament have the right to express their opinions in either House without reservation and without being questioned therefor in any other place. This important privilege has been established by a long line of cases. It is stated explicitly in the Bill of Rights and has been repeatedly confirmed by the courts. Either House, however, may call its members to order for unparliamentary language. In a large number of cases members have been censured, imprisoned, or even expelled for offensive utterances. In most cases the member using unparliamentary language is called to order, and satisfies the House by an apology or an explanation. In other cases a more severe punishment follows.

The principle of the privilege of freedom from arrest is practically as old as the government of England. The reasons for the privilege are obvious, and it is accorded to all free legislatures. A long line of court decisions has confirmed this privilege and has defined its limitations in some respects. The duration of the privilege of freedom from arrest, however, has never been defined. As a matter of ancient custom, the privilege holds for forty days before the meeting of Parliament and for forty days after, as well as during the session. This construction was put upon the privilege in the case of Mr. Fortescue Harrison in 1880. The historical reason for allowing forty days before the meeting was that writs for the meeting of Parliament were issued forty days in advance. The servants of members also enjoy a certain immunity from arrest for obvious reasons.

Each House also has the power of deciding cases of contested seats, but the House of Commons, as explained elsewhere, has delegated this right to the courts.

It was formerly held that members need not attend court when subpœnaed as witnesses, but this view was seen to have a bad effect upon the administration of justice; and the privilege, if it ever existed, has now been waived. Parliamentary duties, however, are held to take precedence of those of the jury, and the member may refuse to serve if drawn.

In order to make it easily possible for members of Parliament to attend the meetings, it is customary for both Houses at the opening of a session to instruct the commissioners of police to keep **Obstructions.** the streets leading to the Houses of Parliament "free and open," and to permit no obstruction to impede the free passage of members to and from Parliament.

With the same end in view Parliament has ordered that not more than ten persons shall go in a body to the Houses of Parliament for the purpose of presenting a petition. It is also provided that not more than fifty persons shall assemble, when Parliament is sitting, within one mile of Saint Stephen's for the purpose of drafting a petition to either or both Houses.

A Sunday sitting of Parliament is a very rare occurrence. There have been a few, however, on that day. During the excitement of the so-called "Popish plot," both Houses met occasionally on Sunday. The Reform Bill of 1832 was read a second time on Sunday morning; the royal assent has been given to measures occasionally on Sundays, and the sittings have in some instances been protracted into the Sabbath.

Sunday Sittings.

When a special day of thanksgiving is appointed, such as May 4, 1856, when a treaty of peace was made with Russia, it is customary for the Lords to attend divine services at Westminster Abbey, and for the Commons to go to Saint Margaret's church. These places of worship are situated across the street from the Houses of Parliament and are thus easy of access. Each House selects its own preacher for the occasion, and the choice is closely circumscribed by custom or resolution. The Lords, naturally enough, select a bishop; and the Commons, a dean, or a doctor of divinity, or the Speaker's Chaplain. As long ago as 1699 it was resolved, "That for the future no person be recommended to preach before this House (the Commons),

Special Services.

who is under the dignity of a dean in the Church, or hath not taken his degree of doctor of divinity." An exception was later made in favour of the Chaplain, and, on one occasion at least, a bachelor of divinity was permitted to preach the sermon.

St. Paul's Cathedral is also visited for divine service by the King and Parliament on some special occasions. Such services were held on the recovery of King George III. in 1789; after the notable victories of 1797; after the signing of the treaty of peace in 1814; at the funeral of the Duke of Wellington in 1852; and on the recovery of King Edward VII., then Prince of Wales, in 1872.

Parliament sometimes adjourns, but not regularly, upon the death of a member. Sir Robert Peel and Sir George Cornewall Lewis were honoured in this way, but in the latter case the wisdom of the adjournment was questioned. There was no seeming impropriety in that particular case, but it was felt to be a dangerous plan to honour in this way the "distinguished" members only. There might be a difference of opinion in some cases. Parliament also sometimes adjourns on the death of a member of the Royal Family, and only short sessions are held on Ash Wednesday and Ascension Day. When Queen Victoria's birthday fell on a working-day, it was customary for Parliament to adjourn, and an adjournment has also usually taken place on Derby Day. There has been some opposition in recent years, however, to an adjournment for Derby Day, but there is still a strong sentiment in favour of such a course, and large numbers of dignified lords

Adjournments.

and distinguished commoners still retain their liking for the turf, and are present when the flag falls. The horse in England is an object of very great interest.

It frequently becomes necessary in the course of a session for the Houses of Parliament to communicate with each other. The simplest and most popular method of accomplishing this is by message. Messages are sent daily on various subjects from one House to the other. Since 1855 it has been customary to intrust the message to a clerk, and his appearance does not stop the proceedings of the House to which he is sent. Prior to 1855 the method of sending and receiving messages was more ceremonious and impressive.

Communications between the two Houses.

It sometimes happens that conferences of the two Houses are held in the chamber of the lords. This is the most formal method of communication, and during its progress the business of the two Houses is suspended. Either House may demand a conference upon certain subjects, such as the privileges of Parliament or the amending of bills. By ancient custom the Lords may name the time and place for the meeting, whether it was asked for by themselves or by the Commons.

A more convenient method of communication is by deputations or conference committees. In this case "managers" are appointed to represent their respective Houses, and by "ancient rule" the number of the commoners is twice that of the lords. The managers for the House of Commons arrive at the appointed place first, and having removed their hats, they enter the room and remain standing during

The English Government

the entire conference. The lords then arrive and wear their hats until they go inside the bar of the place of meeting. They then remove them and go to their seats uncovered. After taking their seats they replace their hats upon their heads and remain thus seated and covered during the entire meeting, while the commoners stand uncovered at the table. At the conclusion of the conference the managers make their reports to their respective Houses.

It is also necessary at times for the Crown to send communications to Parliament and *vice versa*. By a fiction of the law the Crown is supposed to be present in Parliament, as he is in the courts of justice. If he were actually present in the legislative halls, an exchange of communications would be a comparatively simple matter. In point of fact, however, the King is now present in Parliament only on a very few special occasions. In ancient times he was frequently present and took part in the debates. Later he came as a spectator merely, and is now present only for the purpose of opening or proroguing Parliament or giving his assent to bills. Queen Anne was the last monarch to attend the debates in Parliament, and she did so for the last time in 1710. The practice fell into disuse at that time and was never revived by the House of Hanover. This being the case more indirect methods of communication must be resorted to on many occasions. One of these methods is by a message from the King under the sign manual. The message is conveyed by a member of Parliament who is at the same time a minister of the Crown or member of the Royal Household. In the House of Lords the member in possession of the message announces that fact from his place in the chamber, whereupon the document is read by the Lord Chancellor, hats being removed. In the House of Commons the member bearing the document appears at the bar and informs the Speaker that he has a message to the House signed by the King. The members then remove their hats and the Speaker reads the message. Such messages relate to important matters and may be considered as postscripts to the King's Speech delivered at the opening of the session. The same message is usually sent to both Houses on the same day. It sometimes happens that messages from the King are delivered orally to Parliament by the ministers.

As indicated above, the answer to the Speech from the Throne is by a formal Address. In the same way,

Replies. a message under the sign manual is usually acknowledged by the House of Lords by an address presented by the "Lords with the white staves" or by others especially selected for the purpose. A direct answer on the part of the House of Commons is not always deemed necessary, since a compliance with the royal request is looked upon as the most satisfactory kind of an answer. If, for example, funds be asked for and an appropriation be promptly made, no other recognition of the message is considered necessary. Messages relating to other than financial matters are usually recognised by an appropriate address. Sometimes a joint address is presented to the Crown, but usually each

House responds singly. In the case of a joint address the presentation is made, by the two Houses in a body, or by two peers and four commoners. The lords always ascertain his Majesty's pleasure in advance and notify the commoners as to the time and place of the presentation. When it is not convenient for the Crown to receive the address, that ceremony is dispensed with. This was done by Queen Victoria in 1880, when she was at Balmoral. When a joint address is to be presented by the two Houses in a body, the Lord Chancellor and Speaker proceed in state to the King's palace, accompanied by the members of Parliament. The members assemble in an apartment adjoining the throne-room, and when the King is ready to receive them, the doors leading to the throne-room are opened. The Lord Chancellor and the Speaker then advance toward the King, followed by the members of their respective Houses. The Lord Chamberlain conducts them to the throne, and the Lord Chancellor reads the address which is presented to the King. The King then responds, and the members retire. Addresses from the Houses acting separately are presented in much the same way. It is interesting to note the nicety and the exactness with which every detail is taken care of. This comes from centuries of experience. The lords attend in levee[1] dress, while the commoners are in their ordinary attire. Walking-sticks and umbrellas

---

[1] Levee dress is a uniform worn by certain officials. It is less splendid than "full dress." In the case of privy councillors' and other civil service uniforms the coat has less gold and the costume includes trousers, instead of white knee-breeches and white silk stockings.

are not permitted in the royal presence. In the time of Demosthenes the use of the walking-stick was obligatory in Athens, and any man appearing upon the street without one was looked upon as a disorderly character and immediately locked up. The Athenian point of view on this matter, however, is quite different from that of the English court and the art gallery.

Although the general principles of parliamentary procedure are familiar, it may be well to notice a few **Methods of Procedure.** of the peculiarities in the practice of the two Houses. It is a peculiar fact that in the House of Lords it is not necessary that a motion be seconded. By usage, however, it is customary to second the Address in answer to the King's Speech. This is the only case in which a second is required. In the House of Commons, however, every motion must be seconded, or it is immediately dropped and no mention of it appears in the records. Again there are some subjects which may not be brought before Parliament by motions. The Houses have placed some very salutary restrictions upon themselves in this respect. It is not permissible, for example, to bring any matter pending in a court of law, before either House by a motion or otherwise. Nor is it permissible to bring up a matter which at a previous time in the same session was decided either in the affirmative or the negative; nor may a member anticipate by motion a matter whose consideration has been set for a future date. A motion may be withdrawn by the mover, but only with the unanimous consent of the House, and a motion can never be withdrawn in the absence of the member who proposed it. The reasons for these provisions are so obvious that a discussion of them seems unnecessary.

The method of ascertaining the will of either House is simple, yet effective. In the House of Lords those voting in the affirmative say, "content," and those in the negative, "not content." The Lord Chancellor, after hearing the voices, says, "I think the 'contents' (or the 'not contents,' as the case may be) have it." If the members acquiesce, the question is resolved according to the opinion of the presiding officer. In the House of Commons those voting in the affirmative say "aye," and those in the negative "nay." The Speaker ventures a tentative opinion upon hearing the voices, and in case of no challenge it stands as the decision of the House. In case of a dispute in either House the matter is determined by a "division," in which the members favouring and those opposing the proposition are accurately counted by tellers. When a division occurs, a member is compelled to vote in the same way that he did when the voices were called for. In at least three instances members voted on one side upon a call of voices and went into the opposite lobby upon a division. The Speaker's attention was called to the fact, and he directed that the votes be recorded as first given. In 1866 when "a member's vote was contrary to his voice" the Speaker declared the practice to be "irregular and unparliamentary," as by it divisions were forced. Attention must be called to the abuse, however, before the result of the division is announced.

Both Houses have ordered that no bill or question

which has been passed upon shall be brought up again for consideration in the same session. Neither is it sufficient that the wording be changed; the bill must be different in substance, or the Speaker will declare it out of order. This rule is sometimes the occasion of inconvenience, and when it is thought best to evade it, means are not wanting. In 1707 Parliament was prorogued for a week in order that a bill rejected by the Lords might be reintroduced; and in 1831 Parliament was again prorogued for a short time in order that the third reform bill might be brought in. In the American Congress a bill lives over from a long to a short session, and the proceedings may be resumed at the point where they terminated; but all bills die at the end of the short session because the body which next assembles is a new Congress. If Parliament acted upon this principle it might logically resume the proceedings upon bills, session after session, during the same Parliament. Proposals looking to this end have been made repeatedly, but have been uniformly rejected. Parliament has been content to meet the embarrassment occasioned by the rule by means of technical but judicious evasions.

As in the American Congress, it is necessary that a bill be read three times before it is finally disposed of by Parliament. Before the invention of printing each bill was actually read aloud three different times in each House. A "reading" now simply means a stage in the progress of the bill, and the Speaker would not allow the reading of the complete text of a measure even if such reading were requested by a member. In these days

The Three Readings of a Bill.

when all bills are printed the only reason for such a request would be to obstruct the proceedings of the House. When the House votes that a bill be read a second time "this day six months," the fate of the measure is sealed. It is not expected at the time that Parliament will be in session six months from date, and if it should be it would not take up the deferred measure. The motion is simply a polite way of defeating the bill. The procedure upon bills is practically the same in the two Houses. A measure is introduced, put through the three readings, sent to the other House, put through the same routine, and then deposited with the House of Lords to await the royal assent. Upon receiving the royal approval it becomes a law.

As a general rule a bill may originate in either House, but there are certain classes of bills which must originate in a particular House. All revenue bills, such as those relating to taxation and appropriations, must originate in the House of Commons; and bills for the restitution of honour and blood must originate in the House of Lords. Bills of attainder and other measures of a judicial character must originate in the Upper House.

Parliamentary bills are of two classes, — public and private. Public bills relate to matters of public policy and involve the general welfare of the whole people, while private bills relate for the most part to the affairs of private individuals or corporations. Public bills are introduced by members of Parliament, while private measures originate from the petitions of the persons interested. A water company, for example, wishes certain privileges. It petitions Parliament for a grant of those privileges, and this petition constitutes a private bill.

When a bill is presented in either House the first reading is allowed without opposition. This is now a mere matter of form. The contest is made at the second reading. This is the most important stage in the progress of the measure. At this reading the House approves or disapproves the principle of the bill. It is not in order to discuss the details of the measure, as the general principle alone is passed upon. It is at this stage in the progress of the bill that an opponent will move that the measure be read a second time three or six months from date. This method, as noted above, is employed to compass the defeat of the measure and is considered more courteous than outright rejection. Motions to reject bills were once common, but are not now made. The House of Commons has not always been so courteous and considerate in its treatment of measures which it did not wish to pass. In the reign of Queen Elizabeth a bill was not only rejected but ordered to be "torn." In 1620 the same method of procedure was unanimously adopted. In 1772 the Lords aroused the ire of the Commons by amending a money bill, and the result was that the measure was rejected by the House, thrown over the table by the Speaker, and kicked out of the chamber by the members. It is much less abrupt to postpone the second reading for six months.

When the principle involved has been indorsed by the second reading, the bill is considered in the "committee of the whole house." Here the details are minutely discussed. The Speaker has left the chair, the mace is "under the table," and the members are no longer restricted to one speech each. After this careful discussion a time is fixed for the third reading. It is still possible to make amendments, but since 1888 it has been held that these amendments must be relevant to the subject-matter of the bill. When the third reading takes place in the House of Commons, the bill has passed that body. In the House of Lords, however, the additional motion is put, "That the bill do pass." Upon resolving this in the affirmative, the passage of the measure in the House of Lords is complete. After the passage of a bill by either House, it is conveyed to the other by a clerk, and there goes through practically the same routine. After being passed by the two Houses, the bill is placed in the custody of the House of Lords, if not there already, to await the royal assent. This assent being given in the old Norman-French phraseology, the bill becomes an Act. It might be noted as an exception to the above statement that money bills remain in the custody of the House of Commons while awaiting the approval of the Crown.

When the monarch comes in person to give his assent to bills, he is met in the robing-room by a clerk and there signifies his approval, which of course cannot be withheld. Henry VIII. was the first monarch to give the royal assent by means of a commission, but that method was much used by the late Queen Victoria. Queen Victoria was also accustomed to give a slight nod of assent when the titles of the bills were read, in addition to the approval given before entering the chamber.

The time consumed in the passage of a measure will vary with the nature of the bill and the general circumstances in Parliament at the time. Instances have been known where a bill was passed by the two Houses and approved by the King in a single day. So rapid a passage is, of course, very exceptional. The course of a bill is more likely to be long, tedious, and stormy.

The above discussion applies to public bills almost exclusively; and since there is no legislation in America which corresponds to the passage of private bills by the English Parliament, it may be well to note the essential difference between public and private measures. A public bill is one which is introduced for the purpose of promoting the general welfare. It has no reference to individuals as such. It has an eye single to the public good. It "affects the general interests of the state." Private bills, on the other hand, " enable private individuals to associate together to undertake works of public utility at their own risk, and, in a degree, for their own benefit." Private legislation is largely judicial and local in character, and applies to such subjects as fisheries, rivers, harbours, floods, charters for railways, gas, tram, and water companies. "Every bill for the particular interest or benefit of any person or persons is treated, in Parliament, as a private bill. Whether it be for the interest of an individual, a public company or corporation, a parish, a city, a county, or other locality, it is equally distinguished from a measure of public policy, in which the whole community are interested; and this distinction is marked by the solicitation of private bills by the parties themselves whose interests are concerned. By the standing orders of both Houses, all private bills are required to be brought in upon petition; and the payment of fees, by the promoters, is an indispensable condition to their progress." [1]

While the distinction between public and private bills is clear in theory, in practice there is no little difficulty in drawing the line. The result of this difficulty has been the recognition of a third or intermediate class of a quasi-public character called "hybrid" bills. In these, as the title indicates, are clauses of a public character, as well as provisions of peculiar interest and value to individuals. A few examples may serve to show the practical difficulties arising in the classification of bills. A bill involving the special interests of a single county is clearly a private bill; and a bill for the benefit of three counties has also been held to be private in character; but a bill involving all of the English counties would clearly be a public bill. When, then, does a bill cease to be a private and become a public measure? What number of counties must it necessarily involve? Again, although bills relating to a single city are looked upon as private measures, those relating to London — the entire city, not to the City proper — have been classified as public bills. London is, in a very large sense, the mother city of England; and

[1] May's "Parliamentary Practice," p. 634.

her interests are more than local, they are national; and for this reason bills relating to the policing and draining of the city have been dealt with as public measures. In 1878, however, a London water supply bill was treated in some respects as a "hybrid" measure because it involved the private interests of certain water supply companies. The rule is, however, that bills relating to the English metropolis are looked upon as public bills. Bills relating to the "City" of London, however, have usually been looked upon as private. The City, presided over by the Lord Mayor, comprises only about one one hundred and twentieth of the area of the entire city, and is thus, in many respects, not as important as many other cities of the United Kingdom. A bill to create a police force for the City was introduced and passed as a private bill. Bills relating to Dublin and Edinburgh have been either public or private according to their contents. For example, bills relating to the port of Dublin have been regarded as public, and those relating to markets and similar subjects in which the residents of the city only have an interest have been passed as private bills.

The proceedings on private bills are of an interesting and thorough character. The principal contest is in the committees of the two Houses. Here the proceedings are, to a large extent, judicial in character. The promoters, or those advocating the passage of the bill, are represented by counsel and the opponents of the measure also. Witnesses are examined, expert testimony is taken, and the general atmosphere of a court-room prevails. Fees also are required of the promoters and the opponents, and the passage of a private bill of importance is a very expensive process. In case the bill be considered prejudicial to the interests of the community, it will be rejected or amended so as to remove the objectionable features. An opposed bill is certain to receive a very searching and critical examination, and the chairman of the Lords' committees and the chairman of the ways and means committee are charged with the critical inspection of bills which are unopposed, and, in fact, with a general revision of all private measures. The committees make their reports to the Houses in the usual way, and the bills are put through the customary routine of the three readings. Private bills in England embrace a large variety of subjects, many of which in the United States would be dealt with by state legislatures and city councils. There are private bills relating to corporations, paving, lighting, and policing cities, ferries, fisheries, markets, canals, bridges, railways, docks, drains, embankments, harbours, piers, sewers, subways, tramways, tunnels, water-works, and a great variety of other subjects.

The theory of public legislation is that it is for the general welfare of the entire people, and no one individual has more interest than another in promoting or opposing it. For this reason no such facilities for advocating or opposing the passage of a public bill are afforded to individuals as are given in the case of private measures. Yet even in the latter case not every one has a right to be heard. His interests must be directly involved. The owners of land which the bill proposes to appropriate have a right to be heard. Lessees and occupiers also possess a similar right. The owners of springs, wells, or water-powers, whose interests might be affected by the proposed bill, may appear before the committee and state their cases. Persons whose interests are not directly affected by the proposed legislation, however, have no right to be heard.

While the promoters of a private bill usually constitute a single corporation, such as a railway, canal, or water-works company, the opponents may be numerous. Cities and individual property owners may petition against the passage of a measure which would accord special privileges to a corporation. The establishment of a new water-works company may be opposed, for example, by cities and individuals whose water supplies and water-powers might be jeopardised. It is not always easy to show, however, that the establishment of a new water-works system, for example, would decrease the water supplies already existing or impair the water-power of existing manufactories. It is in this connection that the expert testimony of engineers is important. For example, certain persons whose water supplies might be affected by the diverting of underground water by a new construction were denied a hearing; but when it was scientifically demonstrated that the underground water followed a certain well-defined channel, they were heard. The rights of owners of surface water have always been recognised in this respect.

Formerly the private bills which could originate in the House of Lords were very limited in number. The House of Commons possessed the right to originate all bills relating to rates, tolls, and duties, but has waived some of its rights in this respect, so that at the present time about one half of the private bills originate in the Upper Chamber. Bills relating to estate, naturalisation, name, divorce, and the peerage, have always originated in the House of Lords. In the matter of private bills the services of the Lords are as important as those of the Commons. This is a fact not ordinarily appreciated in the United States. We are likely to underrate the House of Lords in this even more than in other respects. It is true, however, that the burden of the work on private bills is done by a comparatively few members.

As noted above, it is often a very expensive matter to promote or to oppose a private bill. There are certain fixed fees to be paid by the various parties interested. It should be remembered that in private bill legislation Parliament is acting largely in a judicial capacity, and that these fees are comparable to our court charges. There is a fixed schedule of fees which is printed, and which will be given to any one who may apply for it. There is also a taxing officer in each House whose duty is to assess the costs on the proper parties in the case.

The deliberations of Parliament are governed by the general rules of procedure which obtain in all legislative bodies, but there are some mod- **Practice and** ifications and peculiarities which deserve **Proceedings.** notice. There are certain orders and resolutions, relating to the conduct of business, which are peculiar to Parliament. Some of these are "Standing Orders" of a permanent character, others are "Sessional

Orders," continuing in force during the session only, while still others are "General Orders" and resolutions not defined as to permanence.

These various "orders" constitute the peculiarities in the proceedings of the two Houses. Centuries of experience have settled definitely the practice of many details. In the House of Lords the member speaking addresses his remarks to the House, while in the House of Commons all remarks are addressed to the Speaker. Members deviating from this rule have been called to order on various occasions. A member is not allowed to read his speech from manuscript, but may use notes if he wishes to do so; consequently there are no long tiresome sieges of monotonous reading from manuscript such as occur in the American Congress, the beginning of which causes the assembled members to scatter to various parts of the Capitol. A member may, however, read extracts of various kinds in the course of his speech, but these must be merely incidental. From an English standpoint "any other rule would be at once inconvenient and repugnant to the true theory of debate." "Leave to print" with its attendant abuses is also unknown. When a member of either House wishes to speak he rises in his place and stands uncovered. In case of sickness or infirmity, however, a member may be allowed to speak without rising. When a member speaks during a division, when the doors are closed, he remains seated and covered. This is the only occasion when a member is permitted to speak in this way. It is allowable for a speaker to address the House from

Rules of Debate.

the side galleries, as these are reserved for the use of members, but the position is not a favourable one and is rarely used. A member is not allowed to speak from below the bar, as he is then outside of the House. When a person not a member of Parliament is summoned to either House, he appears at the bar and is sometimes heard from this position, but a member must speak from his place on the floor of the House. In the House of Lords when more than one member rises at the same time to speak, the House decides, by a division, if necessary, which one shall be heard. In the House of Commons, however, the Speaker gives the floor to the member first observed by him. This is sometimes no easy matter, as it occasionally happens that a score of members may jump up in their places almost simultaneously and clamour for recognition. The Speaker must be impartial, and, as a rule, he will recognise speakers from the Government and Opposition ranks, alternately. He is not a partisan, and knows no friends or foes when in the chair. As a matter of courtesy, a new member is usually given precedence over others. When a member wanders away from the topic under discussion and brings in irrelevant matter, the Speaker may warn him to confine his remarks to the subject in hand. Should he persist in the irrelevant discussion, the Speaker may compel him to discontinue his speech. Frequent repetition is dealt with in the same way. It is needless to remark that both discretion and tact on the part of the Speaker are needful in the enforcement of these rules. Both Houses have decreed that a member may not speak twice upon the same question, unless in a committee, or to explain some part of his previous speech which was evidently misunderstood. Even then he must confine his remarks to the explanation and must not bring in any new material. This rule is generally adhered to, but has been set aside in a few instances under very special circumstances. In a "committee of the whole House," however, the Speaker is not in the chair, and the above restriction does not obtain. A member is not allowed to debate a matter already determined upon by the House. Such a matter is considered closed. This rule is not invariably insisted upon, but is sometimes waived at the discretion of the Speaker. Neither is a member at liberty to read, from a book or newspaper, printed extracts of a speech made in the current session, nor to cast reflections upon previous votes of the House. Such a course, if permitted, would serve only to arouse prolonged, angry, and fruitless discussions. The same rule applies to allusions to the debates in the other House. The theory is that since it is a breach of privilege to print the debates, their contents are unknown and hence incapable of discussion. The rule in practice, however, serves to prevent wrangling and recrimination between the two Houses. It is, however, frequently violated. It is not necessary that a debater be surpassingly ingenious and adroit in order to be able to break the rule in spirit while the letter remains intact. From the standpoint of courtesy and common sense the rule has much to commend it. The rule does not apply to "the votes and proceedings of either House as they are printed by authority."[1] It is probably needless to remark that treasonable or seditious language, or the irreverent use of the King's name, is not tolerated in debate. Members have been reprimanded and even sent to the Tower for this offence. And not only is the King of England protected from the irreverent use of his name in the debates of Parliament, but also are the rulers of other countries at peace with Great Britain likewise protected. Neither is it allowable to use the King's name in an attempt to influence the House. The ministers voice the King's recommendations, and any further expression is unnecessary and inconsistent with the independence of Parliament. The King is impersonal in this sense, and has no private opinions aside from those expressed by his ministers.

Neither House will permit the use of language which tends to lower Parliament in the estimation of the people. Remarks derogatory to the character of either House may be punished by reprimand or commitment, in case an apology be not forthcoming.

Both Houses have ordered that members shall be referred to in debate, if at all, not by name but indirectly. It is the "noble Earl" or the "right reverend prelate" in the House of Lords, and the "honourable gentleman, the member for York," in the House of Commons. Other adjectives, formal and empty, but outwardly courteous, are employed in an endeavour to indicate the member referred to without the use of his name. Members in debate are expected to observe the forms of decorum, whatever may be their

[1] May's "Parliamentary Practice," p. 312.

real sentiments. Imputing sinister motives, misrepresentation, or charging with misrepresentation or deception, is unparliamentary, and the offender may be checked by the Speaker. The rule is the same in the two Houses. On one occasion when Mr. Fox and Mr. Wedderburn indulged in heated language in the House of Commons, they were not allowed to leave the chamber until they promised that the matter was at an end. Having thus given bond to keep the peace, they were allowed to depart.

Undue obstruction of parliamentary business is not tolerated. The Englishman is essentially fair and honest, and is desirous of giving abundant opportunity for the discussion of all important matters, but cannot abide undue obstruction. Obstructionists may be punished by censure, suspension, or commitment, as the House may determine.

There are some rules of a very general character which are deserving of passing notice. The members of Parliament are expected to conduct themselves in an orderly manner, to avoid going needlessly from place to place within the chamber, and not to stand in the passageways. Members of the House of Commons are expected to remove their hats when entering or leaving the chamber, and to make an obeisance to the chair when passing. This obeisance is now so slight, however, that it is scarcely perceptible. It is irregular in either House to pass between the presiding officer and the member who has the floor. Such passage is held to be permissible, however, if the member is speaking from the third or a higher bench. The reading of books, newspapers,

The English Government

and letters is forbidden, but the Speaker enforces this rule with some elasticity and discretion. Members preparing to speak may consult books and letters upon matters connected with the debate. Silence is also enjoined in both Houses. Any interruptions by hissing or otherwise intended to disconcert the debater are considered unparliamentary. However, the Speaker often finds it impossible to enforce this rule when it is being violated simultaneously by scores of members.

At the close of the debate comes the "division." All important matters in the two Houses are decided in this way. This piece of machinery has been in operation so long in the English Parliament that its details are worked out to a nicety. In order to be entitled to vote upon any matter it is essential that the member be within the folding doors of the House, and hear the question put by the Speaker either the first or the second time. Votes have been stricken from the list by order of the Speaker when it appeared that this regulation was not complied with.

Divisions.

Formerly all strangers were required to withdraw before a division took place in either House. For nearly half a century, however, strangers have been ordered to withdraw only from below the bar in the House of Commons, and have been allowed to remain in the galleries of the House of Lords and in the space within the rails of the throne. In short, strangers are now allowed to remain in those parts of the chambers where their presence does not interfere with the division.

When the debate on any matter is finished, the Speaker puts the question, and, after hearing the voices, announces his tentative decision. If a division be called for, the Speaker orders the strangers to withdraw. A two-minute sand-glass is then inverted by one of the clerks, and while the sand is running the electric bells are kept ringing in all parts of the great buildings to summon the members to the division. When the sand has run through, the doors are promptly closed and locked by order of the Speaker. Those members who arrive late cannot enter, and those on the inside are not allowed to leave until the division is taken. The question is now put by the Speaker a second time, in order to enable those to vote who came in since it was first put. During the division the chamber must be entirely empty. All present must participate except under some very special circumstances. The breaking of this rule in 1881 was followed by the suspension of twenty-eight refractory members of the House of Commons. In case a member of the House of Commons does not wish to vote he may retire to the rooms behind the Speaker's chair before the question is put for the second time. A peer not desiring to vote withdraws to the woolsack. He is then outside the chamber and is not included in the division. The vote of the presiding officer in the House of Lords is taken first, and in the case of a tie he has no casting vote, and the "not contents" prevail. The Speaker of the House of Commons never votes except to break a tie. When the House is in the "committee of the whole" the Speaker may vote and speak as

The English Government

other members do, but in recent years he has not generally availed himself of this privilege. Tellers are appointed in the usual way, and a member thus chosen is compelled to act. If it is not possible to find two tellers for each party the division does not occur. Those voting in the affirmative go to the lobby at the right of the presiding officer, and those voting in the negative go to the left. Each section is counted by the tellers, and the result is duly announced by the presiding officer. The members, however, know in advance of the Speaker's announcement which side has prevailed, as the tellers for the majority walk at the right in advancing toward the Speaker's chair to deliver the division paper. Two members may force a division, and it is needless to remark that that power is sometimes abused and that restraint has been necessary.

"Pairs" are made for a sitting or even for weeks or months at a time. This is a matter of custom and private arrangement, and no parliamentary recognition has ever been taken of it. In one instance an effort made to condemn the practice failed.

There is a very high sense of honour and dignity in both Houses of Parliament, and any soliciting for votes which might appear undignified is frowned upon. The distribution of a circular intended to influence votes was condemned by the Speaker as "contrary to the best usages and traditions of the House." No member of either House having a pecuniary interest in the success or failure of a certain bill is allowed to vote in a division upon that measure. The interest, however, must be " immediate and personal," and not general in character. Members have been held in numerous instances to be ineligible to vote because of this pecuniary interest in measures. The votes of certain members were not received on one occasion on a bill for the incorporation of a manufacturing company, because it was shown that they were financially interested in the matter. In most cases, however, the member will not offer his vote if there is any doubt at all of its acceptability. There is usually a feeling of delicacy which restrains him from precipitating a discussion upon this point.

The work of Parliament is expedited by committees of various kinds. In fact, the committee seems indispensable in all large legislative bodies.

Committees.

The "Committee of the whole House" is important because it permits a freer discussion of the various features of a bill than would be possible at a regular sitting of the House. The Committee is, in reality, the House of Commons with the Chairman of Committees, instead of the Speaker, presiding. With the Speaker in the chair each member may speak but once upon a question, but in a Committee of the whole House there is no such restriction. This arrangement permits of a more minute and detailed discussion than would otherwise be possible.

Since 1883 there have been certain "standing committees" to which bills relating to law, courts of justice, trade, shipping, and manufactures have been referred. The House of Lords also has its "standing committees," and in each House the members are nominated by "committees of selection" and not by the presiding officers.

A "Select Committee" is appointed for the purpose of investigating any matter of importance and reporting its findings to the House. Many of these reports are exceedingly important documents. When the committee is made up of efficient, energetic, and interested men, the results are likely to be of great and permanent value. The subject for investigation may be any one upon which either House desires detailed and reliable information. Select Committees were formerly not allowed to report their opinions to the House, but were compelled to confine themselves to an exposition of the facts. They are now permitted, however, to append any opinions and inferences which they wish. The Select Committee usually consists of fifteen members.

After a contest which had extended over centuries, it was decided that the right to levy taxes and grant supplies lay with Parliament. "The Crown demands money, the Commons grant it, and the Lords assent to the grant." *Taxation and Supply.* The above is the concise statement of May in reference to grants of money for the expenses of the government. The demand is made by the King through the Cabinet, the appropriation is made by the Commons and assented to by the Lords without amendment. The Commons will not increase the amount asked for by the ministers, nor will they impose any tax or increase the taxes which obtain, unless such a step be recommended by the ministers. Estimates of the probable expenditure of the government are made by the Chancellor of the Exchequer, and the House of Commons is expected to accept these estimates without alteration. A rejection or material revision would mean a want of confidence in the government, on the part of the House. The supplies asked for by the Crown are now almost invariably granted. Formerly they were sometimes withheld in order to compel the Sovereign to redress certain grievances. No such reason now exists for refusal, and this weapon "lies rusty in the armoury of constitutional warfare."

The House of Commons for centuries has had full control of money bills in Parliament. The control of the Commons in this respect is even more absolute and complete than that of our House of Representatives. In taxation and appropriation of supplies the function of the Lords is to concur and not to mutilate or amend. This is now a settled principle of the English Constitution, and is strictly adhered to by one House and insisted upon by the other. It was explicitly stated in 1678, "That all aids and supplies, and aids to his Majesty in Parliament, are the sole gift of the Commons; and all bills for the granting of any such aids and supplies ought to begin with the Commons, and that it is the undoubted and sole right of the Commons to direct, limit, and appoint in such bills the ends, purposes, considerations, conditions, limitations, and qualifications of such grants, which ought not to be changed or altered by the House of Lords." This rule still obtains and is rigidly insisted upon by the Commons.

Owing to their inviolable character, it was formerly the custom of the Commons to "tack" objectionable clauses to money bills in order to coerce the Lords to indorse them. This custom has been condemned as "unparliamentary," and the practice of "tacking,"

The English Government

analogous to our method of appending "riders," has not been resorted to in recent years. In 1807, however, the Lords rejected two bills on the ground that they contained "multifarious matter."

It might be interesting to note in this connection that the revenues of the English government all pour into the "Consolidated Fund," and that all disbursements are made from this source. Prior to the reign of George III. there were innumerable funds, and the business of the government was needlessly complicated by maintaining distinctions among them. In that reign, however, steps were taken to provide a fund "into which shall flow every stream of the public revenue, and from whence shall issue the supply for every public service." The Consolidated Fund grew from this movement, and its establishment has greatly simplified the administration of English finances.

The hereditary revenues of the Crown are now paid into the Consolidated Fund, and the allowances for the maintenance of the Royal Family are made from that source. At the accession of a new sovereign it becomes necessary for Parliament to vote these allowances. In 1901 the annual royal income was fixed as follows: —

The Civil List and Royal Grants.

Their Majesties' Privy Purse	£110,000
Salaries of H. M. Household, and Retired Allowances	125,800
Expenses of H. M. Household	193,000
Works	20,000
Royal Bounty, Alms, and Special Services	13,200
Unappropriated Moneys	8,000
	£470,000

Parliament has also granted annual allowances to other members of the Royal Family as follows: —

Prince of Wales	£20,000
Princess of Wales	10,000
His Majesty's daughters	18,000
Duke of Connaught	25,000
Princess Christian of Schleswig-Holstein	6,000
Princess Louise, Duchess of Argyll	6,000
Princess Henry of Battenberg	6,000
Duchess of Saxe-Coburg and Gotha	6,000
Duchess of Albany	6,000
Duchess of Mecklenburg-Strelitz	3,000
Duke of Cambridge	12,000
Total	£118,000

The expense of sustaining the Royal Family in England must seem prodigious to those accustomed to the less ostentatious republican form of government; yet many English writers find satisfaction in the fact that the income of their King is exceeded by that of several of the monarchs of continental Europe. The Civil List of the present King is considerably greater than that of the late Queen Victoria. It can never be charged that England has been parsimonious in the support of the Royal Family. It would seem to a foreigner that she has been liberal to a fault. A comparison of the Civil List of the King with the salary of an American President serves to intensify the contrast.

There are a large number of other grants and pensions which have been made to members of the Royal Family from time to time. When Prince Albert came to England in 1840, Parliament gave him a liberal annual allowance. It was proposed to give him £50,000 a year; but Mr. Hume, a thrifty Scotch member, considered it bad policy "to set a young man down in the streets of London with so much money in his pockets." The allowance was very considerably reduced to £30,000. In addition to this, however, the Prince was given several offices yielding good salaries with but little work.

In addition to the parliamentary grants certain members of the Royal Family enjoy funds from other sources. For example, the King receives the revenues from the Duchy of Lancaster Estates, which amounted to £61,000 in 1900; and the Prince of Wales enjoys an income from the Duchy of Cornwall Estates, which amounted in 1900 to more than £70,000.

The net income from the Crown lands which is now turned into the Consolidated Fund amounted to £500,000 in 1900-1901. Minor sources of hereditary revenue yielded £29,000 in the same time. Thus the income from the Crown Estates is approximately equal to the amount of the Civil List.

Although the process of impeachment is now well-nigh obsolete, no case having occurred since 1805, and there having been but two cases in the last century and a half, a brief discussion of the matter may serve to illustrate a once powerful feature of the English government.

Impeachment.

The method of impeachment in England is similar to that which obtains in the United States. In England the charges are brought by the House of Commons, and the case is tried before the House of Lords acting as a jury. In the United States the charges are preferred by the House of Representatives, and the case is heard and determined by the Senate.

While the crimes for which impeachment may be resorted to in England have never been specifically listed, the practice has been to confine the process to those of an extraordinary character. It has also been reserved, for the most part, for the cases of persons of high official position.

The initiative in the matter rests with the House of Commons. When a member of that body wishes to institute impeachment proceedings against an individual, he rises in his place and makes charges of treason or other high crime or misdemeanour, submitting proof of his statements at the same time. He concludes by moving the impeachment. Should the House determine to take up the matter, the mover is directed to go to the House of Lords, "and at their bar, in the name of the House of Commons, and of all the commons of the United Kingdom, to impeach the accused; and to acquaint them that this House will, in due time, exhibit particular articles against him, and make good the same." The member, accompanied by others of the House, then carries out the above directions. A committee is then appointed by the Commons to draw up articles of impeachment, which are forwarded to the Lords after approval by the Commons. Further articles may be added from time to time. "Managers" are appointed by the Commons to prepare the evidence and to conduct the case, and the Lords fix a day for the beginning of the trial. The trial is usually held in Westminster Hall.

This hall is now almost entirely devoid of furnishings, and is occupied, as Moses Coit Tyler said, only by "centuries of reminiscences," but it is properly fitted up on occasions of this kind. The Lord Chancellor presides except when a peer is impeached for treason. In that case the Lord High Steward, appointed by the Crown, is the presiding officer. The case is then conducted in the usual way by the managers, the accused being allowed the service of counsel and the benefit of witnesses in his behalf. The case is then "given to the jury," and the Lords proceed to determine by vote the guilt or innocence of the accused. Each article is voted on separately. The Lord High Steward submits the question on the first article to each peer in succession. The peer rises, removes his hat, places his right hand upon his breast, and answers, "guilty, upon my honour," or, "not guilty, upon my honour," as the case may be. Each article is submitted to vote in like manner, and the results are ascertained and made known by the Lord High Steward. If the finding be "not guilty," the case is dismissed; if "guilty," the Commons will demand that the Lords pronounce penalty, unless they wish to pardon the offender by dropping the case at this point. The Lords may not pronounce judgment until it has been demanded by the Commons. Sentence is then pronounced by the Lord High Steward, or by the Lord Chancellor upon the convicted man standing at the bar of the House of Lords.

When Parliament has entered upon an impeachment, the proceedings cannot be stopped by adjournment, prorogation, or even dissolution. A dissolution puts an end to the existence of a Parliament and a new one must be chosen in its stead, but it does not terminate impeachment proceedings. The case continues until a decision is reached.

The impeachment of Warren Hastings is the most memorable trial of the kind in the history of modern England. It began on the 13th of February, 1788, and lasted for seven years. Some of the most noted men in England at the time took part in the proceedings. Miss Fanny Burney[1] was an eye-witness of the famous trial, and her account of it is interesting in the extreme. She did not, however, view the proceedings with unprejudiced eyes, as she had become acquainted with Hastings and his wife, and had a very warm admiration for both of them. Miss Burney describes in some detail the arrangement of Westminster Hall, and the respective places of the lords, commoners, and others who were present either as participants or spectators. The trial began about twelve o'clock with the entry of the "Managers of the Prosecution." "I shuddered," she writes, "and involuntarily drew back, when, as the doors were flung open, I saw Mr. Burke, as Head of the Committee, make his solemn entry." Other members of the committee, including Fox and Sheridan, followed, and took their places in the committee box. Then the other members of the House of Commons entered and took the green benches put in place for them. "Then began the

Trial of Warren Hastings.

---

[1] See Seeley's "Fanny Burney and her Friends," pp. 189-200. Also Madame d'Arblay's "Diary and Letters," vol. ii. pp. 86-153.

procession, the Clerks entering first, then the Lawyers according to their rank, and the Peers, Bishops, and Officers, all in their coronation robes; concluding with the Princes of the Blood, — Prince William, son to the Duke of Gloucester, coming first, then the Dukes of Cumberland, Gloucester, and York, then the Prince of Wales; the whole ending by the Chancellor with his train borne." After all had taken seats, a sergeant-at-arms arose and commanded silence. "Then," says Miss Burney, "some other officer in a loud voice called out, as well as I can recollect, words to this purpose: 'Warren Hastings, Esquire, come forth! Answer to the charges brought against you; save your bail, or forfeit your recognisance!'" Then the accused came forth, preceded by the Gentleman Usher of the Black Rod, and made a low bow to the Chancellor and the court. He went slowly to the opening of the defendants' box and bowed again. He then advanced to the bar, and with his hands upon it dropped on his knees. Being given permission to rise, he stood up and bowed low to the court for the third time. The Crier then proclaimed "That Warren Hastings, Esquire, late Governor-General of Bengal, was now on his trial for high crimes and misdemeanours, with which he was charged by the Commons of Great Britain; and that all persons whatsoever who had aught to allege against him were now to stand forth."

"A general silence followed, and the Chancellor, Lord Thurlow, made his speech."

Hastings then bowed again to the court, and leaning over the bar answered: "My Lords, — impressed, deeply impressed, — I come before your Lordships equally confident in my own integrity, and in the justice of the court before which I am to clear it." The case was then opened by the reading of the charges against the accused, and was continued from day to day in the usual way. Miss Burney attended the trial at other times than the opening and was captivated by the eloquence of Burke but rather repelled by the fury of Fox. Yet she listened to his violent eloquence on one occasion for five hours.

Suffice it to say that Hastings was acquitted in 1795, after a memorable and protracted trial lasting for seven years. Although there has been one impeachment case in England since that time, the trial of Hastings did much to convince the English people that impeachment, as Anson puts it, is "out of date."

Petitions. The right to petition the Crown and Parliament for a redress of grievances is fundamental in the English Constitution. This right, which John Quincy Adams championed so strenuously and so successfully in the American Congress during the period of slavery agitation, is in England as old as Magna Charta at least. Yet, although an ancient and honoured right, its exercise has always been attended with some restrictions. As noted above, the number of persons who may present a petition in person to Parliament is limited, and so is the number allowed to congregate within one mile of Westminster Hall for the purpose of drafting a petition when Parliament is in session. The form of introduction to the petition is specified, and so is its conclusion in a general way. After the stereotyped introduction comes the recital of grievances, the redress of which is desired. Next comes the "prayer," in which the object of the petition is set forth. No petition will be received without the prayer. It is also necessary that the petition be written. If printed or lithographed, it will not be received by Parliament. One signature at least must be on the same sheet with the body of the petition. The document must be in the English language or accompanied by an English translation whose correctness is vouched for by the member presenting the petition. Petitions may not have interlineations or erasures, the signatures must be the original ones, not copies, and must be written upon the petition and not pasted upon it. The chairman of a public meeting is not competent to sign a petition in behalf of those present, although he may have been instructed by the meeting to do so. A petition thus signed is looked upon by Parliament as the petition of the chairman only, and not of the assembly. Forgery or fraud in the preparation of a petition renders the offender liable to punishment by Parliament, as such an act is looked upon as a breach of privilege. The language of the petition, too, must be respectful and must not cast reflections upon Parliament, upon either House, or upon an individual member. In 1848 a petition was objected to because it prayed for the abolition of the House of Lords. This objection, however, was not pressed, and the petition was eventually received. In 1849 a petition was presented by one W. S. O'Brien and others "attainted of treason," and the objection was made that a petition could not be received from persons "civilly dead." The petition, however, owing "to the peculiar and exceptional circumstances of the case," was subsequently received.

It is essential that the petition be presented by a member of the House to which it is addressed, and this member must place his name with his own hand at the beginning of the document. In order to facilitate the redress of grievances, it is provided that petitions may be sent through the mails, free of postage, to members of either House, in case they be sent in open covers and do not weigh more than thirty-two ounces.

The freedom with which the right to petition is exercised in England will be evident from a few statistics. Since 1833, nearly a million petitions upon all conceivable subjects have been presented to the House of Commons. The number of petitions gradually increased from 1833 to 1872, but since that time there has been a decrease. In 1843, 34,000 petitions were presented at a single session. The whole history of petitioning furnishes a good illustration of that spirit of freedom and justice which pervades the entire government of England.

CHAPTER XV

IMPRESSIONS OF PARLIAMENT

THAT famous legislative body which Carlyle sarcastically termed, "The great talking shop at Westminster," has a peculiar interest for American travellers in Europe. The English Parliament is in itself an important body, representing as it does one of the greatest of the modern world powers; but it possesses a peculiar attraction for the American tourist, since his institutions are of English origin and are still strikingly similar in many respects to those of the mother country. Few Americans, then, will fail, if opportunity offers, to look in upon that great legislative body which represents not only the Witan of Anglo-Saxon times, but also the original House of Commons established by Simon de Montfort in 1265. The history of the English Parliament, its present importance, and its kinship to our institutions invest it with a peculiar interest from the American standpoint.

The visitor soon finds that it is somewhat more difficult to gain admission to the English Parliament than it is to the American Congress. He may enter the spacious galleries of the Senate or House of Representatives without ticket, but before entering those of the Lords or Commons

Cards of Admission.

he must obtain an order signed by a member of the House to which admission is sought. It is usually not very difficult to obtain the requisite order, and many Americans have been admitted through the courtesy of Mr. James Bryce, the well-known author of the "American Commonwealth." Even when fortunate enough to obtain the necessary order, however, the visitor is often obliged to await his turn before being admitted. He is also scrutinised with great care by the practised eyes of the officials, and is not allowed to carry a hand bag or a parcel of any kind into the Houses. These precautions have been made necessary by the various gunpowder plots and dynamite episodes which have centred about the Houses of Parliament. The same precautions are taken at other public places in London, notably at the Tower, where the Crown jewels to the value of £3,000,000 are deposited. When we consider the small size of the various galleries, and the fact that no little damage was done to the Houses of Parliament by a dynamite explosion during the Fenian agitation of a few years ago, we can readily see why restrictions are placed upon the admission of visitors.

The visitor will usually go to the House of Commons first, and to the House of Lords later, if at all.

House of Commons. The House of Commons is now the real governing power in England. The power of the Crown has practically vanished, and that of the Lords is by no means co-ordinate with the power of the popular branch. Since 1832 the Lords have not been able to defeat a measure which the Commons have been determined to pass. Since the House of Commons can dictate to the Crown and coerce the Lords, greater interest attaches to its proceedings. Before being admitted, the visitor must wait until the Speaker has been conducted from his residence — which is in the Houses of Parliament — to the chamber of the Commons. That official is preceded by the Sergeant-at-arms carrying the mace, the symbol of authority, and his coming is announced in loud tones by the heralds in the corridors. After he has taken the chair and prayers are over, visitors are admitted; not, however, until they have signed their names and written their addresses, together with the names of the members whose orders they bear, in a book provided for that purpose. Then having obtained the printed order of the day from an official whose palm has been properly crossed, the visitor soon finds himself in the gallery overlooking the floor of the Commons. Here is the storm centre of English politics. Here a sovereign legislative body is deliberating which "can do anything but make it rain." Here are those men who shape the destiny of the British Empire. The interior of the chamber is not impressive. The room is not large, — seating only four hundred and eighty-six members, — and the decorations while rich are rather sombre, and anything but startling. The seats are long benches, upholstered in dark green leather, are somewhat elevated, and extend the length of the room. Between the banks of benches and at one end of the room the Speaker sits in a somewhat conspicuous position. The historic "bar" is at the opposite end of the chamber, and the bar in the House of Lords is similarly located. The visitor who is familiar with the spacious galleries at Washington will feel himself somewhat cramped in the narrow quarters provided for strangers in the House of Commons. One of these galleries, — probably the smallest, — elevated only a short distance above the floor of the chamber, will accommodate only eight persons. However, the galleries provided for the use of men are very commodious in comparison with that for the use of women. The latter gallery is located at one end of the chamber, immediately beneath the high ceiling, and is screened with a lattice-work, apparently of iron. From that lofty position the women of England are certainly unable to influence the trend of parliamentary legislation. The representatives of the press are well cared for. The reporters are favourably and conspicuously placed in the front row of the gallery, although, as has been said, there are at the present time orders upon the journals of the House prohibiting the publication of the debates. It is needless to say that these orders, although never repealed, are not now enforced.

The House assembles at two o'clock in the afternoon, and the visitor will probably be surprised at
Time of Meeting. the comparatively small attendance. There are now six hundred and seventy members in the House of Commons, but the attendance will not exceed one hundred and fifty or two hundred, unless an unusually interesting debate is in progress, or a vote is being taken. Forty members constitute a quorum to do business, and the attendance is fre-

quently not much in excess of that number. There is a reason for this, however, which will appear presently.

The American familiar with the legislative halls at Washington will be impressed upon entering the House of Commons with the business-like atmosphere of the place and the lack of useless display. *Good Order.* Business is carried on in a much more quiet and dignified way than in our House of Representatives. In the latter chamber each member has his own desk, and while business is going on, is likely to be writing letters, conversing with a neighbour, or reading a book or daily paper. In the House of Commons there are no desks, no writing is allowed, and no books or papers permitted except the printed order of the day. Messengers are not allowed upon the floor, and hence are not an element of confusion as the pages are at Washington. Pages and others not members of the House of Representatives go about upon the floor of the House with great freedom; but the floor of the House of Commons is sacredly guarded, and no one but a member is allowed to put foot upon it while the body is in session. There is a railing at each end of the room beyond which the attendants may not venture. When a note or card is sent in, the attendant hands it to a member who happens to sit near the railing, or waits until some member comes to relieve him of the article. It is noticeable, however, that when a member sits only a short distance from the railing, the attendant will step inside and hold out the message or card in one hand while grasping the railing with the other. As long as he holds to the railing, the law seems to be complied with, although he may be entirely within the sacred precincts of the Commons. The fact that the floor of the House of Commons is reserved exclusively for members makes for good order in that body. The absence of desks is more important still. It has been proposed at different times to remove the desks from the legislative chambers at Washington, and to do so would certainly eliminate a vast amount of confusion. The congressmen, however, are loath to part with these convenient articles, and the reform is not likely to be effected in the near future.

It is somewhat surprising to see the majority of the members sitting with their hats on. This custom **Hats on.** has survived from the time when the members of Parliament wore hats, long boots, spurs, and swords during their deliberations. In the process of evolution the swords, spurs, and long boots have vanished, but the hats still remain. When a member rises to speak, and when he enters or leaves the room, his hat is removed and a slight bow is made in the direction of the Speaker, but under ordinary circumstances the hat remains upon the head of its owner.

The attendance in the chamber on ordinary occasions seems small in comparison with the membership. **Attendance.** There are now six hundred and seventy members in the Lower House, and only a minority of these are expected to be present in the chamber at any given time. The seating capacity of the House is only four hundred and eighty-six, so that

The English Government

the entire membership could not be accommodated if present. Since most of the discussions are rather prosy affairs and have little influence upon the voting, many members prefer to take refuge in other parts of the House while the debate is in progress, and to appear at its conclusion to cast their votes. The actual attendance at any given time may be comparatively slight, but if a vote or a division takes place, the members flock into the chamber in astonishing numbers. When a division is called for, the Speaker reverses a little sand-glass, which stands on the table in front of him. It takes exactly two minutes for the sand to run through, and this is the time allowed for the assembling of the members. Electric bells connected by sixty miles of wire are set ringing in all parts of the great building, which covers eight acres of ground, and "whips" hurry out to notify the members of their respective parties, who flock in from the library, the dining-room, the smoking and committee rooms, and other parts of the Houses. When the sand has run through, the doors are closed and no one may enter. In the division the "ayes" go to the lobby at the Speaker's right and the "noes" to the one at his left, where the counting is done by the tellers. In this way a member may vote on all important matters and attend but few or no debates. He may also know what is going on in the House. An electrical apparatus in each of the important rooms where members congregate, prints the name of the man speaking, the time when he began, and also indicates the subject under discussion. When another gets the floor the change is duly indicated. The Englishman, by the way, instead of "getting the floor," is said to "get on his legs" to speak; as if, as Charles Dickens remarks in his "Sketches by Boz," it were sometimes customary for members to stand on their heads while speaking by way of diversion.

The manner of speaking is quite different from that in vogue at Washington. The conversational style **Manner of Speaking.** prevails with no attempt at oratorical display. The lofty rhetoric so often heard in Congress is seldom inflicted upon the House of Commons. A member sometimes becomes eloquent because he cannot help it, but never with "malice aforethought." Members are not allowed to deliver speeches from manuscript, but may use notes if they wish. The result is that most of the speeches are short, business-like talks, while some are rambling and contain many repetitions. The average member of the English Parliament is not fluent, but speaks in a hesitant way. He will not rush on, but will wait for the word which he wishes to express his idea. The result is that he usually speaks with precision, saying exactly what he intends to say. His speech reads much better than it sounds. This hesitant manner of speaking is much affected in some quarters in America. There are some who wish to imitate the English manner of speaking, and others who think that readiness in utterance must accompany superficiality in thought. This, unfortunately, is too often true, but it is also true that fluency in delivery often results from a thorough mastery of the subject in hand. There have been great masters of parliamentary oratory in England, —

The English Government

there are a few such at present,—but the average member of Parliament is far from being an orator in the popular sense of that term. He is a very effective speaker, nevertheless.

The manners of the House of Commons are an interesting study. The individual member is the personification of courtesy; but the House, as a whole, is hard, unsympathetic, and at times rude. *(Manners of the Commons.)* While speaking, the member is scrupulously careful not to impute to a fellow member motives even in the slightest degree dishonourable. Should he do so, he is called to order instantly and apologises promptly. The House, as a whole, however, is not so courteous. When a man makes a long and tiresome speech or utters unpopular sentiments, all courtesy seems to vanish. It would be difficult to imagine a more disagreeable body to face. There is no applause by clapping of hands or evidence of disapproval by hissing, as in the United States Congress, but the words "hear! hear!" are uttered in such a way as to express approval, disapproval, contempt, or ridicule. The tone of voice is the indicator, and there is no mistaking it. When the cry, "hear! hear!" is not effective, noises of all conceivable kinds may be resorted to. It was a chorus of this kind which Burke characterised as the "yelping of a parcel of boys," and which O'Connell called the "beastly bellowing" of the members. When an Irish bill is being discussed, or when Sir William Vernon-Harcourt, "the fighting Ajax of his party," is attacking the Government, or when Joseph Chamberlain is defending his administration of the Colonial Office, there is no lack of excitement. The words "hear! hear!" are then used in all their different shades of meaning. The Irish question has been especially prolific of sensations. The English government of Ireland has not been like a placid stream. Opposition rather than co-operation has been the rule with the Irish members. I heard on one occasion a member of the House of Lords making complaint to that body that a law of Parliament affecting Ireland was being ignored. It seems that the Act provided that certain notices regarding the provisions of the law be posted in various parts of Ireland. The noble Earl who was voicing the complaint reported that the Irish official whose duty it was to post these notices had taken care to post them in every instance with the printed side toward the wall. This antagonism on the part of the Irish people has given rise to many spirited debates in the House of Commons, and has also served to emphasise the collective discourtesy of that body. The late Moses Coit Tyler, writing from England in 1866, differentiates clearly between the courtesy of the individual and the discourtesy of the House as a whole. "Standing," says Tyler, "he must observe the gracious amenities of debate; sitting, he may do what he likes. Standing, he must not breathe the slightest suspicion against his antagonist; sitting, he may bellow at his antagonist, bray at him, bark at him, mew at him, squeal at him, crow at him, whistle at him, laugh aloud at him. Standing, he must illustrate the manners of an English gentleman; sitting, he is at perfect liberty to illustrate the manners of a ruffian, a cow, a cat, a dog, an ass, a South Sea

Islander, or a baboon." All of these noises Tyler likens in character and variety to those heard in Regent's Park at feeding time. Miss Martineau mentions the fact that Brougham was on one occasion "interrupted by a peculiar cry, heard amid the cheers of the House, but whether a baa, or a bray, or a grunt, Hansard does not inform us." Brougham stopped long enough to pay his respects to his assailants. "By a wonderful disposition of nature," said he, "every animal has its peculiar mode of expressing itself, and I am too much of a philosopher to quarrel with any of those modes." However, it would not be fair to dwell too long upon this phase of the manners of the House, since disorder of this kind is entirely exceptional, and order and decorum as a rule prevail.

The *personnel* of the House is also a matter of interest. The members supporting the Government sit at the Speaker's right, and the Opposition members at his left. Members of the Cabinet and some other ministers occupy the front bench on one side, and the leaders of the Opposition are similarly placed on the other. The man who by virtue of his office has been the most conspicuous figure on the Government side is Mr. Arthur J. Balfour, First Lord of the Treasury and Leader of the House of Commons, and later Premier. Mr. Balfour is a man slightly beyond middle age, the nephew of Lord Salisbury, and has been a familiar figure in parliamentary politics for many years. He is of a literary turn of mind, decidedly unsensational in manner, and impresses one as being a man of great candour, sincerity, and stability. He is a good, forcible speaker, very unassuming and unpretentious in manner. The man, however, who has attracted the most attention during recent sessions is Mr. Joseph Chamberlain, the Colonial Secretary. Mr. Chamberlain was brought into prominence by his management of the South African affair, as well as by the great ability which he displayed in other matters. He is tall, striking, and intellectual in appearance, apparently about forty-five years of age, but in reality sixty-six. He is a man of action rather than a logician, and probably represents the English nation of to-day better than any other man, with the possible exception of Lord Salisbury. He is fearless in action, and has an all-abiding faith in the destiny of the Anglo-Saxon race in general, and of the British Empire in particular. He was frequently mentioned by the London press as the probable successor to Lord Salisbury when the latter's retirement from the Premiership seemed imminent. Politics certainly makes strange bedfellows. Only a few years ago Mr. Chamberlain was in Mr. Gladstone's Cabinet, and was one of the most persistent and virulent foes of the Conservative party. He gave no quarter. There is now no more staunch supporter of that same party than he. Light was not miraculously shed about him while on the road to Damascus, but he found himself entirely out of sympathy with the Home Rule ideas of Mr. Gladstone, and during the last few years has been acting with the Conservative party. Lecky, the well-known historian, representing Dublin University, sits with the Government party, as did Sir John Lubbock, the famous scientist and

The English Government

author, before his elevation to the peerage on New Year's Day, 1900.

On the opposite side of the chamber we notice Sir Henry Campbell-Bannerman, the Leader of the Opposition; Mr. James Bryce, well known to Americans; John Burns, the great labour leader; Henry Labouchere, the courageous and sarcastic editor of "Truth," and the scholarly John Morley, the author of many worthy volumes, including the authorised biography of Mr. Gladstone. It is quite evident to the observer that the Opposition at the present time lacks unity and leadership. Since Mr. Gladstone passed away there has been no one in the Liberal party to take his place. His shrewd leadership and masterful personality are sadly missed. Sir Henry Campbell-Bannerman, the present Leader of the Opposition, is certainly not master of the situation. Possibly no man could be. The disintegration of the party was quite marked even while Mr. Gladstone was in command. The Liberals, Radicals, and Irish Nationalists, who make up the Opposition, are often pulling in three different directions at the same time. Strong leadership on the part of any man under the present conditions would probably lead to disruption. There is a unity of purpose in the Government party at present which presents a striking contrast to the jarring elements of the Opposition. The present Leader is probably as efficient as any other would be under the existing conditions.

I would like to add a word to what was said above concerning John Burns, the famous labour leader of Battersea. Here is a truly remarkable man. At the age of fourteen he began his apprenticeship as an engineer, and was employed before that time in a candle factory and in another manufacturing establishment in London. His early education was thus obviously neglected, but his self-improvement has been remarkable. He is a stranger to academic halls, but a man of wonderful vigour of mind and tenacity of purpose. During a parliamentary contest in East St. Pancras I attended a political meeting at which John Burns was one of the speakers. His argument was forcible and convincing. It would certainly be difficult to find a more effective political speaker. His services in the House and in the committee rooms are also highly valued. Organised labour on both sides of the Atlantic would profit greatly, if such sane leaders could be multiplied.

In comparing the *personnel* of Parliament with that of Congress, one must be impressed with the large number of literary and scientific men who hold seats in the English legislative chambers. In the American Congress we have very few, almost none, of this class of men. In England the practical politician has no such monopoly of legislative honours as he enjoys in America.

A visit to the House of Lords will not prove so attractive. The chamber itself is much more gorgeous than that of the Commons, but the business of the Upper House is not so important. The interior decorations are quite elaborate and striking, yet in good taste. The benches are upholstered in red leather, and the wood-carving, statuary, and paintings add to the attractiveness of the

<small>House of Lords.</small>

scene. At one end of the room is the ornate throne of the King, which, by the way, he would not be allowed to occupy except on very special occasions. The House usually convenes at four-fifteen o'clock in the afternoon, and its sessions are generally short and uneventful. There are nearly six hundred members at the present time, and three of these constitute a quorum. A larger quorum would probably be embarrassing. Scores of members almost never attend the sessions. Many, like Lords Roberts and Kitchener, have duties elsewhere, while others appreciate the honours of the membership, but do not assume the responsibilities.

Lord Salisbury, the recent Premier, and Lord Rosebery, his predecessor in office, are probably the best-known men now in the chamber of the Lords. The Lord Chancellor presides, sitting on the famous "woolsack," which is now a large ottoman upholstered in red. The debates are likely to be rather perfunctory in character, owing to the predominance of the House of Commons. The real strength and importance of the House of Lords appear in the work of its committees.

The archbishop and bishops of the Church of England, clad in their clerical robes, are present and participate in the business of the session. There has been an agitation for a number **Spiritual Peers.** of years tending toward the disestablishment of the Church of England and the removal of the spiritual peers from the House of Lords. The change is destined to be made sooner or later, and when made will benefit the Church and State alike.

Although American institutions are offshoots from the English stem and are English in substance, yet **Forms and Ceremonies.** there are some peculiar forms and ceremonies connected with the English Parliament which cannot fail to attract the attention of the American observer.

There is evidence of extreme vigilance and suspicion on the part of those officials whose duty is to care for the safety of the Royal Family and the members of Parliament. The search which is instituted before the formal opening of a session of Parliament gives evidence of this feeling. In 1605 it was found that Guy Fawkes and others had placed barrels of gunpowder in the basement of the Houses of Parliament with the intention of blowing up the King, Lords, and Commons, when they assembled on the fifth of November of that year. The discovery frustrated the designs of the plotters, and has caused the officials about the buildings to be abnormally careful and vigilant ever since. A few hours before the opening of the session a search is made through the basements and other dark recesses of the buildings, where by any chance a villain might be lurking or a quantity of explosives stored. Four high officials, with four of his Majesty's yeomen superbly armed and carrying lanterns, go in solemn procession through the lonely and unfrequented cellars of the Houses. They flash their lights into every dark corner, but never find anything and never expect to; yet the search has been made regularly for nearly three hundred years, and the custom shows no symptoms of ever ending. After making the search and finding

The English Government

no signs of plots, the Sovereign is informed by telegraph that he would incur no risk by attending at the opening of Parliament. After having her fears thus allayed, it was the custom of the late Queen to send a commission to represent her at the opening of the session.

The opening of a new session of the English Parliament is always an interesting scene, and will be either impressive or absurd, according to the standpoint of the individual observer. Should the individual be intensely modern and coldly practical in his views, the ceremonies attending the formal opening of the session cannot fail to strike him as being empty and ridiculously pompous. On the other hand, should the observer possess that sympathy and historical background which result from a thorough knowledge and appreciation of the history and theory of English politics, he cannot fail to be impressed with some features at least of the elaborate ceremonies. The careful observer, viewing the scene before him in its true historical perspective, will not expect to find republican simplicity in the government of that country, where the forms of monarchy, if not the essence, still survive. He will see that the old forms and ceremonies have survived in some instances at least for a good purpose.

It was formerly the custom for the King or Queen to be present at the opening of a session, and to participate in the attendant ceremonies. The late Queen, however, did not attend, **Opening of Parliament.** but intrusted the duty of opening Parliament to a Royal Commission constituted for the purpose. The ceremony is interesting and quaint, especially when a Speaker is to be chosen. These commissioners, conscious apparently of the important function which they are to perform, enter the House of Lords in great state with their cocked hats and showy robes of ermine and scarlet, and take their seats in front of the throne. A messenger repairs to the House of Commons and requests that body to appear in the Lords' chamber to learn the pleasure of the Queen. Had the Queen been present in person the messenger would have *demanded* the presence of the Commons. In the present instance he can only *request* such attendance. The messenger to whom this duty is intrusted is the Gentleman Usher of the Black Rod. He is arrayed in a very elaborate manner, and is resplendent in his black silk knickerbockers, his coat of peculiar design, and his ruffles, which suggest the fashion-plates of centuries long past. He moves with a stately punctiliousness quite in keeping with his mission and his raiment. The doorkeeper of the House of Commons knows of his coming, and when he appears that official shuts and bars the door to show this emissary of the Crown that he has no right to invade the sacred precincts of the Commons' chamber except by the permission of that body. That permission is always granted, however, after a show of resistance, and the Gentleman Usher of the Black Rod is admitted after knocking three times. His arrival is announced, all business is suspended, the members remove their hats, and Black Rod approaches the Speaker's chair, bowing impressively three times. He makes known his message; and the

The English Government

Chief Clerk of the Commons, followed by the members, or a part of them, repairs to the chamber of the Lords. Here they listen to the Royal Commission and then return to their own chamber to elect a Speaker. A programme previously arranged is quickly carried out. The Chief Clerk in the absence of a Speaker is the presiding officer, and at the proper moment he points three fingers at the member, who has been accorded the honour of placing in nomination the name of the man previously agreed upon for Speaker. The individual thus designated makes a brief nominating speech, and a member similarly designated by the Clerk seconds this nomination. There is usually no opposition, and the man thus nominated is speedily elected upon motion. He expresses his appreciation of the honour conferred upon him, and receives the congratulations of the Leader of the House, and an adjournment takes place until twelve o'clock, at which time the Speaker-elect "presents himself with all humility for his Majesty's gracious approbation." The approval of the Crown is announced by the Lord Chancellor, whereupon the Speaker makes the customary claim for freedom of speech, freedom from arrest, and the right of access to the person of the Sovereign. No one disputes these claims, and the Speaker returns to the chamber of the Commons to begin the work of the session.

Then, too, a member after being duly elected cannot resign his seat in Parliament. This is a well-settled legal principle. In view of this fact, when a member wishes to re- *Relinquishing a Seat.*

linquish his seat he applies for an office under the Crown, usually the Stewardship of his Majesty's Chiltern Hundreds. This office is merely nominal, having no definite term, and no duties. It is granted as a matter of course, and by accepting it the member vacates his seat in the House of Commons. An attempt was made as long ago as 1775 to obtain the passage of an Act enabling members to vacate their seats directly, but English conservatism has prevented such an innovation.

In such matters as these the American observer will note a difference between English and American practice. The difference, however, is one of externals rather than of essentials. English conserva-

English Conservatism. tism prevents change in form even after a change in substance has actually occurred. It is this conservatism which causes the old bell in the "Tom Tower" at Oxford to peal out one hundred and one strokes at five minutes after nine each night, although the original significance of those strokes has entirely vanished. Neither is this conservatism without its advantages. The history of the English government shows that it pays to make haste slowly. Conservatism has been the secret of English success in various lines, and the bulwark of the English Constitution, notwithstanding the fact that it has many absurd features. England is certainly well governed. In Parliament the visitor is impressed with the intensely practical nature of the proceedings. The Englishman cares very little for the logic or the political theory of the matter so long as his institutions work well. They certainly have done this. It is in this line that the English people have made their most notable contribution to the civilisation of the world. It is for this reason more than for any other that the people of the world and of America in particular have a vital interest in English institutions.

BIBLIOGRAPHICAL NOTE

ALTHOUGH the literature relating to the history and development of the English Constitution is exceedingly voluminous, that relating to the actual working of the government at the present time is remarkably scanty. The theoretical and historical phases of the subject have been exhaustively discussed, while the present practical aspects have been neglected. There are, however, some works which treat certain phases of the subject in a very satisfactory way. Some of these are enumerated below.

1. Alpheus Todd: "Parliamentary Government in England: its Origin, Development, and Practical Operation." 2 vols. London: Sampson Low, Marston and Company, 1892. This is the most satisfactory work on the subject. The last edition has been much improved by the editing of Spencer Walpole.

2. Sir Thomas Erskine May: "A Treatise on the Law, Privileges, Proceedings, and Usage of Parliament." London: William Clowes and Sons, tenth edition, 1893. This work, better known by its briefer title, "Parliamentary Practice," is the standard authority for the subjects of which it treats. It is indispensable to students of the practice of Parliament, and has no rival in its field. It contains innumerable details and exceptions which the general reader will omit, but is a thorough and masterly piece of historico-legal work.

3. Sir William R. Anson: "The Law and Custom of the Constitution." 2 parts. Oxford: The Clarendon Press,

1896-97. A piece of scholarly work by the Warden of All Souls College, Oxford. It is particularly strong on the historical side.

4. Walter Bagehot: "The English Constitution." London and Boston, 1873. One of the most brilliant and incisive books ever written on the English Constitution. The author had a rare insight into constitutional forms and a wonderful power of expression. Although written a generation ago, the book is still one of the most valuable and stimulating works upon the subject.

5. A. V. Dicey: "Lectures Introductory to the Law of the Constitution." London, 1885. The work of a master. The book is both scholarly and readable. The first eighty pages are especially applicable to the subject.

6. L. O. Pike: "The Constitutional History of the House of Lords." London: Macmillan & Co., 1894. Valuable in connection with the recent agitation against the House of Lords.

7. William C. Macpherson: "The Baronage and the Senate; or the House of Lords in the Past, the Present, and the Future." London: John Murray, 1893. An able defence of the House of Lords.

8. A. C. Ewald: "The Crown and its Advisers; or the Queen, Ministers, Lords, and Commons." London, 1870. Four popular lectures delivered in London. The book is elementary, but accurate on the theoretical side, and extremely lucid. The distinction between the theory and the practice of the government, however, is not clearly made. Although written over thirty years ago, the book is by no means antiquated.

9. Albany de Fonblanque: "How we are Governed; or, the Crown, the Senate, and the Bench." London, 1879. An elementary and interesting sketch.

10. Reginald F. D. Palgrave: "The House of Com-

mons." London, 1878. An interesting and accurate sketch, somewhat anecdotal in character, by a clerk of the House of Commons.

11. H. D. Traill: "Central Government." London: Macmillan & Co., 1892. An excellent little book by an eminent scholar. It is one of the volumes of the "English Citizen" series. It is satisfactory on the historical side, but its treatment of the actual working of the government is inadequate.

12. Spencer Walpole: "The Electorate and the Legislature." London: Macmillan & Co., 1892. This is also one of the volumes of the "English Citizen" series, and is a good short account, but too historical to be satisfactory.

13. G. Lowes Dickinson: "The Development of Parliament during the Nineteenth Century." London and New York: Longmans, Green, and Co., 1895. The author is a Fellow of King's College, Cambridge, and is opposed to the present agitation against the House of Lords. He shows that Parliament has become "democratised" during the nineteenth century. He is not a "democrat," and is apparently losing confidence in the House of Commons as now constituted. He would not have "the will of the people" prevail in all instances. The minority is often right. He would strengthen the House of Lords.

14. J. H. Rose: "The Rise of Democracy." London: Blackie and Son, 1897. "Victorian Era Series." A work upon an important subject by a well-known scholar. It is essential that the student have an adequate conception of the great democratic movement in England in the nineteenth century in order to understand the present practice of the English government.

15. E. A. Freeman: "Growth of the English Constitution." London: Macmillan and Co., 1876, and reprinted 1894. A scholarly exposition of the origin and early devel-

opment of the Constitution. It does not deal with the more recent development or with the machinery of the government.

16. Sheldon Amos: "Fifty Years of the English Constitution." London: Longmans, Green & Co., 1880. The book deals with that important transitional period extending from 1830 to 1880. The work is well done, and forms an indispensable supplement to the works of Stubbs, Hallam, and May.

17. T. A. Spalding: "The House of Lords: A Retrospect and a Forecast." London: T. Fisher Unwin, 1894. The book is a plea for the reconstruction of the House of Lords. It contains an historical sketch, intended to show the necessity for such reconstruction, and a proposed plan of reform. The author is much opposed to the House of Lords in its present form, and writes with some feeling in regard to its attitude toward reform measures. The book is forcibly written and very readable, especially the latter chapters.

18. Wakeman and Hassall: "Constitutional Essays." London and New York: Longmans, Green, and Company, 1891. Good brief sketches on a variety of subjects.

19. C. A. Houfe: "The Question of the Houses." London: Constable and Company, 1895. A book of 130 small pages published as a contribution to the "current controversy." It is a theoretical and somewhat unsatisfactory defence of the House of Lords. The author would preserve the principle of heredity, but not of perpetual heredity. He suggests certain changes in the constitution of the Upper Chamber.

20. Acland and Ransome: "A Handbook in Outline of the Political History of England to 1896." London and New York: Longmans, Green, and Company, 1897. An exceedingly useful chronological compilation of the facts of

English political history. Not in narrative form, but very convenient for reference.

21. Justin McCarthy: "A History of our own Times." 3 vols. London and New York: 1878 and later. An interesting narrative by a man who has been in public life in England for many years. The third volume of the American edition is particularly valuable for an account of recent events. It brings the narrative down to 1897, and gives many interesting sketches of men now prominent in English politics.

22. David Syme: "Representative Government in England: Its Faults and Failures." London: Kegan Paul, Trench, and Company, 1882. A critical study of the theory of the English government.

23. William E. Gladstone: "Gleanings of Past Years." 7 vols. London: John Murray, 1879. The first volume is of especial value in a study of the English government.

24. Moses Coit Tyler: "Glimpses of England." New York: G. P. Putnam's Sons, 1898. A series of short, sketchy papers written in England in the years 1863–66. The papers are political, social, and literary, and most of them appeared in "The Nation" or in "The Independent." The style of the author is brisk and entertaining.

25. "A Sussex Peer": "Drifting towards the Breakers." 1895. An alarmist book of no especial value. It illustrates the absurd extreme to which some minds go in a controversy. The author thinks that civil war will result from the present agitation against the House of Lords, and urges the latter to organise to meet the attack.

26. Joseph Grego: "A History of Parliamentary Elections and Electioneering from the Stuarts to Queen Victoria." London: Chatto and Windus, 1892. Not a book of great value; however, it contains a recital of a vast number of amusing incidents connected with election methods.

27. George H. Jennings: "An Anecdotal History of the British Parliament, from the Earliest Periods to the Present Time, with Notices of Eminent Parliamentary Men, and Examples of their Oratory." London and New York: 1881. The book contains some few passages of interest and value, but is rather stupid as a whole.

28. Richard Harding Davis: "Our English Cousins." New York: Harpers, 1894. Chapter II., pp. 48 to 105, contains an interesting, popular sketch of a general election in England.

29. Richard Grant White: "England Without and Within." Boston: Houghton, Mifflin, and Company, 1881. A gossipy and interesting book. Chapters VIII. and XIII. are of interest in connection with a study of the English government.

30. John R. Seeley: "Fanny Burney and Her Friends." The book contains a good contemporary description of the impeachment of Warren Hastings. It is well worth reading in connection with a study of the process of impeachment.

31. Madame d'Arblay: "Diary and Letters." For the trial of Warren Hastings see Vol. II. pp. 83-153.

32. Dod: "Parliamentary Companion." London: Whittaker and Company. Published annually. Contains alphabetical lists of the members of the two Houses together with brief biographical sketches. It also contains tables and summaries of great value. It is indispensable to the student of current English politics.

33. G. Barnett Smith: "History of the English Parliament." London: Ward, Lock, Bowden, and Company, 1892. A comprehensive work in two large volumes covering the entire history of the English Parliament. The work is based on the standard histories of Stubbs, Freeman, Hallam, and others.

34. Leonard Courtney: "The Working Constitution of

the United Kingdom." Macmillan & Co.: New York and London, 1901.

35. H. Whates: "The Third Salisbury Administration." 1895-1900. London: Vacher & Sons, n. d. A volume of over 500 pages containing the history of five important years. The author has had access to ministerial and other dispatches, and has prepared a book of great value. It contains a large number of important state papers in the appendices.

The list of books bearing upon the subject in an indirect way might be extended almost indefinitely. The great constitutional histories of Stubbs, Hallam, and May will be of almost constant use to the student for reference in regard to the historical development of the Constitution. The less comprehensive work of Taswell-Langmead, covering the entire constitutional history of England, will often serve as a convenient work of reference. The articles in the Encyclopedia Britannica upon "Nobility" and "Peerage" by Professor Freeman, and those by the late John Fiske in Lalor's Cyclopedia, upon the "House of Commons" and the "House of Lords," are good brief sketches by two great masters.

"The Statesman's Year Book," "Financial Reform Almanack," "The Constitutional Year Book," "Whitaker's Almanack," and other publications of a similar character, contain vast storehouses of statistical information relating to the British Empire.

The magazine literature upon the subject is voluminous. "Current History" is of great value to any one who would keep abreast of current political movements in England. "Subjects of the Day," an English quarterly review, which was suspended in 1891 after the publication of four numbers, contained some valuable material. The last number was entirely devoted to the House of Lords. The "North American Review" for January, 1900, contains an interesting and valuable article by Sidney Brooks entitled, "Congress and Parliament: A Contrast." Bowen Graves argued against the present constitution of the House of Lords in the "Fortnightly Review," Vol. XIII. (N. S.), 1873. The following articles are also worthy of mention: "Shall Indian Princes sit in the House of Lords?" by the Earl of Meath, "Nineteenth Century," May, 1894; "The House of Lords as a Constitutional Force," by Lord Halsbury and others, "The New Review," March, 1894; "Shorter Parliaments," by John Hohns, M. P., "Nineteenth Century," January, 1879; "The Procedure of the House of Commons," James E. Thorold Rogers, "The Contemporary Review," March, 1882; "Parliamentary Obstruction and its Remedies," Henry Cecil Raikes, "Nineteenth Century," December, 1880; "The Deadlock in the House of Commons," Frederic Harrison, "Nineteenth Century," September, 1881; "Business in the House of Commons," Lord Sherbrooke, "Nineteenth Century," April, 1881; "The Business of the House of Lords," Lord Zouche, "Nineteenth Century," April, 1879; "Party Government," Frederick V. Fisher, "The Westminster Review," October, 1893; "Lord Rosebery's Enterprise against the House of Lords," L. A. Atherley Jones, M. P., "Nineteenth Century," December, 1894; "If the House of Commons were Abolished?" Sidney Low, "Nineteenth Century," December, 1894; "Obstruction, or 'Clôture,'" Lord Sherbrooke, "Nineteenth Century," October, 1880. This list of magazine articles might be extended almost indefinitely. I have mentioned only a few of the most important articles which were consulted. Poole's "Index to Periodical Literature" will serve as a valuable guide to literature of this kind.

During political campaigns and on other occasions, pamphlets and leaflets of various kinds relating to problems of government make their appearance. Some of these are

The English Government

valuable. The following are worthy of perusal: "Payment of Members of Parliament," H. Hawken, 16 pp., London, 1892; "Payment of Members," James A. Duncan, M. P., 8 pp., London, 1892; "House of Lords," George Panton, 41 pp., London, 1882 (a defence of the House of Lords, not of great value); "The House of Lords; as it is, and as it should be," "Hinc Solon," 8 pp., London (against the Lords); "Peers or People: Which Shall Rule?" "Demos," 56 pp., Manchester, 1884 (against the Lords); "The House of Lords: Its History, Rights, and Uses," 59 pp., London, 1893 (a defence of the Lords); "Lords and Commons," A. B. Smith, 36 pp., 1894 (against the Lords); "The House of Lords," "A Commoner," 20 pp., London, 1894 (a mild defence of the Lords); "The Nation's Debt to the House of Lords," F. W. Worsey, 14 pp. (a defence of the Lords); "The House of Lords," Harold Spender, M. A., 46 pp., London, 1895 (largely made up of caricatures); "Why should Bishops Continue to sit in the House of Lords?" Geo. A. Denison (Vicar of East Brent), 37 pp., 1851 (against the sitting of Bishops); "Fifty Years of the House of Lords," reprinted from "Pall Mall Gazette," London, 1881 (against the Lords).

Copies of reports of committees and Acts of Parliament and other public documents may be obtained from the Government Printers, Messrs. Eyre and Spottiswoode, East Harding Street, Fetter Lane, London, E. C. These documents are sometimes of great value.

INDEX

Abbey, Westminster, 17, 18, 20, 21.
Abercromby, Lord, 189.
Aberdeen, University of, 235.
Act of Settlement, 16, 18, 35, 94.
Admiralty, First Lord of, 80.
Albert, Prince, 34, 42, 326.
Alfred, 13.
Aliens, in House of Commons, 240.
Anne, Queen, 30.
Anson, Sir W. R., 5, 17, 38, 82, 236.
Appeal, Lords of, 171; salary, 172.
Appointments, 37, 43; ladies of Household, 40; army, 43; navy, 43; diplomatic, 43; judicial, 43; dismissals, 44.
Asquith, H. H., 77, 132.
Assent, royal, to bills, 307.

Bagehot, Walter, 30, 48, 53, 89, 147, 188.
Balfour, A. J., 72, 84, 85, 254.
Balfour, Gerald, 83.
Bill of Rights, 15.
Bills, "hybrid," 310.
——, private, 308.
——, public and private, 305.
Bishops, 170, 190.
Black Rod, Gentleman-Usher of, 177, 354.
Blackstone, 29.
Board of Agriculture, President of, 80.
Board of Trade, President of, 80.
Bright, John, 193.
Brodrick, Rt. Hon. W. St. John, 79, 105, 129.
Brougham, Lord, 36-37.
Bryce, James, 86.
Budget, 73.
Burns, John, 349.
Bye-election, 239.

Cabinet, origin and early development of, 59-67; importance of, 59; origin, 60, 61; early history of, 64, 65; stages in development, 65-67; composition of, 71-89; Prime Minister, 71; First Lord of Treasury, 71; Lord Privy Seal, 72; Chancellor of the Exchequer, 72; Lord Chancellor, 75, 76; Lord President of Privy Council, 76; five Secretaries of State, 76; Home Secretary, 77; Foreign Secretary, 77; Colonial Secretary, 78; War Secretary, 79; Secretary for India, 79; First Lord of the Admiralty, 80; President of the Board of Trade, 80; Lord Lieutenant of Ireland, 80; Chief Secretary for Ireland, 80; President of the Local Government Board, 80; President of the Board of Agriculture, 80; Lord Chancellor of Ireland, 80; Chancellor of the Duchy of

Lancaster, 80; Secretary for Scotland, 80; Postmaster-General, 80; First Commissioner of Works, 80; Vice-President of Committee of Council on Education, 81; size of, 82–83; fundamental principles of, 93–101; members of, in Parliament, 93; members re-elected, 94, 108–109; members in House of Lords, 95; unanimity of, 95; collective resignation, 97; subordination to Prime Minister, 98; miscellaneous provisions, 105–115; apportionment of members between the two Houses, 105; meetings of, 110–112; salaries, 113–114; pensions, 115; responsibility to Parliament, 119–133; vote of censure, 120; resignation, 121; appeal to the country, 121–122; resignations of Lord Salisbury and Mr. Gladstone in 1886, 124; fall of the Rosebery Ministry, 1895, 126; voluntary dissolution, 130; Lord Salisbury's resignation, 1892, 131; in Parliament, 137–151; King's Speech, 137; control of legislation, 141; answers to questions, 146; theory *versus* practice, 150.

Cambridge, University of, 235.

Campbell-Bannerman, Sir Henry, 79, 86, 129.

Campbell, Rt. Hon. J. A., 236.

Canterbury, Archbishop of, 17, 19.

Catholics, Roman, ineligible to throne, 16.

Chamberlain, Joseph, 79, 84, 85.

Charles II., 11.

Chief Justice of King's Bench, 44.

Chiltern Hundreds, 356.

Church of England, 17.

Civil List and Royal Grants, 325.

Coke, Sir Edward, 290.

Colonial Secretary, 78.

Commission, Royal, 76.

Committee of Council on Education, 81.

Committee, of the Whole House, 306.

Committees, of House of Commons, 322.

Committees, Select, 323.

Commons, House of, 26; Leader of, 144; importance of, 221; origin of, 222; evolution of, 225; representation in, 226; "rotten boroughs," 227; Reform Bill, 1832, 230; present representation, 232; university members, 234; contested seats, 237; vacancies, 238; disqualifications, 239; clergymen, 241; contractors excluded, 241; disabilities removed, 244; expulsion of members, 245; franchise, 246; disqualifications, 248; nominations, 249; campaign speeches, 250; women in politics, 252; oath of office, 254; Oaths Act, (1888), 255; Test Roll, 257; places and seats, 261; time of meeting, 262; long sessions, 263; quorum, 264; "count out," 265; attendance, 266; payment of members, 268; strangers, 271; Speaker, 273; Sergeant-at-Arms, 275; "Votes and Proceedings," 275; "Journal," 276; parties, 276; *personnel*, 277, 347; authors in, 282; power of, 284; present status, 338; order, 341; hats on, 342; manner of speaking, 344; manners, 345; the Opposition, 349; relinquishing a seat, 355.

Commonwealth, the period of, 11.

# Index

Conservatism, English, 356–357.
Consolidated Fund, 325.
Consort, Prince, 34; *see also* Albert, Prince.
Coronation, 17–22; Oath, 19–20; chair, 20–22.
Corrupt Practices Act (1883), 242.
"Count out," 265.
Cranbourne, Viscount, 105.
Cromwell, Oliver, 21, 128.
Crown, power of, 25; "Fountain of Justice," 28, 34; theoretical prerogatives, 27–28; as executive, 30; veto of, 30; in Parliament, 31; when present in Parliament, 31–32; present by commission, 32; and Foreign Secretary, 33; pardons, 35; appointments, 37; private secretary, 41–42; Head of Church, 43, 47; salaries and pensions, 44; Commander-in-Chief of army and navy, 45; power to declare war, 46; treaty-making power, 46; "Fountain of Honour," 48; sign manual, 48; moral influence of, 52–55; Speech from Throne, 137; Civil List, 325; jewels, 338.

Debates, rules of, in Lords, 179; in Commons, 314.
Defoe, 157.
Devonshire, Duke of, 76.
Dicey, Prof. A. V., 25.
Dickinson, G. L., 213.
Dilke, Sir Charles, 81, 211.
Disabilities, removal of, 244.
Disraeli, Benjamin, 82, 106.
Divisions, in Lords, 180; in Commons, 319.
Dod, "Parliamentary Companion," 278.
Dublin, University of, 235.
Duchy of Lancaster, 80.

Edgar, 14.
Edinburgh, University of, 235.
Edward I., 20.
Edward II., 15.
Edward VII., 12, 16, 18, 26.
England, contribution to civilization, 3; Church of, 17.
Ewald, A. C., 27, 82.
Exchequer, Chancellor of, 72.
Expulsion of members of House of Commons, 245.

Financial Reform Almanac, 201–202.
First Lord of Treasury, 71.
Foreign Affairs, Secretary of State for, 46, 72, 77–78.
Foster, Sir Michael, 236.
Fox, C. J., 78, 239, 318.
Franchise, 246.
Freedom from arrest, 294.
—— of speech, 294.
Freeman, Prof. E. A., 12, 151.

George I., 82.
George II., 45.
George III., 8, 42, 48, 82, 96, 139.
George IV., 36, 45, 49.
Gladstone, W. E., 81, 84, 95, 124, 132, 189, 254, 270.
Glasgow, University of, 235.
Goschen, Rt. Hon. G. J., 80.
Government, English, nature of, 3–8; theory *versus* practice, 49–50.
Government, party, 149.
Green, J. R., 26.
Gully, Speaker, 273.

Hamilton, Lord George, 79–80.
Hanover, House of, 16.
Hardy, Gathorne, 30.
Harold, 14.
Hastings, Warren, 330.
Hawken, H., 269.

Index

Henry IV., 15.
Henry VIII., 47.
Hicks-Beach, Sir Michael, 75, 85.
Home Secretary, 36, 77.

IMPEACHMENT, 327-332.
India, Secretary for, 79; princes of, 210.
Ireland, Lord Lieutenant of, 80, 81, 82; Chief Secretary for, 80, 81; Lord Chancellor of, 80; representative peers of, 167; union with England, 165.

JAMES II., 15.
Jebb, Prof. Sir R. C., 235.
Journal, of House of Commons, 276.
Judges, appointment of, 35.
Judiciary, independence of, 35.

KEBBEL, T. E., 214.
Kelvin, Lord, 163.
Kensington Palace, 18.
Kimberly, Earl of, 192.
King, *see* Crown.
Kitchener, Lord, 166.
Knollys, Lord, 42.

LABOURERS AND LORDS, 200.
Lands of peers, 182.
Lansdowne, Marquis of, 72.
Law Officers, 149.
Law, unconstitutional, 5.
Lecky, Rt. Hon. W. E. H., 236.
Levee dress, 301, note 1.
Lewes, battle of, 223.
Liberal Unionists, 96.
Lindhurst, Lord, 189.
Liverpool, Lord, 45.
Local Government Board, President of, 80.
London, "City" of, 310.
——, "Gazette," 86.
——, University of, 235.
Lord Chancellor, 43, 75, 138, 176.

Lord Privy Seal, 81.
Lords, House of, 155, 350; Leader of, 143; importance of, 155; origin of, 157; composition of, 161; three classes of members, 163; creation of peers, 163; archbishops and bishops in, 170; Lords of Appeal, 171; precedence, 173; disqualifications, 173; growth of, 174; Lord Chancellor, 176; woolsack, 177; Sergeant-at-Arms, 177; Clerk, 177; Gentleman-Usher of the Black Rod, 177; Yeoman-Usher, 178; time of meeting, 178; quorum, 178; prayer, 179; rules of debate in, 179; divisions, 180; privileges, 180; powers and functions, 181; proposed reforms of, 187-217; reform advocated by lords, 190; Lord Rosebery's proposed reform, 191, 203; Lord Salisbury's plan, 192-205; Earl of Pembroke's plan, 192; theoretical objections, 193; attitude toward Reform Bill (1832), 196; since 1832, 198; tactics of lords, 199; Spalding's attitude, 198; fifty years of, 200; and labourers, 200; proposed changes, 203; Spalding's plan, 206; Indian princes, 210; one chamber, 211; views of Sir Charles Dilke, 211; defenders of, 212; Macpherson's views, 212; views of Lord Wemyss, 212; Dickinson's views, 213; Kebbel's views, 214; views of "A Sussex Peer," 215; general conclusion, 217.
Lords, spiritual, 169.

MACAULAY, LORD, 47, 197.
Macpherson, W. C., 212.
Marlborough, Duchess of, 41.

Index

Marlborough, Duke of, 163.
McCarthy, Justin, 248, 255.
Meeting, time of, in Lords, 178.
Melbourne, Lord, 40.
Message, royal, 32.
Ministers, responsibility of, 29; appointment of, 85.
Ministry, 83.
Montfort, de, Simon, 222.
Morley, John, 86, 189.

NATIONALITY, English, 12.
Nicolas, Sir Harris, 63.
Nominations, 249.

OATH, coronation, 19-20; for House of Commons, 254.
Oaths Act (1888), 255.
Occupations of members of House of Commons, 278.
O'Connell, Daniel, 139.
Office, kingly, continuity of, 11.
Opposition, 147, 349.
Order of the Day, 146.
Orders, Standing, Sessional, General, 313-314.
Oxford, University of, 235.

PAIRS, 321.
Palgrave, R. F. D., 267.
"Pall Mall Gazette," 200.
Pardoning power, 35.
Parliament in Tudor period, 6; questions in, 146; composition, 289; sovereignty of, 289; annual meetings, 292; privileges, 292; obstructions, 295; sundry sessions, 296; special services, 296; adjournments, 297; communication between the two Houses, 298; communication between Parliament and Crown, 299; replies, 300; procedure, 302; three readings, 304; public and private bills, 305; "Committee of the Whole House," 306; royal assent, 307; private bills, 308; "hybrid" bills, 310; practice and proceedings, 313; rules of debate, 314; divisions, 319; tellers, 321; pairs, 321; committees, 322; taxation and supply, 323; "tacking," 324; cards of admission, 337; forms and ceremonies, 352; opening of, 353.
Parliaments, duration of, 131.
Parties, political, 276.
Patronage, abuse of, 46.
Pauncefote, Sir Julian, 164.
Payment of members, 268.
Peel, A. W., 164.
Peel, Sir Robert, 45, 82, 87, 88.
Peers, Scotch, representative, 167; creation of, 163; Irish, 165, 167; introduction of, 166; estates of, 182; spiritual, 351; and Reform Bill (1832), 196.
Pembroke, Earl of, 192.
Pensions, 44, 115.
Pepys, 18.
Personnel of House of Commons, 277.
Petitions, 332.
Pitt, William, 82, 96.
Postmaster-General, 80.
Prayer, in Parliament, 179.
Prerogative, royal, 25-55; definition of, 25.
Prime Minister, 38, 71, 81, 83, 112, 140; selection of, 83; either peer or commoner, 86; as First Lord of Treasury, 87; a busy man, 88; origin of office, 99; power of, 101; relation to Crown, 112.
Primrose League, 252.
Princes of Royal Blood, 166.
Private Bills, 308.
Privileges of Lords, 180.

Privy Council, 60, 62–64; present status of, 63, 64.
Privy Councillor, oath of, 60, 61; term of, 61.

QUEEN. *See* Crown.
Quorum, in Lords, 178; in Commons, 264.

REALM, Estates of, 8.
Reform Bill (1832), 230.
Reid, Sir Wemyss, 18, note 1.
Reply to King's Speech, 140–141.
Reporters, 271.
Residences, official, 113.
Revolution of 1688, 26.
Richard II., 15.
Richmond, Duke of, 189.
Ritchie, Rt. Hon. C. T., 77.
Roberts, Lord, 163.
Rosebery, Lord, 76, 78, 85, 126, 191.
Royal Household, officers of, 39.
Royal prerogative, 25–55.
Russell, Lord John, 239.

SAINT ANDREWS, University, 235.
Saint Paul's, Cathedral, 297.
Salaries, 44.
Salisbury, Lord, 72, 79, 84, 87, 124, 126, 129, 130, 131, 192.
Scone, Abbey of, 20.
Scotland, Secretary for, 80; representative peers of, 167; union with England, 165.
Seats, contested, 237.
Secretary, King's private, 41–42.
Selborne, Earl of, 80.
Selden, 156.
Select Committee, 323.
Septennial Act, 291.
Sergeant-at-Arms, 177, 275.
Settlement, Act of, 16, 18, 35, 94.
Sign manual, 48.
Smith, Goldwin, 3.

Smith, Sydney, 197.
Sovereign. *See* Crown.
Spalding, T. A., 198, 206.
Speaker, 142, 265, 273; elevated to peerage, 45.
Speeches, campaign, 250.
Steward, Lord High, 329.
Stone of Fate, 20.
Strangers in Commons, 271.
"Subject of the Day," 191, 214.
Succession, 11–17.
Supremacy, Act of, 47.
"Sussex Peer," 215.

TACITUS, 12.
"Tacking," 324.
Taswell-Langmead, 12, 27.
Taxation and supply, 323.
Taxes, 74.
Tellers, 321.
Test Roll, 257.
Throne, succession to, 11–17.
Titles by courtesy, 240.
Todd, Alpheus, 27, 29, 33, 35, 51, 52.
Tyler, Prof. M. C., 50, 271, 346.

UNIVERSITY members, 234.

VACANCIES, in House of Commons, 238.
Vernon-Harcourt, Sir William, 75, 84, 126.
Veto, royal, 30; last use of, 30.
Victoria, Queen, 16, 18, 42, 49, 51, 54, 55; coronation of, 18–22.
"Votes and proceedings," 275.
Voting, plural, 235, 248.

WALPOLE, ROBERT, 95–96, 98, 100.
War, Secretary of State for, 46, 79; power to declare, 46.
Watson, William, 225.
Wellington, Duke of, 36, 45, 78.

Index

Wemyss, Lord, 212.
Westminster Abbey, 17, 18, 20, 21.
—— School, 19.
Whips, 145.
William IV., 18, 138.
—— and Mary, 15, 22.

Witan, 13, 158–161.
Women, in politics, 252.
Woolsack, 177.
Works, First Commissioner of, 80.

YEOMAN-USHER, 178.